The Key to

Understanding
REVELATION

An Easily Grasped Structure of a Complex Book

Books by Arthur E. Bloomfield

Before the Last Battle—Armaggedon

The End of the Days

How to Recognize the Antichrist

The Key to Understanding Revelation

The Key to

Understanding
REVELATION

An Easily Grasped Structure of a Complex Book

Arthur E. Bloomfield

BETHANYHOUSE
MINNEAPOLIS, MINNESOTA

The Key to Understanding Revelation
by Arthur E. Bloomfield

Copyright © 1959, 2002
Bethany House Publishers

Originally titled *All Things New*

Published by Bethany House Publishers
A Ministry of Bethany Fellowship International
11400 Hampshire Avenue South
Bloomington, Minnesota 55438
www.bethanyhouse.com

Printed in the United States of America by Bethany Press International

Library of Congress Cataloging-in-Publication Data

Bloomfield, Arthur E. (Arthur Edward), b. 1895.
   [All things new]
   The key to understanding Revelation : an easily grasped structure of a complex book / by Arthur E. Bloomfield.
     p.   cm.
Originally published: c1959.
Includes index.
   ISBN 0-7642-2593-6 (pbk.)
   1. Bible. N.T. Revelation—Criticism, interpretation, etc. I. Title.
BS2825.2 .B58   2002
228'.06—dc21

                                          2001008129

FOREWORD

The Key to Understanding Revelation was first published by Bethany Fellowship in the late 1950s under the title *All Things New*. The author, the Reverend Arthur E. Bloomfield, was an ordained Methodist minister and served several years as a pastor. As he studied and taught the Bible, he found himself drawn to the prophetic books: Revelation, Isaiah, and Daniel, along with Christ's prophetic discourse in Matthew 24 and 25. The discoveries he made about Bible prophecy drew more and more of his time and attention, and he began teaching, writing, and further expanding his findings.

Bethany Fellowship's founder and director, the late T. A. Hegre, had seen information in a Christian periodical about Bloomfield's booklet on Revelation and ordered a copy. Convinced that the structure presented in those few pages was valid, even revolutionary, Hegre invited Bloomfield to speak on the subject at a Bethany conference, the first of many such invitations. Eventually the original booklet was expanded into a book-length work, along with further volumes on the other prophetic sections of Scripture.

I served on the faculty of Bethany's College of Missions for almost forty years, and with much personal delight I used this material to teach the book of Revelation. Because the author passed on to his reward some years ago, I have taken the liberty to make minor editorial updates to this new edition.

Bloomfield's exposition of this rather complex book is as eye-opening as it was when originally penned, and it provides lay readers and biblical scholars alike with valuable tools and insights—*The Key to Understanding Revelation*!

Harold J. Brokke
Dean Emeritus/Bethany College of Missions
January 2001

PREFACE

More books have been written on Revelation than on any other book in the Bible. Why another one? Revelation is still a mystery to most people, yet it is the only book that the church is commanded to hear. Why would Jesus send His church a message that it could not understand? Yet it has not been understood for nearly two thousand years.

It is quite evident that Revelation was prepared in advance for a certain time in the experience of the church, and when that time comes, then "blessed is he that readeth and they that hear, for the time is at hand."

One who reads or teaches Revelation when the time is at hand will have an advantage over those who have labored in times past. We have done something in this book that has not been done in previous expositions; we have based the whole interpretation on a structure that keeps the entire book before you while the details are being studied.

If you will master the structure and the simple diagrams, you will not become lost in the mass of detail which has baffled so many teachers. Revelation is designed to be taught in a class. "Blessed is HE that readeth and THEY that hear." This book, for the first time, makes a Bible study class in Revelation feasible. "I, Jesus, have sent mine angel to testify unto you these things in the churches." This puts an obligation on all pastors, teachers and leaders.

Arthur E. Bloomfield

TABLE OF CONTENTS

LIST OF CHARTS AND MAPS

INTRODUCTION

The first thing Revelation says about itself is that it is a prophecy. "Blessed is he that readeth and they that hear the words of this prophecy." Prophecy is more than history written in advance; it is the completion of a story. The Bible deals with time—all time—beginning with the creation as recorded in Genesis and ending with the new heaven and the new earth which includes the Holy City that comes down out of heaven from God, the "long home" of the saints.

The story of time had to be written in the middle of that time; therefore, some of it would have to be written before the events took place. This is prophecy. The book of Daniel completes the story of the nations; the book of Ezekiel completes the story of the Jews; the book of Revelation completes the story of the church.

When the prophetical historian passes from the past into the future, he sometimes has to change his methods because new situations arise which cannot be described in ancient words. It is then that types and symbols are employed. If we consider the seven churches described in the second and third chapters as types of the church in different eras of its history, then the church at Ephesus would represent the church at about the time of the end of the book of Acts. Revelation is a continuation of the book of Acts. It continues the story of the church through the ages of its earthly history, into heaven at the Resurrection, returning with Christ to reign for a thousand years, then finally receiving the many mansions prepared in the Holy City. Revelation is a completion of the story of the church.

Revelation is for the church. It was sent to show unto His servants the things which must shortly be done. It is directed to the seven churches and it has a seven-times repeated command: "He that hath an ear, let him hear what the Spirit saith unto the churches."—Rev. 2:7, 11, 17, 29; 3:6, 13, 22.

A blessing is pronounced to those who read; we are commanded to hear; and the Lord pleads with us to take the Word to heart. "I, Jesus, have sent my angel to testify unto you these things in the churches." The churches *should* study the other books; they *must* study Revelation. Sometimes people make the excuse, "I cannot understand it." The Holy Spirit cannot tell you what the Bible means until you know what the Bible says. Our responsibility lies in knowing what Revelation says. Teachers of this book may lean hard upon the Holy Spirit. Revelation is a message direct from Christ to His church after His ascension.

Revelation is not only *for* the church; it is *about* the church. This is probably the most important thing we could say at the beginning of this study. It has been said that Revelation is for the church but about the Jews. However, the Jews are not once mentioned in the book, except the 144,000 who have become Christians. The return of the Jews is not mentioned; they are not mentioned in the account of the return of Christ, the battle of Armageddon, nor the kingdom reign.

On the other hand, the churches are mentioned in the first chapter, in the second and third chapters, and in the last chapter. The saints are mentioned or referred to by some means in every chapter. We do not have in Revelation the complete biography of Antichrist. He is mentioned only in his relationship to the saints and the false church; not one word is said about his relationship to the Jews, except in connection with the two witnesses, and even then the Jews are not mentioned.

"Church" is an earthly name for the organization of the saints of God. The name is not applied to the saints after the Rapture. Other names are used to indicate the particular work that the saints will do at that time: such names as Elders, Living Ones, Horsemen, Angels, Bride of Christ, Kings, and Priests. Most of the confusion in the interpretation of Revelation has been caused by a failure to recognize the saints in their heavenly organization and work.

Revelation differs from the other books of the Bible in the way it was revealed. It was all directly revealed by vision. John was told exactly what to write and what not to write. This is true to such an extent that even the rules of grammar are made to work for the author. Some have thought that John could not have been the writer because the vocabulary and grammar are so unlike his other books. This difference may be accounted for by the way this book was given to John.

Prophetic Language

We may divide the methods of expression into two groups: literal and figurative. Of these two kinds of language the figurative is the easier and the literal is the more difficult to understand. We will, therefore, consider first the figurative language. This may in turn be divided into two groups: types and symbols.

FIGURATIVE LANGUAGE

Types

The difference between types and symbols is the manner of their interpretation. A type is interpreted by similar features. A type must be like the antitype in some respects. It is in those respects only that it is a type. Usually there is only one fulfillment of each type because of the fact that a type cannot be understood until the antitype arrives. For instance: Adam may be considered a type, with Christ the antitype. However, we would not be able to judge in what respects Adam was like Christ until after Christ had come. In the same way we may consider Eve, the bride of Adam, a type of the church, the bride of Christ. There are few types in the New Testament. In Revelation the seven churches are types because they are like the churches which they prefigure and which have since come upon the scene. It is possible that John himself was a type when he was caught up into heaven and when he ate the little book (Rev. 4: 1; 10: 10).[1]

Symbols

Symbols, on the other hand, have a given meaning with no reference to similarities. The fulfillment may occur many times or only once.

Symbols may be understood before their fulfillment; however, a symbol cannot be understood unless its meaning is indicated in some way. Examples of symbols are leaven, which is a symbol of evil, and good seed, which is a symbol of the children of God. There are actually few symbols in Revelation. The principal ones are candlesticks, stars (1: 20); woman, man-child, dragon (12); beasts (13); scarlet woman (17). In every case the explanation is given or may be determined from the context, or from the use of the same symbol elsewhere in the Bible. Heavenly things are not symbolized. For instance, the man-child was caught up unto God and to His throne. Man-child is a symbol; God and His throne are not.

---

1. "After this I looked, and, behold, a door was opened in heaven: and the first voice which I heard was as it were of a trumpet talking with me; which said, Come up hither, and I will shew thee things which must be hereafter" (Rev. 4:1). "And I took the little book out of the angel's hand, and ate it up; and it was in my mouth sweet as honey: and as soon as I had eaten it, my belly was bitter" (Rev. 10:10).

LITERAL LANGUAGE

Literal language may also be divided into two groups: first, that which deals with things of earth; second, that which deals with things of heaven. When we are dealing with literal language concerning earthly things, we must read with understanding. The prophets had to use words known only in their day to express things known only in our day. That is why literal language is sometimes more difficult to follow than figurative language. Words change their meaning but symbols do not.

When heavenly things are in view, we encounter words which at first sight seem to be symbols. Some of the confusion in the interpretation of Revelation is due to an attempt to interpret literal heavenly things as though they were symbols of earthly things. John was caught up into heaven and saw things that never have appeared on earth. These things have to be reported in earthly words. We must understand them as being literal but not earthly.

The horsemen are literal. Whatever in heaven corresponds to the means of locomotion of an earthly army is what John saw. The trumpets, the vials, the robes, the crowns, the thrones are all literal; but when we see them they may not look at all like those which are manufactured upon the earth. All knowledge must come to us by experience, that is, through our senses. We have never experienced any heavenly scene. We do not know one heavenly word. The best John could do was to find something on earth that corresponded as nearly as possible to what he saw, and to express those heavenly things in our earthly words. They are not symbols. They are literal, but heavenly.

Rules of Interpretation

Revelation may be interpreted largely by rule. We would expect this to be so because of the nature of God. He is the

Creator, and all creation runs by fixed laws. A scientist may make nature work for him to the extent that he can discover and apply the laws involved. All modern science is based upon the one fact that God never changes. If we could find all the rules of interpretation which undergird Revelation, we could find the meaning of every sentence. It will, therefore, be a great help if we can find some of the rules. However, it is not enough simply to know the rules of interpretation; they must be continually and consistently applied. A rule may not be considered established unless it is always true and unless its application adds to our understanding of the book and keeps us from going astray in our interpretation.

We present here six rules of interpretation:

1. In symbolical language the action is always literal; only the subject matter is symbolic. Therefore, the method of interpretation will be to discover the meaning of the symbol and then apply the action literally. For instance, Jesus said, "The kingdom of heaven is like unto leaven, which a woman took, and hid in three measures of meal." Whatever the woman stands for *took* whatever the leaven stands for and *put it into* whatever the meal stands for. Again, in the 12th chapter of Revelation, whatever the woman stands for *gave birth* to whatever the man-child stands for; and whatever the man-child stands for *was caught up* into heaven. In every case the action is literal.

2. Events numbered occur in succession and in the order numbered. This is axiomatic. There would be no other reason for numbering them. When the seven trumpets are blown, one after the other, the events that follow are successive events and take place in order as they are numbered. This sounds like a simple rule, yet it is violated in many modern interpretations. There are no "parenthetical chapters."

3. When Christ is mentioned throughout the book, reference is made to some feature in the first chapter. Thus

Christ may be identified whenever He appears, even though He may be called an angel.

4. Christ has various names, according to His work: Lamb, Lion, Angel.

5. The saints have various names, according to their work or position: Elders, Living Ones, Horsemen, Angels, Bride.

6. Saints may be identified by their clothing, crowns, thrones, work, and songs. Angels are not said to sing; only the saints have a song. Singing in Revelation is confined to redemption themes, which only saints can sing.

USE OF NUMBERS

Revelation is consistent in its use of numbers. Sometimes there seems to be an inconsistency. In such cases we have failed to grasp the full meaning of the text. The principal numbers which have meanings peculiar to themselves are these:

ONE. This is the number of God. Deut. 6:4, "I, the Lord, thy God, am one God."

THREE. The Trinity. The triangle is the smallest unit in geometry and is therefore a proper symbol of the Triune God (Matt. 28:19;[1] Rev. 1:4–6). This number is prominent when redemption is involved. God was revealed as a Trinity only in the process of redemption. It requires the Father, the Son, and the Holy Spirit to save one sinner.

FOUR. The world number is four: four directions, four winds, four seasons. This number is in evidence when God is dealing with the world. The four world empires of Daniel are symbolic of man's rule over the earth from Nebuchadnezzar to Christ. The four Gospels record the life of Christ

---

1. "Go ye therefore, and teach all nations, baptizing them in the name of the Father, and of the Son, and of the Holy Ghost" (Matt. 28:19).

on earth. The cherubim of Ezekiel (four in number) are a presentation of the heavenly organization for the judgment of the earth. The four Living Ones of Revelation relay the judgments written under the seals to the four Horsemen, who in turn transmit them into action upon the earth.

SIX. The number of evil. This is Satan's number (Daniel 3: 1; Rev. 13: 18).

SEVEN. The number of completeness (not perfection). The dragon has seven heads, indicating his complete reign over the whole earth, typified by the seven great world empires. Seven shows the subject in its entirety, from beginning to end: seven churches, the whole church of all time; seven spirits, the Holy Spirit. If, for instance, the seven-sealed book has in it the consummation of redemption, it must all be completed in the opening of the seven seals and the blowing of the seven trumpets, which occur under the seventh seal.

TEN. Ten is an indefinite number or a round number, or a number that is subject to change. Examples: "ten thousand times ten thousand" (Dan. 7: 10;[1] Rev. 5: 11), ten virgins (Matt. 25: 1), ten days (Rev. 2: 10).

TWELVE. The number of the redeemed. In the Old Testament they were represented by the twelve tribes; in the New Testament by the twelve apostles; in the Holy City there are the twelve gates and the twelve foundation stones named for the saints of the Old and New Covenants.

The Text

In this book we have followed basically the Authorized Version. In many cases, but not all, some of the revised versions are undoubtedly better. The various new versions do not agree among themselves. Some of the best new versions

---

1. "A fiery stream issued and came forth from before him: thousand thousands ministered unto him, and ten thousand times ten thousand stood before him: the judgment was set, and the books were opened" (Dan. 7:10).

follow the Authorized Version in places where the American Standard Version differs.

This is not as serious as it sounds because in no instance does a change affect the interpretation. Usually it is only a matter of a choice of words that have the same over-all meaning. Because it is called "revised" does not of itself prove that it is better.

As an illustration, in Revelation 1:11 we read these words: "What thou seest, write in a book, and send it unto the seven churches which are in Asia." The words *which are in Asia* are omitted in the American Standard Version. They do not appear in the best manuscripts nor in any of the ancient versions.

Turkey was called Asia in Bible times. We know the exact location of all the churches mentioned. They were in Asia. These words in question do not add anything to our knowledge, and nothing is lost by omitting them. They in no way affect our interpretation.

Wescott and Hort say: "We are by no means sure that we have done all for the text of the Apocalypse that might be done with existing materials. But we are convinced that the only way to remove such relative insecurity as belongs to it would be by a more minute and complete examination of the genealogical relations of the documents than we have been able to accomplish, *nor have we reason to suspect that the result would make any considerable change*" (italics ours).

There are instances where the Authorized Version, though not as exact a translation, gives the meaning more clearly than the newer versions. Translations may be tricky. A literal translation may not give the sense as well as a free translation.

For instance, Revelation 1:6 is as follows: "And hath made us kings and priests unto God and his Father." Most revised versions follow the Greek and translate it "kingdom, priests" or "a kingdom of priests." In support of this change the *Pulpit Commentary* remarks: "Christians are nowhere said to be kings." But for that matter, Christians are not called priests.

Peter calls the church a royal priesthood (I Pet. 2:9). This does not mean that saints are all priests and live in a realm that is ruled over by a king. It means they are both kings and priests. This is in harmony with the teachings of Jesus and Revelation.

Well, thou good servant: because thou hast been faithful in a very little, have thou authority over ten cities.—Luke 19:17

Well done, thou good and faithful servant: thou hast been faithful over a few things, I will make thee ruler over many things.—Matt. 25:21

Verily I say unto you, That ye which have followed me, in the regeneration when the Son of man shall sit in the throne of his glory, ye also shall sit upon twelve thrones, judging the twelve tribes of Israel.—Matt. 19:28

And he that overcometh, and keepeth my works unto the end, to him will I give power over the nations: and he shall rule them with a rod of iron.—Rev. 2:26, 27

To him that overcometh will I grant to sit with me in my throne.—Rev. 3:21

And I saw thrones, and they sat upon them, and judgment was given unto them: and I saw the souls of them that were beheaded for the witness of Jesus, and for the word of God . . . and they lived and reigned with Christ a thousand years.—Rev. 20:4

And they shall reign for ever and ever.—Rev. 22:5

Notice that in several instances the functions of judge and king are combined. Paul asked: "Do ye not know that the saints shall judge the world?"—I Cor. 6:2.

The expression "a kingdom of priests" can have only one meaning—that is, we shall be kings and priests. Many revised versions have to be explained because the words themselves convey no meaning. The Authorized Version needs no explanation. It may not be as literal a translation, but it gives the exact meaning.

There are many grammatical errors in the original text. These have been corrected in the translations. An easy explanation is that John was writing in a foreign language and under stress. He had no time to consider the niceties of grammar, which he would do if he were writing under favorable conditions. This alone would be enough to account for the difference in composition between Revelation and the Gospel of John.

But there are other considerations. The deeper we go into the prophetic Scriptures the more we are convinced of the verbal inspiration of the Bible. The accuracy of statement is astounding. Prophecy has a language of its own. There are certain peculiarities of expression that are characteristic of the prophetic method. God uses grammar for His purpose. He seems to take the attitude that grammar was made for man, not man for grammar.

When Moses asked what name he should give for the God of his fathers, God said, "Thou shalt say unto the children of Israel, I AM hath sent me unto you."—Ex. 3:14.

There is a good example in Ezekiel 39:2 of how the prophets use grammar: "And I will turn thee back, and leave but a sixth part of thee." This has a variety of renderings: one for each translator. "I will put six hooks in thy jaws." "I will plague thee with six plagues." These are not literal translations because a literal translation would not be grammatical. Ezekiel uses a noun for a verb. A literal translation would be: "I will six you," meaning "I will do something to you with the number six," or "I will apply to you, in some way, the number six."

Sometimes the solecism is so obvious it seems almost impossible that it could be an accident. For instance, Revelation 1:4 reads: "From him which is, and which was, and which is to come." The *Pulpit Commentary* remarks: "The designation of the Deity in this verse is, when grammatically considered, very remarkable. It may be literally rendered: The *being* and the *was* and the *coming*."

A very useful version for Bible students would be one that always uses the same English word to translate the same original when the construction and meaning are the same. Robert Young points out that in the Authorized Version no less than 49 Hebrew words are translated by the one word *destroy*. On the other hand, a number of English words are sometimes used to translate the same Hebrew or Greek word.

Apokalupsis is translated in the Authorized Version by these words: *appearing, coming, manifestation,* and *revelation*. The American Standard Version translates it *revelation* in each place. The saints will return with Christ. His revelation is also their revelation. Paul refers to it in Romans 8:19, but the sense is lost because of the use of a word that nowhere else is used for revelation. "For the earnest expectation of the creature waiteth for the *manifestation* of the sons of God."

One of the most unfortunate translations is Revelation 4:6, where *zoon* is translated *beast*. The American Standard Version has *living creatures*. *Living ones* would be still better. The emphasis is on the word *living*. An entirely different word ("therion") —wild beast—is used in chapter 13.

The Authorized Version is quite inconsistent in its translation of the Greek *thronos* by *seat,* as well as by *throne*. In a single verse the same word is translated throne and seat. "And round about the throne were four and twenty seats." —Rev. 4:4.

So in some cases the American Standard Version helps; in others it does not. On the whole, the Authorized Version requires no more critical comment than does the American Standard Version. Differences of consequence will be noted, but there is little to be gained by a change in the wording unless the change adds something to our understanding.

The Theme

The theme of Revelation is redemption. Redemption involves the restoration of everything that was lost by sin, including man's soul, his body, the human race, and the earth. As we shall see in the first chapter, the qualifications of Christ to be the Redeemer of the world include His suffering and death, as well as His power to judge and reign. He is both the Lamb of God and the Lion of Judah.

The process of redemption has been committed to the church. The history of the church is the history of redemption as it applies to the souls of men. This is not the day of redemption for the physical earth or even the human race as such. That is why all reforms fail and all efforts for world peace come to naught. The church is not now "working with God for a brave new world." This is the day of redemption of individual souls, not the redemption of the earth. It is the first part of the whole process of redemption.

Redemption involves the soul, the body, and the earth.

And not only they, but ourselves also, which have the firstfruits of the Spirit, even we ourselves groan within ourselves, waiting for the adoption, to wit, the redemption of our body.—Rom. 8:23

And grieve not the Holy Spirit of God, whereby ye are sealed unto the day of redemption.—Eph. 4:30

When these things begin to come to pass, then look up and lift up your heads: for your redemption draweth nigh.—Luke 21:28

Jesus spoke of the Rapture as "your redemption." Following the custom of the prophets, Jesus addressed His people at the time of the prophecy. "Your" does not refer to the four disciples to whom Jesus was talking but to the people involved in the prophecy. There is nothing unusual about this. It is a common prophetic device.

For instance, Jeremiah commands: "Flee out of the midst of Babylon, and deliver every man his soul: be not cut off in her iniquity; for this is the time of the Lord's vengeance; he will render unto her a recompence."—Jer. 51:6.

This was spoken long before Babylon was destroyed; in fact, the whole prophetic picture is still future. It was not the people of Jeremiah's day that were warned to flee Babylon. They were just about to be taken captive. It would be seventy years before any would be allowed to leave, and then Babylon would already have fallen into the hands of the Persians.

The people addressed are those living when the prophecy is fulfilled and who are directly involved. There will be a city which, in the last days, will be to our world what Babylon was to its world. It may well be on the same site and it could be called by the same name. Its great wealth will attract many people. Those are the ones the prophet warns. The prophecy is addressed to a specific people at a specific time in a specific place.

Paul also uses this method when he says, "Then we which are alive and remain shall be caught up."—I Thess. 4:17. It does not follow that Paul expected the Rapture before he died; in fact, the context shows that Paul simply follows the prophetic principle of stating the prophecy in the words of those to whom it is spoken.

Jesus did the same thing when He said, "Verily, verily, I say unto you, The hour is coming, and now is, when the dead shall hear the voice of the Son of God: and they that hear shall live."—John 5:25.

These instances could be multiplied. It is an important principle of interpretation. Prophecy is often couched in the words of those to whom it is addressed or to whom it is directly spoken. The fact that God can do this is one of the marvels of prophecy. Still it is in keeping with the nature of God. Eternity is timeless. The time element is often lacking in prophecy. God speaks of future things as though they were already happening. "Babylon is fallen, is fallen" is the way of predicting the future end of the prophetic Babylon. The recognition of this principle will aid materially in understanding all prophecy. "Your redemption" is not the redemption of Peter, James, John, and Andrew, but the redemption of those who will be living when these things begin to come to pass.

"Redemption" here does not mean salvation. Those who are told to look up and lift up their heads are already saved. Redemption is the restoration of everything that is lost; therefore it may be applied to the soul, the body, or the earth. In this case it is the redemption of the body that Jesus means. The same use of the word is found in Romans 8:23: "And not only they, but ourselves also, which have the firstfruits of the Spirit, even we ourselves groan within ourselves, waiting for the adoption, to wit, the redemption of our body." The redemption of the body is the Rapture.

Jesus made two statements concerning His own predictions. First He said: "When these things *begin* to come to pass, then look up, and lift up your heads; for your redemption draweth nigh."—Luke 21:28. Second: "When ye see these things come to pass, know ye that the kingdom of God is nigh at hand."—Luke 21:31. "When ye shall see *all* these things, know that it is near, even at the doors."—Matt. 24:33.

In other words, Jesus said that when these things *begin* to happen, the Rapture is near; when they *all* take place, the kingdom is at hand.

The greater part of Revelation concerns that time between the Rapture and the return of Christ in glory.

REGENERATION

The two great prophetic words are Regeneration and Redemption, although these words are usually applied in such a way as to limit their meaning to that which is now past (but which was once prophecy). Many people who take no stock in prophecy are continually dealing with Bible truths which were once future and were proclaimed before they happened. By type, symbol, and direct statement, God told the whole story in advance. You cannot deal with any part of regeneration or redemption without dealing with prophecy.

The whole story may be expressed in three words: generation, degeneration, regeneration.

Regeneration is the process of restoring to its original *state* something that has gone through the process of degeneration.

The word appears only twice in the Bible. Once it refers to the soul: "Not by works of righteousness which we have done, but according to his mercy he saved us, by the washing of regeneration, and renewing of the Holy Ghost."—Titus 3:5.

Once it refers to the earth: "And Jesus said unto them, Verily I say unto you, That ye which have followed me, in the regeneration when the Son of man shall sit in the throne of his glory, ye also shall sit upon twelve thrones, judging the twelve tribes of Israel."—Matt. 19:28.

Regeneration is applied to the soul because there has been a degeneration, and there must be a restoration to the original perfect state, a washing and a renewing. Regeneration is applied to the earth because it has degenerated far below the perfection of original creation, and it has to be restored.

Regeneration is not applied to the bodies of the saints. They are not to be restored to their original state, for then they would be subject to death again. Instead, they are to be changed and glorified. "It is sown a natural body; it is raised a spiritual body."—I Cor. 15:44. That is something over and beyond regeneration.

REDEMPTION

Redemption is the process of restoring to the original *owner* something that has been lost or sold.

The soul is redeemed; it is restored to God. The body is to be redeemed, restored to man (changed and glorified). The earth is to be redeemed, taken from Satan and restored to the people of God.

The soul: "Christ hath redeemed us from the curse of the law."—Gal. 3:13.

The body: "Waiting for the adoption, to wit, the redemption of our body."—Rom. 8:23.

The earth: "The redemption of the purchased possession."—Eph. 1:14.

A large part of prophecy is concerned with the redemption of the earth, and that includes everything on the earth that can be redeemed. That which cannot be redeemed will be destroyed. Even the human race will be redeemed. "For the earth shall be filled with the knowledge of the glory of the Lord, as the waters cover the sea."—Hab. 2:14.

The Scope of Prophecy

The prophetic method differs from the method of the historian. The historian deals only with what has happened. In prophecy the entire story is in view all at once. The historian records events in the order of their occurrence. The prophets had no such limitations. They could talk about the last things first; not necessarily one thing at a time, but the whole picture at once is the prophetic method. One of the first prophecies to be made is one of the last to be fulfilled: that the seed of the woman would bruise Satan's head.

History is a matter of development; we have to wait and see what comes next. Prophecy is a matter of revelation from One who is as familiar with the end as with the beginning. Prophecy is more concerned with what will happen than with when it will happen. The end is certain; the time is relatively unimportant, for one day is with God as a thousand years. (The relative time is important: that is, the time of fulfillment of one prophecy in reference to another.)

The scope of prophecy is governed by what is to be accomplished. Prophecy began with the fall of man and involves all that was lost by the Fall, plus whatever else may be gained in the process of restoration. Probably the simplest and, at the same time, the most comprehensive statement of the scope of prophecy is found in Rev. 21:5: "And he that sat upon the throne said, Behold, I make all things new."

At the end of the church age God's people will be removed from earth to heaven. This is called the *Rapture*. There will be gathered together all those who have been redeemed by the blood of Christ. They will be the administrators of God's judgments and God's grace during the time of tribulation and judgment.

All redemption involves cleansing. The Bible recognizes only two purging agents: one is blood, the other is fire. People may be redeemed by blood, the blood of Christ, because they can believe in Him; but this physical earth must be redeemed by fire. The fire is coming. It will be sent from heaven and will be administered by the saints from heaven after the Resurrection.

Those things which cannot be redeemed either by blood or by fire must be destroyed; so we are given one section of Revelation which is taken up entirely with the destruction of those things which cannot be redeemed: namely, Satan's church, Satan's man, Satan's kingdom, and Satan himself (Rev. 17 and 18).

COMPLETING THE STORY

Revelation is the last book in the Bible and so brings to a close the Word of God. It is the only book in the Bible which could serve in this capacity. The Gospels do not complete the story of redemption. The book of Acts picks up the story where the Gospels leave it and tells about the founding of the Christian church and the progress of Christianity in the world. But the book of Acts does not finish its story; it closes abruptly, almost in the middle of a sentence. No other book of the New Testament adds anything to the narrative until we come to Revelation.

In Revelation the story continues, beginning at the place where Acts closes and by the use of typical churches, traces the course of the church down through the years to the very time of the Resurrection. The Revelation rehearses the activities of the saints in heaven after the Resurrection and tells what will take place on earth during those days of judgment. It records the second coming of Christ with His saints to reign on the earth and the appearing of the Holy City, the final home of the saved.

Revelation records the last days of *time.* By *time* we mean that period between creation as recorded in Genesis, and the new heaven and the new earth of Revelation. Revelation completes the story that Genesis begins. Genesis tells how the earth became subject to a curse because of sin, and Revelation allows us to see a new earth where there is no more curse. In Genesis we have light coming from the sun. In Revelation the Lord God is the light of the Holy City. In Genesis dominion is given to man, only to pass into the hands of Satan. In Revelation dominion is restored and the saints inherit the earth. In Genesis the tree of life appears, of which a man may eat and live. In Revelation the tree of life is seen growing again, and the leaves are for the healing of the nations. In Genesis Satan appears and is victorious. In Revelation he appears again and is defeated.

Revelation is the last chapter of a love story, for the Bible may be considered as a great love story—the story of the love of God for the world, a love which reached its grand climax when He sent His only begotten Son to die for sinners. This is a great all-consuming love which will stop at nothing until the resources of an infinite God are placed at the disposal of those He loves. The true church is the object of this love. She will become the bride of Christ, the highest, most glorious position in all heaven, the envy of angels, and the brightest gem in God's crown. Revelation tells about the marriage of the Son of God and His Bride, the Church, and the new home with many mansions, where the saved will "live happily ever after."

Music of Revelation

I wonder that someone has not written a great oratorio on Revelation. It would begin with the soft music representing the washing of the waves against the barren rocks on the Isle of Patmos, and would gradually blend into a medley of the crusading hymns of the church as it marches through the centuries, going forth conquering and to conquer.

The Church's one foundation is Jesus Christ her
        Lord;
She is His new creation by water and the word:
From heaven He came and sought her to be His
        holy bride;
With His own blood He bought her, and for her life
        He died.

'Mid toil and tribulation, and tumult of her war,
She waits the consummation of peace for evermore;
Till with the vision glorious her longing eyes are
        blest.
And the great Church victorious shall be the Church
        at rest.

Then the trumpet call, loud and clear, resounds around the world to announce the coming of the Lord to raise the dead and to transform the living saints and to call them to meet the Lord in the air.

When the trumpet of the Lord shall sound,
　　and time shall be no more,
And the morning breaks, eternal, bright and fair;
When the saved of earth shall gather
　　over on the other shore,
And the roll is called up yonder, I'll be there.

On that bright and cloudless morning
　　when the dead in Christ shall rise
And the glory of His resurrection share;
When His chosen ones shall gather
　　to their home beyond the skies,
And the roll is called up yonder, I'll be there.

Then the scene would change and we would see the throne of God, a judgment throne, established in the heavens. This throne is not for the purpose of judging the church that is now in heaven, for that judgment took place on Calvary when Christ paid the penalty of sin. This is the judgment of the nations of the world that have rejected Jesus Christ. It is the purging and renovation of a sin-cursed world. The saints will have a part in this judgment. Paul says, "Do ye not know that the saints shall judge the world?" This is a scene of the saved of all the earth gathered about the throne of God immediately after the Resurrection, and we see a quartet standing before the throne of God: four living ones singing, "Holy, holy, holy, Lord God Almighty, which was, which is, and which is to come."

Holy, holy, holy, Lord God Almighty!
Early in the morning our song shall rise to Thee;
Holy, holy, holy, merciful and mighty!
God in Three Persons, blessed Trinity!

Holy, holy, holy! all the saints adore Thee,
Casting down their golden crowns around the glassy
    sea;
Cherubim and seraphim falling down before Thee,
Which wert, and art, and evermore shalt be.
Holy, holy, holy, Lord God Almighty!
All Thy works shall praise Thy name, in earth, and
    sky, and sea;
Holy, holy, holy, merciful and mighty!
God in Three Persons, blessed Trinity!

This song is answered by the four and twenty elders
who represent all the saved of all the earth singing the new
song of the redeemed. "And they sung a new song, saying,
Thou art worthy to take the book, and to open the seals
thereof: for thou wast slain, and hast redeemed us to God
by thy blood out of every kindred, and tongue, and people,
and nation; and hast made us unto our God kings and priests:
and we shall reign on the earth."—Rev. 5: 9, 10.

I love to tell the story of unseen things above,
Of Jesus and His glory, of Jesus and His love.
I love to tell the story, because I know 'tis true;
It satisfies my longings as nothing else can do.

I love to tell the story, for those who know it best
Seem hungering and thirsting to hear it like the rest.
And when, in scenes of glory, I sing the new, new
    song,
'Twill be the old, old story that I have loved so long.

I love to tell the story, 'twill be my theme in glory
To tell the old, old story of Jesus and His love.

The theme is taken up by the angels around the throne
saying, "Worthy is the Lamb that was slain to receive power,
and riches, and wisdom, and strength, and honour, and glory, and blessing."—Rev. 5: 12. And then the whole chorus
and orchestra would come in on the refrain, as it is record-

ed: "And every creature which is in heaven, and on the
earth, and under the earth, and such as are in the sea, and
all that are in them, heard I saying, Blessing and honour,
and glory, and power, be unto him that sitteth upon the
throne, and unto the Lamb for ever and ever."—Rev. 5: 13.
"And the four living creatures said, AMEN."

> Ten thousand times ten thousand in sparkling
> raiment bright,
> The armies of the ransomed saints throng up the
> steeps of light:
> 'Tis finished! all is finished, their fight with death
> and sin:
> Fling open wide the golden gates, and let the victors
> in!

We would then expect a pause while we prepare for the
second part of the oratorio. The second part begins with
the orchestra playing a song of conquest as the four horsemen leave their posts and ride to battle. We would hear the
rumble of war and thunder, the sea and the waves roaring.
The world is in commotion. There is no peace, there is no
safety, the heavens present fearful sights, and the earth reels
like a drunken man until great buildings topple and mountains are moved into the sea. Brave men hide in the rocks
and call upon God to take their lives in that great day of His
wrath. Then comes, as from an angel, the only ray of hope
to a stricken world—a gospel message. "And I saw another
angel fly in the midst of heaven, having the everlasting gospel to preach unto them that dwell on the earth, and to every
nation, and kindred, and tongue, and people, saying with a
loud voice, Fear God, and give glory to him; for the hour of
his judgment is come: and worship him that made heaven,
and earth, and the sea, and the fountains of waters."—Rev.
14: 6, 7.

The Son of God goes forth to war, a kingly crown
  to gain;
His blood-red banner streams afar: who follows in
  His train?
Who best can drink His cup of woe, triumphant
  over pain,
Who patient bears His cross below, who follows in
  His train.

The martyr first, whose eagle eye could pierce
  beyond the grave,
Who saw his Master in the sky, and called on Him
  to save:
Like Him, with pardon on His tongue in midst of
  mortal pain,
He prayed for them that did the wrong: Who follows
  in His train?

Thousands will respond to the angel's message, although
to be a Christian in that day of Satan's power will mean
death. There have been martyrs in days gone by; there will
be more in days to come. The angel's voice will be a welcome
sound to thousands of distressed and discouraged people, and
they will willingly give their lives that they may enter the
promised "Haven of Rest." "And I heard a voice from heaven
saying unto me, Write, Blessed are the dead which die in
the Lord from henceforth: Yea, saith the Spirit, that they
may rest from their labours; and their works do follow
them."—Rev. 14:13.

My soul, in sad exile was out on life's sea,
So burdened with sin, and distressed,
Till I heard a sweet voice saying, "Make Me your
  choice."
And I entered the Haven of Rest.

I've anchored my soul in the Haven of Rest,
I'll sail the wide seas no more;

The tempest may sweep o'er the wild, stormy deep,
In Jesus I'm safe evermore.

Then we would hear the sounding of seven trumpets announcing the seven judgments of God upon a wicked world.
When the seventh trumpet sounds, the four and twenty elders will fall down upon their faces and sing, "We give thee
thanks, O Lord God Almighty, which art, and wast, and art
to come; because thou hast taken to thee thy great power,
and hast reigned. And the nations were angry, and thy wrath
is come, and the time of the dead, that they should be judged,
and that thou shouldest give reward unto thy servants the
prophets, and to the saints, and them that fear thy name,
small and great; and shouldest destroy them which destroy
the earth."—Rev. 11:17, 18.

Again the scene would change in order that we might
hear the song of those who were saved out of the great tribulation. "A great multitude, which no man could number, of
all nations, and kindreds, and tongues, stood before the
throne, and before the Lamb, clothed with white robes, and
palms in their hands; and cried with a loud voice, saying,
Salvation to our God which sitteth upon the throne, and
unto the Lamb." The angels take up the chorus and say,
"Blessing, and glory and wisdom, and thanksgiving, and
honour, and power, and might, be unto our God for ever and
ever. Amen."—Rev. 7:10, 12.

Then we would see another group, a smaller group this
time, made up of Jews, 144,000 in number, standing on Mount
Zion; while up in heaven an orchestra of harps and a great
organ plays the accompaniment for the 144,000 as they sing
their song of redemption. We would hear the sound of music
and the sound of the voices, but we would not hear the words,
for "no man could learn that song but the 144,000 which
were redeemed from the earth."

Again the scene would change and the note of rejoicing would turn to a note of sorrow as we listen to the wailing over the great city of Babylon. "Alas, alas that great city of Babylon, that mighty city! for in one hour is thy judgment come. And the merchants of the earth shall weep and mourn over her; for no man buyeth their merchandise any more."—Rev. 18:10, 11. "Alas, alas that great city, that was clothed in fine linen, and purple, and scarlet, and decked with gold, and precious stones, and pearls! For in one hour so great riches is come to nought."—Rev. 18:16, 17.

"Almost persuaded," harvest is past!
"Almost persuaded," doom comes at last!
"Almost" cannot avail;
"Almost" is but to fail!
Sad, sad, that bitter wail,
"Almost, but lost."

Although the destruction of Babylon brings sorrow to the merchants of the earth, it produces great rejoicing in heaven because it means that the nations are brought to the feet of Jesus and henceforth He will reign supremely on the earth. And so we would listen to the "Hallelujah Chorus" as the voice of a great multitude and as the voice of many waters and as the voice of many thunderings singing, "Alleluia: for the Lord God omnipotent reigneth." Then would come the song of the victor returning from battle to claim his bride, and we would hear the strains of the song "Here Comes the Bride" and the voices from heaven saying, "Let us be glad and rejoice, and give honour to him: for the marriage of the Lamb is come, and his wife hath made herself ready." —Rev. 19:7.

He comes, He comes, Lo! Jesus comes,
    The promised King of glory;
The Hope of all the ages past,
    Foretold in song and story;

He comes the pris'ner to release;
   He comes, and wars and tumults cease;
He comes to reign, the Prince of Peace,
   Lo! Jesus comes.
Then sing, O sing, ye ransomed, sing hallelujah!
Praise His name whom angels in glory adore;
Hail, all hail the conquering Lion of Judah!
He shall reign forever and evermore.

We would hear the soft music played during the wedding supper, and then we would be taken in song to be given one glorious view of the Holy City "that comes down from God out of heaven prepared as a bride for her husband." The oratorio would close with the singing of "The Holy City."

THE STRUCTURE

Revelation has a structure. It is not a series of disconnected prophecies. It is not a pile of stones. It is a well-designed building. If you were going to buy and furnish a house, the first thing you would be interested in is the floor-plan. You would want to know how the rooms are arranged; then you could plan the appropriate furniture for each room. Revelation is like a well-planned furnished house. Each room has its proper furniture. But in order to understand the details, you must first know the ground plan. The first essential is to put the right events in the right place.

There are seven main divisions, represented on the chart by seven squares. You will notice that three of these squares are parallel. The parallel squares indicate that the events of those sections occur during the same period of time. It has been recognized by many students that there are certain portions of Revelation which seem to run parallel or duplicate each other. First we will discover what sections are parallel, and then we must find the reason for it.

To do this we will consider Revelation as a building with various rooms and the chart as a blueprint of the floor-

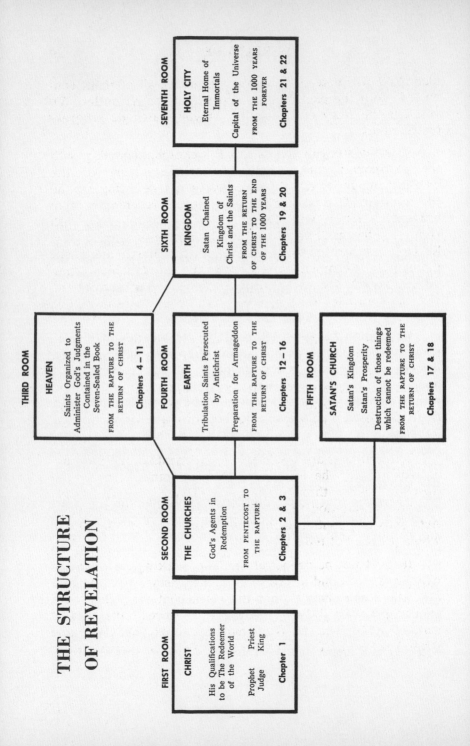

THE STRUCTURE
OF REVELATION

FIRST ROOM

CHRIST

His Qualifications
to be The Redeemer
of the World

Prophet   Priest
Judge   King

Chapter 1

SECOND ROOM

THE CHURCHES

God's Agents in
Redemption

FROM PENTECOST TO
THE RAPTURE

Chapters 2 & 3

THIRD ROOM

HEAVEN

Saints Organized to
Administer God's Judgments
Contained in the
Seven-Sealed Book

FROM THE RAPTURE TO THE
RETURN OF CHRIST

Chapters 4 – 11

FOURTH ROOM

EARTH

Tribulation Saints Persecuted
by Antichrist

Preparation for Armageddon

FROM THE RAPTURE TO THE
RETURN OF CHRIST

Chapters 12 – 16

FIFTH ROOM

SATAN'S CHURCH

Satan's Kingdom

Satan's Prosperity

Destruction of those things
which cannot be redeemed

FROM THE RAPTURE TO THE
RETURN OF CHRIST

Chapters 17 & 18

SIXTH ROOM

KINGDOM

Satan Chained

Kingdom of
Christ and the Saints

FROM THE RETURN
OF CHRIST TO THE END
OF THE 1000 YEARS

Chapters 19 & 20

SEVENTH ROOM

HOLY CITY

Eternal Home of
Immortals

Capital of the Universe

FROM THE 1000 YEARS
FOREVER

Chapters 21 & 22

plan. You will note there are seven rooms, all of them connected, with the exception of one which has no outlet. We
will tell the story of Revelation as you watch its progress
on the chart.

It is the story of Christ and His church, beginning with
the first church, and revealing the whole history of the
church through its earthly experiences: its gathering around
the throne of God to continue the work of redemption from
heaven, its return with Christ to the earth, its reign with
Him for a thousand years, and its final home—the Holy City.
Revelation is written to the church, for the church, and about
the church. It completes the story of the church which began
in the Gospels. Its whole purpose is to tell the future of the
church—on earth, in heaven, on earth again with Christ, and
in the Holy City forever.

Revelation mentions the Jews only if they become Christians. It tells of Antichrist only in his relationship to the
church. Such matters as the return of the Jews and the kingdom of David are omitted. It begins and ends with an appeal to the church to heed its words. It is the one book that
is specifically appointed to be read and studied in the
churches.

The churches are God's appointed agents in the program
of redemption. The history of that program begins in the
Gospels, follows through the book of Acts, and then ends
abruptly. Revelation takes up the story where the book of
Acts ends and continues it through to the completion of the
whole program of redemption.

It must not be supposed that the work of the churches
will come to an end at the time of the Resurrection. At that
time the scene changes, but the work continues. Our work
is not finished until the whole world is restored to its original
state of perfection. This is the teaching throughout the whole
Bible. Paul said, "Do ye not know that the saints will judge

the world?"—I Cor. 6:2. We are told that Christ must reign until He has put all enemies under His feet, and that the saints will reign with Him. Not only the preaching of the gospel, but the whole program of redemption has been committed to the churches.

The First Room

CHAPTER 1

In the first room of our structure we see Christ, the Redeemer and principal character in the drama that is about to begin. It is not so much a portrait of Christ as to His actual appearance as it is a picture of His qualifications to be the Redeemer of the world. He is the hero of the story. His qualifications are these:

PROPHET. He is called the Faithful Witness. Jesus had much to say about the future, much more than is usually realized. He told His disciples that He would come again to receive them; that He would come in glory with all His holy angels with Him; that He would come to reward His servants and punish His enemies; that He would come in a day of distress and judge the nations.

PRIEST. Redemption must include atonement and so requires a Saviour. Christ is the first begotten of the dead. He stands in the midst of the candlesticks. He is clothed with a priestly robe and His hair is white. These qualifications refer to the priestly and sacrificial work of Christ.

KING. He has eyes like fire and feet like brass, a voice as the sound of many waters, a sharp sword, and a countenance as the sun. One of the duties of a king is to sit in judgment. This requires two special characteristics: (1) perfect knowledge, insight, the ability to read even the thoughts of the hearts; and (2) the power to enforce punishment.

Whenever Christ is mentioned throughout the book, some part of this first chapter is repeated. This makes it easy to identify Christ even though He is called an angel. The saints also have identifying marks by which they may be recognized.

The Second Room
CHAPTERS 2 AND 3

Now the scene changes and the subject changes. This room is devoted to the churches. These seven portraits constitute not only a picture, but a history of the churches throughout the ages.

The churches are God's servants and agents in the program of redemption and the principal characters in the following story.

This second room has three outlets. One door opens downwards from the wicked woman, Jezebel, of the Thyatira Church, to the scarlet woman of chapter seventeen.

Another door opens into a room which features Antichrist and the experiences of those who are left behind at the Rapture.

The third door leads to the room which we will enter first, the one which shows the scene in heaven immediately after the Resurrection.

The Third Room
CHAPTERS 4–11

You will notice that there are three rooms occupying the same space as to time. The events in these three rooms are happening at the same time. Of course they have to be related one after the other, and that might make it seem as though one followed the other. But as you will see, the same items appear in all three, only the viewpoint is different. For instance, the 6th chapter relates that the saints are persecuted and killed, but it is only in the 13th chapter that we find out how they are killed and by whom.

At the close of the church age "the Lord himself shall descend from heaven with a shout, with the voice of the archangel, and with the trump of God: and the dead in Christ shall rise first: then we which are alive and remain shall be caught up together with them in the clouds, to meet the Lord in the air: and so shall we ever be with the Lord."—I Thess. 4:16, 17. No longer are the saints divided into churches. The church on earth was God's army, but churches do not go to heaven; only individuals are saved. After the Rapture the army of God will again be divided into groups to carry on the work of redemption.

These groups are called by names that seem strange when we first read them, but there is a reason for each designation. The saints are divided into groups called Elders, Living Ones, Horsemen, and Angels (messengers). Each separate group has its own task to perform in the great events of that day. These duties are the preaching of the gospel from heaven to every kindred, tongue, people, and nation. This will be accompanied by judgments: peace taken from the earth, famine, pestilence, falling stars, and earthquakes. Out of it will come a great multitude of saved people from every nation, including the Jews. These are known as Tribulation Saints.

The trumpets will be blown which send forth upon the earth the seven last plagues, and then we arrive at the exit door which leads directly to the second coming of Christ when the kingdoms of the earth become the kingdoms of our Lord. As we pass through this door, we see the lightnings and we hear the voices and thunderings, the earthquake, and the great hail. These are the things that will accompany the return of Christ.

The Fourth Room

CHAPTERS 12–16

Now we must retrace our steps and go back to the Church Room to go through the second doorway (chapters 12 to 16), in order that we may follow the experiences of those who are left behind upon the earth at the time of the Rapture. Now the scene changes completely; even the language changes from the literal to the symbolical. In the Upper Room the viewpoint of the writer was as one in heaven looking down upon the earth and seeing the things which happen as a result of the activities in heaven. Now the viewpoint of the writer is as one upon the earth. The man-child is caught up into heaven just as the saints were caught up at the Rapture; but this time we do not go with them into heaven, but we remain upon the earth to read the story of the woman who was left behind to face the persecution of Antichrist. Antichrist was not pictured in the Upper Room because he does not come out of heaven. He rises from the earth to become the leader of a large group of nations. Now we see the gospel being preached by angels from heaven, and finally we see Antichrist marshaling the armies of the world against the Lord.

Now we come to the same scene that we witnessed near the exit of the Upper Room—those things which will happen at the return of Christ: the voices and thunders and lightnings, the earthquake and the great hail.

The Fifth Room

CHAPTERS 17 AND 18

Once more we must retrace our steps to the Church Room, for there sprang up within one of the churches a false church, conceived by Satan, which existed through the years and finally became Satan's instrument in the persecution of the Tribulation Saints. In this room there will be revealed to us the mystery of evil and its final destruction. There is no outlet to this room. Everything there will be destroyed.

The Sixth Room

CHAPTERS 19 AND 20

We now enter the Kingdom Room (chapters 19 and 20) where we are allowed to gaze upon the climax of the ages, but before the revelation of Christ to the earth, there is a ceremony in heaven which involves the saints. Now their work as Elders and Living Ones and Horsemen and Angels is past, and they find themselves, for the first time, all united in one group, the Bride of Christ. It is as His Bride that they will reign with Him during the Millennium and forever.

The Seventh Room

CHAPTERS 21 AND 22

At last we enter the final and most glorious room, the very sanctuary of God. Here is pictured in detail the eternal home of the saints. But the details are read with difficulty, for eye has not seen, nor ear heard, neither has it entered the heart of man, the glories that God has reserved for that day.

Chapter One

THE REDEEMER

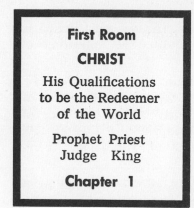

First Room

CHRIST

His Qualifications
to be the Redeemer
of the World

Prophet Priest
Judge King

Chapter 1

The first chapter is probably the most important one in the book. It contains the keys that unlock all the other rooms. If you master this first chapter, the rest of the book will be easy to understand.

It tells what the book is, where it came from, what it is about, whom it is about, how to identify the various characters. It gives the outline of the book, illustrates the rules of interpretation, and pronounces a special blessing on those who give heed to it at the time of fulfillment.

Revelation 1

1 The Revelation of Jesus Christ, which God gave unto him, to shew unto his servants things which must shortly come to pass; and he sent and signified it by his angel unto his servant John:

2 Who bare record of the word of God, and of the testimony of Jesus Christ, and of all things that he saw.

3 Blessed is he that readeth, and they that hear the words of this prophecy, and keep those things which are written therein: for the time is at hand.

THE REVELATION OF JESUS CHRIST. The word "revelation" means an unveiling. It could mean that this book is itself a revelation of Christ, or it could mean that it is about the revelation of Christ, His second coming. Just as John put the whole gospel in one verse—John 3:16—so he puts the whole of Revelation in one verse: "Behold, he cometh with clouds; and every eye shall see him, and they also which pierced him: and all kindreds of the earth shall wail because of him. Even so, Amen."—Rev. 1:7.

Although the word "apokalupsis" is used in more than one sense in the New Testament, its connection with the return of Christ is quite striking. The same construction is used in I Peter 1:13 to refer directly to the appearing of Christ at His return.

"Wherefore gird up the loins of your mind, be sober, and hope to the end for the grace that is to be brought unto you at the *revelation of Jesus Christ.*" Other instances of the same meaning given to "apokalupsis" are I Peter 1:7; I Cor. 1:7; II Thess. 1:7.[1] It is translated "appearing," "coming," and "revealed."

The traditional name of the book is "The Revelation of Saint John the Divine." This is the name found in your Bibles. However, the inspired name is found in the first verse: "The Revelation of Jesus Christ." It has nothing to do with John except that John was the writer. The revelation of Christ is the second coming of Christ. The heavens will part and He will be revealed to the world. "Behold, he cometh with clouds; and every eye shall see him." That is His revelation. I have in my library a book called *The Last of the Mohicans*. That book is not the last of the Mohicans. It is merely written about them, so this book is called "The Revela-

---

1. "That the trial of your faith, being much more precious than of gold that perisheth, though it be tried with fire, might be found unto praise and honour and glory at the appearing of Jesus Christ" (I Pet. 1:7). "So that ye come behind in no gift; waiting for the coming of our Lord Jesus Christ" (I Cor. 1:7). "And to you who are troubled rest with us, when the Lord Jesus shall be revealed from heaven with his mighty angels" (II Thess. 1:7).

tion," not because it is in itself a revelation, but because it is about the revelation of Christ.

This book, The Revelation of Jesus Christ, is a special gift from God through Christ to the church. The matter of His second coming was very dear to Jesus. "When the Son of man shall come in his glory" was His favorite topic of conversation. Nearly all the parables were told to illustrate some phase of this event. Now it is possible for Him to give His servants the complete story of those wonderful times leading up to and following His return.

SHORTLY COME TO PASS. Time is relative. A one-minute pause between words in a lecture would be unbearably long, but a thousand years is a brief time in eternity. Revelation closes a history that began with creation. Although the events recorded may cover a period of two thousand years or more, still, as compared to the whole of time, they are things which must shortly come to pass.

A PECULIAR BLESSING. A special blessing is pronounced upon those who read or teach this book as well as upon those who take its teachings to heart. The reason given is that the time is at hand. This is literally true in two ways.

First. Revelation is a prophecy of things "which must shortly come to pass." This does not mean that everything in the book was to take place immediately after John saw the vision. But the time was at hand for the beginning of a series of events.

The first church of Revelation is the church that was just beginning to leave its first love. Therefore, the first part of this prophecy was being fulfilled even as John wrote. The time was at hand.

Second. Sometimes prophecy is written for a given time. Some portions of the Bible are not meant to be understood until the time of their fulfillment. All of Revelation except that part which deals with the churches (chapters 1–3) is still future. Martin Luther thought Revelation should not be in the Bible. It had no message for him. It was not understood in his day. The time was not at hand. But blessed is he that readeth and they that hear when the time is at hand. This time is mentioned in Daniel: "But thou, O Daniel, shut up the words, and seal the book, even to the time of the end. . . . Go thy way, Daniel: for the words are closed up and sealed till the time of the end. . . . None of the wicked shall understand; but the wise shall understand."—Dan. 12: 4, 9, 10.

At the time of the end when the words are unsealed, then the wise shall understand. Then the time is at hand. Down through the ages, the greater part of Revelation has been sealed. It has been a closed book to the most consecrated Bible students. Today the seal is broken, the book is open, the wise shall understand. "The time is at hand," and "Blessed is he that readeth, and they that hear."—Rev. 1:3.

No other book pronounces such a blessing. No other people could obtain such a blessing but those who are living when the time is at hand for the understanding of the book and the fulfillment of its prophecies.

Revelation 1

4 John to the seven churches which are in Asia: Grace be unto you, and peace, from him which is, and which was, and which is to come; and from the seven Spirits which are before his throne;

5 And from Jesus Christ, who is the faithful witness, and the first begotten of the dead, and the prince of the kings of the earth. Unto him that loved us, and washed us from our sins in his own blood,

6 And hath made us kings and priests unto God and his Father; to him be glory and dominion for ever and ever. Amen.

7 Behold, he cometh with clouds; and every eye shall see him, and they also which pierced him: and all

kindreds of the earth shall wail because of him. Even so, Amen.

Revelation is addressed to the seven churches in Asia. Seven is an all-inclusive number. It shows the subject in its entirety, from beginning to end. It is the number of completeness. The seven churches mentioned here were not the largest or most important churches of their day. They were chosen not because of their prominence but because of their representative nature. It is even doubtful if the churches addressed were entirely like the description given. The picture seems to be more concerned with the future churches than with the typical churches of Asia. These seven churches are types of seven kinds of churches and types of the church in seven periods of church history.

It seems almost impossible that churches so different could exist so close together. Smyrna—poverty-stricken, persecuted almost unto death—is only a hundred miles from Laodicea, a church so wealthy that it thought it had need of nothing. These churches were all in a radius of eighty miles.

A church harboring a wicked element called Jezebel, so bad that it is threatened with the gravest punishment, exists next to a church so good that not one thing is said against it. There is no doubt that the churches had elements in them that corresponded to the pictures painted by John, but the picture was itself a prophecy of what the outcome of that particular situation would be if it were not corrected.

These are true types and follow the law of types. A type is never like the antitype in all respects. It does not have to be in order to be a type. It is a type if it has certain features like the antitype. In this case more attention seems to be paid to the fulfillment than to the type. The thing the church represents is described in detail rather than the church itself.

If they are types, of what are they types?

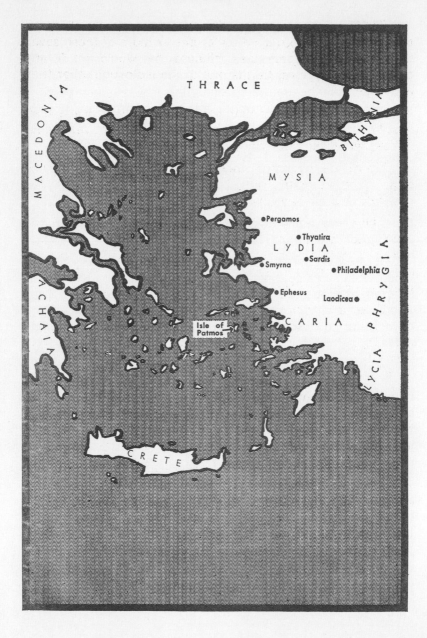

FIRST, they are types of seven kinds of churches. All churches could be grouped under one or more of these seven heads. There are some false religions that would not fit any of these descriptions; that is one of the indications that they are false.

There are churches that have only begun to leave their first love. The defection is so slight that it does not yet appear in their work, their doctrine, or their earnestness.

There are churches undergoing persecution and hardship. They are found only in certain countries today, but somewhere there have always been such churches.

There are churches that have allowed the deeds of the Nicolaitans to become doctrines. They are "churchy." Their leaders consider themselves great churchmen. They are taking in the world and trying to be great world leaders, but they are "blind leaders of the blind."

There are churches that have been taken over almost entirely by the enemy and have become even morally corrupt. There are churches that have partially freed themselves from these corrupt practices, but only in part. They still cling to the forms of paganism and are spiritually dead.

There are churches that have been so completely filled by the Spirit that they have entered open doors all over the world and have earned for themselves the promise of immunity from the time of trouble that is in store for the world.

There are churches that have become so saturated with unbelief that they are poor, blind, and naked spiritually, although rich in worldly goods.

SECOND, they are types of the dominant church in each age. Prophetically, these churches represent seven periods of church history. They form a history of the church. Each church is a type of the church of a certain period. It shows the dominating characteristics of that period.

Ephesus was the church of the first love that was beginning to grow cold.

Smyrna represents the time of world-wide persecution
which was to follow.

Pergamos notes the beginning of Romanism. "Nicolaitans" suggests priestly conquerors of the people. It marks
the beginning of the division of a common brotherhood into
priests and laity. As early as the Ephesus period we note
the deeds of the Nicolaitans. They now become doctrines, and
the church is definitely taking on the form of the Romish
system.

Thyatira sees Romanism thoroughly established. It
is the church of the Dark Ages. The prophecy concerning
Jezebel is fulfilled in the 17th and 18th chapters. She is the
Scarlet Woman of Babylon.

Sardis pictures a reformed church, a great improvement
over Thyatira, yet far from perfect. It made a great and lasting name for itself but was sadly lacking in evangelism and
spiritual warmth. It held the truth but remained very formal.

Philadelphia brings us to the greatest period of church
history: a time when revivals swept over whole countries,
when the doors were opened into the mission fields of all
lands. But the devil sows his tares; leaven is mixed into the
gospel meal. A change comes over the church and the world,
and the Philadelphia period passes into that of the Laodiceans.

Laodicea represents the church of the last days. The
Bible has much to say about this period of church history.

When a certain type of church once starts, it continues
to the end; so in the end time there will be all kinds of churches in the world. These seven periods of church history are
the periods when each of these seven kinds of churches has
its beginning.

SEVEN. We will encounter this number many times, always with the same meaning. It should be noted that Revelation is consistent with the rest of the Bible in its use of numbers and other highly descriptive words. If a meaning or usage is determined here, it may be equally applied to all the prophetic Scriptures. Conversely, if the meaning of a number or symbol is determined anywhere in the Bible, it may be applied here. There is nothing that more thoroughly demonstrates the unity of the Scriptures than the study of prophecy.

Seven has been called the number of perfection; this is true only in the sense of completeness. There is no moral or spiritual quality involved. Satan has seven heads. It involves seven sides of one thing, which constitutes the whole, or seven events which make up the whole story.

It may be illustrated by the week. There are seven days in a week—never any more. The whole week is complete in the seven. Then a new week starts. Seven always shows the thing in its completeness. Nothing more is added after the seven. Something new starts. So when the number seven appears, you are dealing with one subject in its fullness. The seven churches show the whole story of the church on earth, from beginning to end. There is nothing after the Laodicean Church. That brings us to the end. No new movement or new kind of church will rise. All that is done in this age will be done by these seven churches. New movements and religions outside of these seven are false. There will be many of them in the last days. Jesus called them deceivers.

The Seven Spirits. The Holy Spirit is the Comforter. He is God present in the church. Isaiah 11:1–3 speaks of the Spirit of the Lord as the Spirit of (1) wisdom, (2) understanding, (3) counsel, (4) might, (5) knowledge, (6) fear of the Lord, (7) quick understanding (refreshing).

THREE. The number three is especially prominent when redemption is involved. The triangle is the smallest unit of geometry. God is revealed as Father, Son, and Holy Ghost.

John's salutation is from

A. *God the Father,* (1) "which is, and (2) which was, and (3) which is to come."

B. *The Holy Spirit.* "The seven Spirits which are before his throne."

C. *Jesus Christ,* "who is (1) the faithful witness, and (2) the first begotten of the dead, and (3) the prince of the kings of the earth."

"Unto him that (1) loved us, and (2) washed us from our sins in his own blood, and (3) made us kings and priests unto God and his Father; to him be glory and dominion for ever and ever."

THREE TENSES OF REDEMPTION

REDEMPTION	PAST	PRESENT	FUTURE
Christ In God Rev. 1:4	Which Was Col. 1:15–17 John 8:58	Which Is Heb. 7:25	Which Is To Come Rev. 1:7
Jesus Christ Rev. 1:5	The Faithful Witness John 14:1–3 John 8:14	First Begotten of the Dead Col. 1:18–20	Prince of the Kings of the Earth Rev. 19:16 Matt. 25:31, 32 I Cor. 15:24, 25
Unto Him That Rev. 1:5	Loved Us Gal. 2:20 John 3:16	Washed Us From Our Sins In His Own Blood Heb. 9:14 Heb. 7:25	Made Us Kings and Priests I Pet. 2:9 Luke 19:17 Rev. 5:10 Rev. 20:4 Rev. 2:26, 27 Rev. 22:5
Write Rev. 1:19	The Things Which Thou Hast Seen (Christ) Rev. 1:12–18	The Things Which Are (The Churches) Rev. 2 and 3	The Things Which Shall Be Hereafter (After the Church) Rev. 4 to 22

Revelation is in three main sections. This general outline is stated in verse 19: "Write the things (1) which thou hast seen [the vision of Christ], and (2) the things which are [the churches], and (3) the things which shall be hereafter [after the church age]."

Redemption is always expressed in three tenses when the complete process is in view. It has its roots in the past, it is a present process, and its consummation is in the future.

Past: "For God so loved the world, that he gave his only begotten Son,

Present: "That whosoever believeth in him

Future: "Should not perish, but have everlasting life." The gospel without prophecy is an emaciated gospel.

THE FAITHFUL WITNESS. It seems as if the first seven verses were written last, after John had seen the vision. They were written by one who had already beheld the scenes that follow. Sixty years before, John had given up his own work for the service of Christ. He had listened as Jesus told of the glory that was His before the world was, of the blessedness of the coming kingdom, of the mansions that He would prepare. And then John had seen his hopes shattered when Jesus bowed His head and died. But that was only the first of a long series of disappointments and discouragements. One by one the companions of John had lost their lives in the service of Christ, and now John was left, and he had been banished to the Isle of Patmos to die.

I wonder if John in those dreary days did not become discouraged and question whether Jesus had not painted too glowing a picture of the future; if He were really coming again as He said; if there ever could be a Kingdom of Heaven on earth; if after all it had been worth while. And then came this vision. John saw Jesus in His glory. He saw how, out of the imperfect churches of all ages, God was gathering a great company of saints. He saw thrones set up and judgment given to the saints of the Most High. He saw the judgments of God and the end of the wicked.

He saw the heavens open and Christ appear to the world with a multitude of white-robed saints. He heard the angel in accents of victory repeat the solemn words of Christ upon the cross: "It is finished." He saw his Lord actually reigning upon the throne of David, with all nations serving Him. He saw the Holy City—the New Jerusalem—as a bride adorned for her husband, and containing the many mansions that Jesus had promised, and John said, "All that He said is true; He is the Faithful Witness."

The Coming of Christ

Revelation 1

7 Behold, he cometh with clouds; and every eye shall see him, and they also which pierced him: and all kindreds of the earth shall wail because of him. Even so, Amen.

This is the key to the book and its subject. Note the attitude of the world toward the return of Christ: "And all the kindreds of the earth shall wail because of him." A man's inner relationship to Christ can usually be determined by his attitude toward the second coming of Christ. A person who really loves Christ rejoices in the hope of seeing Him. There is a reason for a man's dreading or hating the coming of Christ.

He will come with clouds. Compare Acts 1:9–11: "A cloud received him out of their sight," and they were told that He would "so come in like manner" as they had seen Him go. He will come with all His saints. They will be in white robes. It may be that the clouds, instead of being clouds of vapor, will be clouds of white-robed saints.

Revelation 1

9 I John, who also am your brother, and companion in tribulation, and in the kingdom and patience of Jesus Christ, was in the isle that is called Patmos, for the word of God, and for the testimony of Jesus Christ.

10 I was in the Spirit on the Lord's day, and heard behind me a great voice, as of a trumpet,

11 Saying, I am Alpha and Omega, the first and the last: and, What thou seest, write in a book, and send it unto the seven churches which are in Asia; unto Ephesus, and unto Smyrna, and unto Pergamos, and unto Thyatira, and unto Sardis, and unto Philadelphia, and unto Laodicea.

THE LORD'S DAY

"I was in the Spirit on the Lord's day." The *Pulpit Commentary* says, "The expression occurs here only in the New Testament, and beyond all reasonable doubt it means 'on Sunday.' This is, therefore, the earliest use of the phrase in this sense." However, this vision would require more than one day, and there is no particular reason for mentioning the day of the week or for using a name which had never been applied to Sunday before.

Dr. Seiss says: "What is meant by this *Lord's day?* Some answer, *Sunday*—the first day of the week; but I am not satisfied with this explanation. Sunday belongs indeed to the Lord, but the Scriptures nowhere call it 'the Lord's day.' None of the Christian writings, for 100 years after Christ, ever call it 'the Lord's day.'

"But there is a *'Day of the Lord'* largely treated of by prophets, apostles, and fathers, the meaning of which is abundantly clear and settled. It is that day in which, Isaiah says, men shall hide in the rocks for fear of the Lord, and for the glory of His majesty—the day which Joel describes as the day of destruction from the Almighty, when the Lord shall roar out of Zion, and utter His voice from Jerusalem, and the heavens and the earth shall shake—the day to which the closing chapter of Malachi refers as the day that shall burn as an oven, and in which the Sun of Righteousness shall arise with healing in His wings—the day which Paul proclaimed from Mars' Hill as that in which God will judge the world, concerning which he so earnestly exhorted the Thessalonians, and which was not to come until after a great apostasy from the faith, and the ripening of the wicked for destruction—the day in the which, Peter says, the heavens shall be changed, the elements melt, the earth burn, and all present orders of things give way to new heavens and a new earth—even 'the day for which all other days were made.'

"And in that day I understand John to say, he in some sense was. In the mysteries of prophetic rapport, which the Scriptures describe as 'in Spirit,' and which Paul declared inexplicable, he was caught out of himself, and out of his proper place and time, and stationed amid the stupendous scenes of the great day of God, and made to see the actors in them, and to look upon them transpiring before his eyes, that he might write what he saw, and give it to the Churches. This is what I understand by his being in 'the Spirit on the Lord's day.' "

Weymouth translates: "In spirit, I found myself present on the day of the Lord."—Rev. 1: 10.

John was banished to the Isle of Patmos, a rocky island off the coast of Turkey, because of his preaching the Word of God. The Greek could mean that he deliberately went to the Isle of Patmos for the purpose of receiving the testimony of Jesus and the Word of God. This book is the testimony of Jesus. "The testimony of Jesus is the spirit of prophecy."—Rev. 19: 10.

However, this expression is used twice in Revelation, meaning "because of" witnessing to the Word. "I saw under the altar the souls of them that were slain for the word of God, and for the testimony which they held."—Rev. 6: 9. "And

I saw the souls of them that were beheaded for the witness of Jesus, and for the word of God."—Rev. 20: 4.

A Portrait of Christ

Revelation 1

12 And I turned to see the voice that spake with me. And being turned, I saw seven golden candlesticks;

13 And in the midst of the seven candlesticks one like unto the Son of man, clothed with a garment down to the foot, and girt about the paps with a golden girdle.

14 His head and his hairs were white like wool, as white as snow; and his eyes were as a flame of fire;

15 And his feet like unto fine brass, as if they burned in a furnace; and his voice as the sound of many waters.

16 And he had in his right hand seven stars: and out of his mouth went a sharp twoedged sword: and his countenance was as the sun shineth in his strength.

17 And when I saw him, I fell at his feet as dead. And he laid his right hand upon me, saying unto me, Fear not; I am the first and the last:

18 I am he that liveth, and was dead; and, behold, I am alive for evermore, Amen; and have the keys of hell and of death.

19 Write the things which thou hast seen, and the things which are, and the things which shall be hereafter;

20 The mystery of the seven stars which thou sawest in my right hand, and the seven golden candlesticks. The seven stars are the angels of the seven churches: and the seven candlesticks which thou sawest are the seven churches.

There is not a single word of description of Jesus in the Gospels. We have not the slightest bit of information about His personal appearance outside of the prophecy of Isaiah: "He hath no form nor comeliness; and when we shall see him, there is no beauty that we should desire him."—Isa. 53: 2.

The only attempt at a portrait of Christ portrays Him not in His humiliation but in His glory. It is not, however, a picture of Christ as He will appear when He comes again.

It is rather His likeness in His present work. Of course some of the features will be visible when He returns, especially eyes as a flame of fire and the sharp sword (Rev. 19: 12, 15).

You will notice the characteristics of a Prophet, Priest, King, and Judge.

> *As a Prophet,* He is the faithful witness and the author of "the words of this prophecy."

> *As a Priest,* He wears the priestly attire of the robe and the girdle.

> *As a Judge,* He has eyes as a flame of fire and feet as burnished brass.

> *As a King,* He has a voice as the sound of many waters and a two-edged sword.

It would be worth while to ponder this description. It holds the key to our understanding of much of Revelation. It illustrates some of the most useful rules of interpretation. It shows the difference between symbols and heavenly or spiritual things. Here we have our first experience with the language of prophecy, a language which we will be using throughout the book.

Symbols are used in connection with earthly things, not heavenly things. I am using the term "symbols" in a restricted sense. Symbols are not like the things they symbolize, or if they are, it is accidental. A head of gold or a lion is entirely different in substance from the empire of Nebuchadnezzar. Children of the kingdom have no resemblance to seed sown in the ground. Anything can be made a symbol simply by declaring it so. No resemblance is necessary or implied.

The Bible is full of similes—"a rhetorical figure, expressing comparison, or likeness by the use of such terms as *like, as, so,* etc."—Dictionary

A simile is not a symbol and is not to be interpreted as a symbol. It is merely a comparison because there are no words to express the idea directly. "The desert shall rejoice and blossom as the rose." "Though your sins be as scarlet." "His eyes were as a flame of fire, and his feet like unto fine brass." These are not symbols. They are literal language using similes.

There are only two symbols in the description. They are concerning earthly things and they are both explained. "The mystery of the seven stars which thou sawest in my right hand, and the seven golden candlesticks. The seven stars are the angels of the seven churches: and the seven candlesticks which thou sawest are the seven churches." —Rev. 1: 20.

John saw Jesus in glory and described in earthly words what he saw. It is just as literal as words can make it. Sometimes a description of things in heaven sounds like a symbol because of the difficulty in finding something that has a resemblance to its spiritual counterpart. It is difficult, sometimes, to translate even from one language to another where customs and modes of living are different.

Missionaries were trying to translate some of our songs into the language of a native tribe in deepest Africa, where there was no home life. The natives lived in mud huts, dirty and infested. The missionaries were trying to translate "Home, sweet home." There was no word for home.

Do you think you could express the glories of the resurrected Lord in words of our vocabulary and do it justice? That is what John was told to do. He uses similes. He used the nearest possible corresponding earthly words. Only the Holy Spirit can reveal the depth of their meaning.

We must understand God's methods and how He uses words. If we insist on making symbols out of heavenly language and applying them to things on earth, not even the Holy Spirit can help us much.

ONE LIKE UNTO THE SON OF MAN. "One like unto the Son of man" is a name of Christ. This is not a portrait of Christ in the sense that it reveals His personal appearance; that would be quite impossible, for we have no words in this world with which to describe heavenly things.

For instance, in one chapter Jesus is spoken of as a Lion and also as a Lamb slain. He could not look like both. There is no reference here to His personal appearance. It means that He brings to this work of redemption and judgment the qualifications of a slain lamb and a kingly lion.

This description of Jesus is a character sketch showing His qualifications and equipment for the work that He is about to do, based upon that which He has done.

The elements divide themselves into two parts: comparable generally to the Lamb (Saviour) and the Lion (King), characteristics of Christ. The first three items refer to the past. They show something already done. They are not mentioned again. The others refer to the work that Christ is now doing or will do when He comes again. They are all mentioned again in succeeding chapters. The first time Christ came, He came as Saviour to give His life a ransom for many. Out of that work of redemption come the first three items of this character study.

CHRIST THE SAVIOUR. The features of this part of the portrait are as follows: the long garment, the golden girdle, and the white hair.

The garment and the girdle. These are priestly attire. God instructed Moses concerning the garments of the high priest in these words: "And these are the garments which they shall make; a breastplate, and an ephod, and a robe, and a broidered coat, a mitre, and a girdle: and they shall make holy garments for Aaron thy brother, and his sons, that he may minister unto me in the priest's office."—Ex. 28:4.

White hair. "His head and his hairs were white like wool, as white as snow." The white hair is in striking contrast to the rest of the picture. Feet like burnished brass, countenance as the sun, voice like the sound of many waters, do not suggest white hair. It cannot mean old age. Although Christ was before the world was, still He is neither old nor feeble. No one gets old in heaven. Jesus was a young man at the time of His resurrection.

Everything else in the picture is in keeping with youth, freshness, and energy. This feature of the vision amazed John and he had difficulty in expressing it. "White like wool, as white as snow." The American Standard Version is still more intense: "White as *white* wool, white as snow." It seems that no words could express the whiteness of that hair.

When the Nazis were trying to annihilate all Jews, some German soldiers came upon a Jewish boy in a field. They asked him where his father was and he refused to tell. The soldiers made a cross, nailed the boy to it, and set it up in the ground. The boy was discovered and rescued, but the reporter said his hair was as white as the driven snow.

There is only one thing that will make a man's hair turn suddenly white. That is intense suffering—mental, spiritual, physical—such as Christ suffered in the garden and on the cross. We see in this picture no mark of the nails or the thorns. We see no spear-pierced side. We see only the hair, once as black as the raven's wing, now as white as snow. Only eternity can reveal to us the magnitude of the suffering of Christ for us.

> See, from His head, His hands, His feet,
> Sorrow and love flow mingled down;
> Did e'er such love and sorrow meet,
> Or thorns compose so rich a crown?

EYES AS A FLAME OF FIRE. This part of the picture refers to the future activities of Christ, and these features are each mentioned again at the time of fulfillment. Eyes as a flame of fire and feet like unto fine brass both have reference to judgment, for judgment requires two special characteristics. The first is perfect knowledge, with insight, ability to read even the thoughts of the heart, and eyes that pierce and cast their own light—"eyes as a flame of fire." The other characteristic required in a judge is ability to pronounce sentence and enforce punishment.

To the Thyatira Church, which was so corrupt that the Judge had to threaten swift punishment, He wrote: "These things saith the Son of God, who hath eyes like unto a flame of fire and his feet are like fine brass."—Rev. 2: 18.

VOICE AS THE SOUND OF MANY WATERS. This is in sharp contrast to the eyes like fire and feet like brass. It is the other side of judgment. The judgments of God are for a purpose. The purpose is redemption. Judgment is a working out of the grace of God. As there is a dark side for the sinner, there is a bright side for the saved, and so there is rejoicing among the redeemed.

John beheld the Lamb standing in the midst of a company of those who had been redeemed from the earth, and they sang a new song to the accompaniment of harps. John says, "I heard a voice from heaven, as the voice of many waters, and as the voice of a great thunder: and I heard the voice of harpers harping with their harps."—Rev. 14: 2.

IN HIS RIGHT HAND SEVEN STARS. The stars are the ministers of the churches. And if they are true to God's Word, they will be held in the right hand of the Lord, as He said to the ministers of the church of Ephesus: "These things saith he that holdeth the seven stars in his right hand, who walketh in the midst of the seven golden candlesticks."—Rev. 2: 1.

Jesus is standing in the midst of His church, holding its ministers in His right hand. But if, through the leakage of love or the inroads of unbelief, the church departs from Christ, He will remove the candlestick. Churches usually do not reform. When they are rejected, they lose their place among the candlesticks and some new movement replaces the old.

OUT OF HIS MOUTH WENT A SHARP TWO-EDGED SWORD. "So shall my word be that goeth forth out of my mouth: it shall not return unto me void, but it shall accomplish that which I please, and it shall prosper in the thing whereto I sent it."—Isa. 55:11.

The sword of the Spirit is the Word of God. By it He made the world, and by it He will overthrow His enemies. The armies of saints that follow Him in that day will wear white robes; they do not fight. The battle of Armageddon is one man against the world. By His sword His enemies will be destroyed.

COUNTENANCE AS THE SUN. Jesus told the Pharisees, "For as the lightning, that lighteneth out of the one part under heaven, ... so shall also the Son of man be in his day." —Luke 17:24.

When He comes again it may be midnight or it may be midday. It will make no difference to His glory, for the brightness of His countenance will outshine the sun (Rev. 10:1).

Every time Christ is mentioned throughout Revelation some portion of the first chapter is repeated. Other references to Christ are as follows:

One like unto the Son of man (14:14)
The first and the last (2:8)
Was dead and is alive (2:8)
Has the keys of hell and death (3:7 and 20:1, 2)
The faithful witness (3:14 and 19:11)
Prince of the kings of the earth (1:4)
Has the seven Spirits (3:1 and 5:6)
Hath made us kings and priests (5:10)

This vision was too much for John and he fell to the ground as one dead, but the comforting words of Jesus were sufficient to restore him to his former alertness. Jesus had used those same words to reassure the disciples when He came to them walking on the water, and again at the Mount of Transfiguration. Spoken now, probably in the same tone of voice, they would remind John that this glorious person before him was the same Jesus that he had known so well and talked to so intimately during those three years of companionship.

"I am he that liveth" should be joined with what precedes: "I am the first and the last: I am he that liveth, and was dead, and, behold, I am alive for evermore, Amen; and have the keys of hell and of death." The word "hell" in this verse does not refer to the place of everlasting punishment, but rather to the place of departed spirits, those who are waiting for the Resurrection or for the judgment.

WRITE THE THINGS WHICH THOU HAST SEEN, AND THE THINGS WHICH ARE. Revelation is a dramatized prophecy. The story is acted out. In spirit, John was transported into the future and saw what was to happen. If we consider it as a drama, the first three chapters are the cast of characters, Christ and the saints. On earth, during the church age (the things which are) the saints are identified with the church.

After the church age the saints are no longer called a church. They are still very active in the work of redemption, but they have other designations. They are organized, but the organizations have new names as well as new functions. In chapters two and three we see the churches as they are today and as they have been throughout the ages. Jesus speaks as a judge.

THE THINGS WHICH SHALL BE HEREAFTER. These "things" will come after the church age. The cast of characters remains the same throughout the book; the scene of action changes a number of times. There is a wide variety of tasks. It is, in fact, a time of intense activity and great accomplishment, but first this age must run its course.

When the disciples asked Jesus, "Wilt thou at this time restore again the Kingdom to Israel?" Jesus answered, "It is not for you to know the times or the seasons, which the Father hath put in his own power. But ye shall receive power, after that the Holy Ghost is come upon you: and ye shall be witnesses unto me both in Jerusalem, and in all Judæa, and in Samaria, and unto the uttermost part of the earth."—Acts 1:6-8.

It took many centuries for the church to reach the uttermost part of the earth. It has now been accomplished, and we approach the end of the church age.

Chapter Two

THE SEVEN CHURCHES

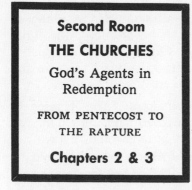

Second Room

THE CHURCHES

God's Agents in
Redemption

FROM PENTECOST TO
THE RAPTURE

Chapters 2 & 3

"For the time is come that judgment must begin at the house of God." Churches are not self-cleansing. They ought to be; the means is provided. The Lord never pleaded with a people as He pleads with the churches to heed these words. No command in the Bible is repeated more times than "He that hath an ear, let him hear what the Spirit saith unto the churches." From the attitude of the churches toward these words, one would think that Jesus had said, "Blessed is he that readeth not, and they who do not hear the words of this prophecy."

These letters are looking glasses, but no church will look at itself. Our government has stood so long because it has built-in cleansing elements. When things get about so bad, the people go to the polls and "vote the rascals out." No government official is above criticism. The government itself can be criticized. Evils in administration can be exposed and corrected. If it were not for this feature, government would soon become tyrannical.

The greatest weakness of all churches is their refusal to allow any machinery for self-cleansing. The doctrine of church loyalty means this: Be loyal to your church leaders whether they are right or wrong. To criticize an evil in the church is considered equivalent to criticizing the church. If the church puts into its course of study or its Sunday school literature some false teaching, it must not be pointed out. No protest may be raised. "Be loyal to your church!"

Conditions in some of the seminaries are almost unbelievable. A young minister told me that in a school in the Midwest, the future preachers sat around between classes, smoking, playing cards, and telling dirty stories. A preacher told me that in the seminary which he attended, the Bible had about as much standing as the *Saturday Evening Post*— just a piece of literature. Yet if you raise your voice in the church against these conditions, you are a troublemaker.

All the prophets were troublemakers. "And it came to pass, when Ahab saw Elijah, that Ahab said unto him, Art thou he that troubleth Israel? And he answered, I have not troubled Israel; but thou, and thy father's house, in that ye have forsaken the commandments of the Lord, and thou hast followed Baalim."—I Kings 18:17, 18.

Jesus was a troublemaker. He made trouble in the synagogues and in the temple.

The apostles were troublemakers. They were men who turned the world upside down. Martin Luther was a troublemaker. The Romish church could tolerate all the evils that Luther pointed out, but they could not tolerate Luther. John Wesley was a troublemaker in the Church of England. The church today needs troublemakers as never before, but the churches have so constituted themselves that they can rid themselves of their critics, but not of the evils which cause the criticism. That is why the effective life of a church is comparatively short, and new ones have to be continually starting.

The crying need of the church through the ages has been machinery for cleansing itself. These seven letters to the churches are that machinery, but the churches will not even consider them. These seven letters show why there has to be a succession of churches.

When a certain type of church once starts, it continues to the end. It may cease to be useful in the thing for which it was intended; it may degenerate into a glorified club, but as an organization it remains to the end. So, at the time of the end of the church age, there will be in the world churches like those described in all seven letters.

ANGEL. "Unto the angel of the church of Ephesus write."

In Revelation the word "angel" is descriptive of office rather than of nature. It means "messenger," that is, one invested with a special commission. In at least two instances saints are called angels. In the 19th chapter, John writes that he attempted to worship the one who brought him the vision and who was called an angel (17:8). The angel replied, "See thou do it not: I am thy fellowservant, and of thy brethren that have the testimony of Jesus."—Rev. 19:10. The angels mentioned in the seven letters are the messengers or ministers of the churches.

Structure

Each of these letters follows the same general outline. This outline has seven points:

1. The name of the church addressed.
2. The identification of the speaker, which is a repetition of some reference to Christ in the first chapter.
3. Praise. Mention of those things of which the Judge approves.

THE SEVEN CHURCHES

CHURCH	EPHESUS	SMYRNA	PERGAMOS	THYATIRA	SARDIS	PHILADELPHIA	LAODICEA
Qualifications of the Judge	Seven Stars Seven Candlesticks	First and Last Was dead Is alive	Sharp Sword with two edges	Son of God Eyes like fire Feet of brass	Seven Spirits Seven Stars	Holy and True Key of David Openeth Shutteth	Faithful Witness Beginning of creation of God
PRAISE	Faithful in Service and belief Hate deeds of Nicolaitans	Faithful under Persecution Poor, but rich	Faithful in belief in spite of Satan	Good Works Some Faith	A Good Name A Faithful Few	An Open Door A little strength A good testimony	
REPROOF	Left first love		Doctrines of Nicolaitans and Balaam	Wicked Woman Jezebel	Works not perfect Spiritually dead		Lukewarm Rich, but poor, blind, naked
SECOND COMING	Remove Candlestick	Crown of Life	Fight against them with the sword of my mouth	Hold fast. Avoid judgment	As a thief without warning	Keep from Tribulation Let no man take thy crown	Church rejected Christ outside Individuals saved
COMMAND TO HEAR	HE THAT HATH AN EAR, LET HIM HEAR WHAT THE SPIRIT SAITH UNTO THE CHURCHES						
PROMISE	Eat of the tree of life	Not hurt of second death	Eat manna White Stone New Name	Power over the nations Morning Star	White Raiment Confess His name	Pillar in Temple New Name	Sit with Me on My Throne

4. Reproof. Mention of the things which should be corrected.
5. Mention of the Second Coming of Christ and its effect upon that type of church.
6. A universal command to hear, repeated in each letter.
7. A promise "to him that overcometh."

After the first three letters the order of the last two points is reversed.

QUALIFICATIONS OF THE JUDGE. Most of the features are taken from the portrait of Christ in the first chapter; some new ones are added. The qualifications connect with what will happen when He comes again. He that stands among the candlesticks will remove the candlestick. That amounts to a rejection of the church.

He that was dead and is alive will give the faithful a crown of life. He that has a sharp sword will fight against His enemies in the church with the sword of His mouth. He that has the seven Spirits will come as a thief in the night. He that has the key of David will open the graves to the dead or close them to the living, thus keeping them from the tribulation. He that is the faithful witness will reject completely the lukewarm, modernist church that has denied the deity of Christ and His authority.

PRAISE. We note the things about the church that please the Judge. The words *faithful* and *faith* predominate. They are faithful in service and belief; they are faithful under persecution; they are faithful in belief in spite of Satan's presence; they have some faith and good works; they have a good name and a faithful few; they have a good testimony and some strength.

REPROOF. Whenever a church is subjected to reproof, there is a warning or an outright condemnation. The church that has left its first love will suffer the removal of its candlestick from among the candlesticks. The church that tolerates the doctrine of the Nicolaitans or Balaam will suffer by the war that Christ himself will wage against those elements in the church. It may not be a pleasant experience.

The church that is plagued by the wicked woman Jezebel is not expected to do much but hold fast and thus avoid a severe judgment. A church whose works are far from perfect because it is spiritually dead will not be ready for the coming of the Lord. The church that has gone into apostasy and has rejected Christ will be rejected as a church, but individuals may still be saved.

PROMISES. Churches that are given no reproof are given special promises rather than a warning. The Smyrna Church is promised a crown of life. The Philadelphia Church also has a crown and will be kept from the tribulation (caught up to be with Christ).

The warning or promise connects with the coming of Christ and is addressed to the church. It shows how the coming of Christ will affect that kind of church.

The final promise of eternal reward is given only to those individuals in the church who are overcomers. In this case it is not the church as a whole that is addressed but the overcomers in the church. To be an overcomer is to overcome in those particular things in which the church has failed. To be an overcomer in the Ephesus Church is to retain one's first love when the church as a whole is departing from it.

To be an overcomer in the Smyrna Church is to be faithful unto death along with the rest of the church. To be an overcomer in the Pergamos Church is to contend against the Nicolaitans and followers of Balaam.

To be an overcomer in the Thyatira Church is to keep separate from the wicked woman Jezebel and not to be contaminated by her. To be an overcomer in the Sardis Church is to maintain a Spirit-filled life in an atmosphere of formality—a rather difficult achievement.

To be an overcomer in the Philadelphia Church is to follow the church through the open doors of service. To be an overcomer in the Laodicean Church is to remain true to the faith in an unbelieving church. There have always been overcomers; every kind of church has them.

Except in such churches as Smyrna and Philadelphia, overcomers will find themselves in the minority and quite unpopular. Although nothing is said about leaving an unfaithful church, that is the way new churches start. In actual practice, overcomers do not always have a choice; they are forced out. If we had more overcomers, we probably would have more churches.

The overcomers from all churches are treated as a unit. They are all in one group. They are the true church. Each of the seven promises applies to all overcomers, and together they constitute a sevenfold promise of eternal reward.

It is with these promises that we begin the subject of the consummation of redemption, which is the burden of Revelation. Redemption is the restoration of what was lost by sin. The primary record of this is Genesis. The first scene in Genesis is the Garden of Eden. God called it good; there was a perfect world and no sin or corruption had entered.

Man was not meant to die, although he was put in a world where death is a natural process. God made man to be above his environment, to have dominion over all created things. He was given the tree of life. He could eat of that tree and never die. The first thing to be lost was the tree of life, so the first thing to be restored is life—eternal life. "To him that overcometh will I give to eat of the tree of life, which is in the midst of the paradise of God."—Rev. 2:7. The paradise of God is the Holy City that comes down out of heaven from

God. It is called "the bride, the Lamb's wife." In it grows the tree of life.

This is somewhat more than restoration of what was lost. The Holy City is a more glorious place than the Garden of Eden. Those who live in the Holy City already have immortality, regardless of where they live. The leaves of the tree of life are for the healing of the nations, but the fruit is only for those who have been redeemed by the blood of Christ and have passed through death and the Resurrection or the Rapture.

When Adam and Eve lost access to the tree of life, the process of death began. This was the second step in the process of degeneration. Spiritually, death came when they sinned; physically, it came when life ran out. So the next promise is concerning immunity from death. "He that overcometh shall not be hurt of the second death."—Rev. 2:11.

The third step in the process of degeneration was twofold: (1) Man lost a perfect world. God cursed the ground for man's sake and made it bring forth weeds and pests. Food came with difficulty and hard labor. All peoples are just one step ahead of starvation.

(2) Man lost his association with God. In the Garden, God came down and talked with Adam. They were partners in developing a new world. God's relationship to perfect man was on a different basis than it was with sinful man. After sin entered, man did not feel easy in the presence of God. Even after the means of salvation was provided, the relationship could not be the same until complete perfection was attained. That meant a new body as well as a clean heart. The complete realization of this objective is stated by Paul: "So shall we ever be with the Lord."—I Thess. 4:17.

The third promise restores this twofold loss: "To him that overcometh will I give to eat of the hidden manna, and will give him a white stone, and in the stone a new name written, which no man knoweth saving he that receiveth it."—Rev. 2: 17.

First, there is the hidden manna. Jesus once said, "I have meat to eat that ye know not of." It is hidden because it is spiritual. "The things which are seen are temporal; but the things which are not seen are eternal."—II Cor. 4: 18.

This manna may be seen and appropriated only by those who have immortal bodies. The Resurrection is strongly suggested by this promise. God works, Jesus works, the saints will always work, but not for a living. There is joy in working, but there is a difference between labor for the purpose of paying bills and work for the joy of accomplishment. The overcomers will not have to work for a living. They have hidden manna.

Second is a white stone and a new name. Both of these suggest a new relationship or association.

Before the days of paper ballots, voting was done with stones or balls. A white stone was a yes vote. A black stone was a no vote. When a new member of an association was being voted on, each member was given a white and a black stone. One or the other was dropped in the box. If a candidate got more white stones than black ones, he was admitted. If he got more black stones than white stones, he was rejected, or blackballed.

Therefore, a white stone stands for admission into a new society. It is emblematic of acceptance into the family of God. The new name carries the same significance.

One of the first things God gave man was dominion over all the earth. "And God said, Let us make man in our image, after our likeness: and let them have dominion over the fish of the sea, and over the fowl of the air, and over the cattle, and over all the earth, and over every living thing that creepeth upon the earth."—Gen. 1: 26.

This dominion was largely lost by sin. Gradually it passed into the hands of Satan until Satan became the prince of this world. A second milestone will be reached when Satan causes all the world to worship the beast. But Jesus said, "Blessed are the meek: for they shall inherit the earth"—Matt. 5:5.

So the fourth promise restores to man the dominion that was lost by Adam's fall: "And he that overcometh, and keepeth my works unto the end, to him will I give power over the nations: and he shall rule them with a rod of iron; as the vessels of a potter shall they be broken to shivers: even as I received of my Father. And I will give him the morning star."—Rev. 2:26–28.

The morning star is Venus. At first sight this seems like an afterthought—something thrown in for good measure—but actually it is the natural sequence of the promise of dominion. This earth is not big enough to provide space for all the promises and prophecies in the Bible.

"Thou hast been faithful over a few things, I will make thee ruler over many things."—Matt. 25:21. How many is "many" to God? If you bring back all the people who have been faithful in a few things in the history of the world, you will need more space than this earth provides to fulfill God's promises. Where will the "many things" come from? Isaiah says, "A little one shall become a thousand, and a small one a strong nation: I the Lord will hasten it in his time."—Isaiah 60:22.

Abraham became the father of a great nation. That, however, is the exception, not the rule. Isaiah sees a time when it will be the rule; every baby born will be the potential head of a new nation. This will take living space beyond anything one planet could provide.

If you put together all the promises and prophecies in the whole Bible concerning possessions, dominion, rulership, authority, power, riches, etc., you will need many worlds to make them all come true. This is all taken care of in the promise: "I will give him the morning star." God will extend His dominion into outer space; He will provide for endless increase.

It is true that there will be no increase among the saints, for they are a fixed number; but God's creatures, the human race, will always be increasing. "Of the increase of his government and peace there shall be no end."—Isaiah 9: 7.

The parable of the mustard seed illustrates this truth.

"The kingdom of heaven is like to a grain of mustard seed, which a man took, and sowed in his field: which indeed is the least of all seeds: but when it is grown, it is the greatest among herbs, and becometh a tree, so that the birds of the air come and lodge in the branches thereof."—Matt. 13:31, 32

The kingdom started with one man; nothing could start smaller than that. It grows now by the spread of the gospel, but there is a limit to this kind of growth. During the Millennium, the kingdom will expand until it covers the earth. The stone, cut out without hand, will become a great mountain and fill the whole world. When this is accomplished, the mustard seed has become a full-grown plant; it has reached its ultimate size as a plant.

But this mustard plant keeps on growing even after it has reached its full size. It becomes a tree, a great tree; the birds of the air lodge in its branches. This was noted to emphasize the great size of the tree or to show that it was a tree and no longer a plant.

So when the kingdom has reached its full-grown size on the earth, it does not need to stop growing; other worlds become available. It is becoming axiomatic that what man can conceive, in time, man can do. Even in a sinful state, man is actually planning space travel. Given a few years of peace and plenty, space travel will become a reality. When we have millennial conditions and the help of God, the spread of the kingdom to outer space will be only a matter of course. Then the plant will have become a tree.

The fifth promise has three parts: (1) Overcomers will be given white raiment; (2) Their names will not be blotted out of the book of life; (3) Christ will confess them before the angels.

This is the second time white has been used in connection with the saints. First was the white stone. White is emblematic of righteousness. It is used in connection with Christ (white hair), God (the great white throne), and the saints (white garments). "For the fine linen [clean and white] is the righteousness of the saints."—Rev. 19:8.

The white garment is the outward evidence of an inward quality. The third promise deals with our relationship to God; this fifth one reveals our relationship to others; and there will be many others in God's great eternity.

What is meant by "I will confess his name before my Father, and before his angels," we can only surmise. It presupposes situations that we never experienced. There is a court of heaven; there are assemblies, governmental functions, tribunals, officials, kings, priests, great convocations; thrilling new adventures in which a host of angels are involved. The greatest men on earth never dreamed of such delegations of power as are commonplace in heaven. Jesus said that John the Baptist was the greatest man who ever lived but that the least in the kingdom of heaven is greater than he.

In all this company of the great, there will be one outstanding group, greater than all the others. They will have special names and badges, dazzling white clothing of special texture, and will be given special recognition in the most august assemblies.

The negative promise, "I will not blot out his name out of the book of life," suggests by inference that those who find themselves in the situation described in this letter are in danger of having their names blotted out. This may apply to some very special set of circumstances. At the great white throne judgment, it is said, "And whosoever was not found written in the book of life was cast into the lake of fire."— Rev. 20:15.

Although the book of life is mentioned in both the Old and New Testaments, it is not explained in either, and we know little about it except that it is a record of names. If Adam had not sinned, we may suppose that all names would be recorded in the book of life, which basically is a record of vital statistics. Twice a reference is made to the beginning, which takes us back to Genesis: "And they that dwell on the earth shall wonder, whose names were not written in the book of life from the foundation of the world."—Rev. 17:8.

The book of life is quite evidently not a single list of the saved of all dispensations; there seems to be more to it than that. Salvation is not a simple matter, and the processes have not always been the same. There may be lists of names of which we know nothing. "Other sheep I have which are not of this fold."—John 10:16.

So if we determine what the book of life means to one generation, it does not follow that another listing could not be made to apply to the people of another dispensation. For instance, those who are living after the Rapture and during the reign of Antichrist would hardly be in the same category as those whom Moses dealt with in Exodus 32:33: "And the Lord said unto Moses, Whosoever hath sinned against me, him will I blot out of my book."

Daniel was told about the Rapture, when the children of his people would be delivered: "every one that shall be found written in the book." God keeps books; He keeps records:

"And the dead were judged out of those things which were written in the books."—Rev. 20: 12.

In the Dispensation of Grace, the book of life would most certainly contain the names of the saved. They are the overcomers. None of these names will be blotted out.

The last two promises look beyond the immediate effects of the fall of man and give us a glimpse into the eternal state of the redeemed ones. "Him that overcometh will I make a pillar in the temple of my God, and he shall go no more out: and I will write upon him the name of my God, and the name of the city of my God, which is new Jerusalem, which cometh down out of heaven from my God: and I will write upon him my new name."—Rev. 3: 12.

The realization of this promise must wait for the coming of the Holy City; yet when the city comes down from God, John says, "And I saw no temple therein: for the Lord God Almighty and the Lamb are the temple of it."—Rev. 21:22. The Holy City is not the temple; saints will go in and out of the Holy City. Our understanding here may be somewhat clouded by our saying, "He is a pillar in the church." John was not using this idiom. Overcoming is a continual process; a pillar is a permanent condition. The fight is over; the victory is won.

The two pillars in Solomon's temple set up in the porch were called *Jachin,* which means "He will establish"; and *Boaz,* which means "In him is strength." Pillars are used as emblematic of strength and durability. "Behold, I have made thee this day a defenced city, an iron pillar."—Jer. 1: 18.

"And I will write upon him ... mine own new name" (A.S.V.). This passage is a promise that when God makes us completely His own by writing His own new name on us, He will admit us into His full glory, which is at present incomprehensible to us. Such comprehension is of the things "which shall be hereafter" and which cannot now be known to us, "for now we see through a glass, darkly; but then face to face; now I know in part; but then shall I know even as also I am known."—I Cor. 13:12.

There is a further contrast with Genesis. In the Garden, God came down to be with Adam. In redemption, man will go up to be with God. Adam gave the animals new names; God will give the redeemed new names.

The last promise is the ultimate, beyond which it is impossible to go. "To him that overcometh will I grant to sit with me in my throne, even as I also overcame, and am set down with my Father in his throne." The full realization of this promise awaits the coming of Christ. The same things that are said of Christ are said of the saints.

Compare Psalm 2:7–9 with Revelation 2:26, 27.

> I will declare the decree: the Lord hath said unto me, Thou art my Son; this day have I begotten thee. Ask of me, and I shall give thee the heathen for thine inheritance, and the uttermost parts of the earth for thy possession. Thou shalt break them with a rod of iron; thou shalt dash them in pieces like a potter's vessel.—Ps. 2:7–9

> And he that overcometh, and keepeth my works unto the end, to him will I give power over the nations: and he shall rule them with a rod of iron; as the vessels of a potter shall they be broken to shivers: even as I received of my Father.—Rev. 2:26, 27

Compare also Daniel 7:14, Daniel 7:27, and Romans 8:17.

> And there was given him dominion, and glory, and a kingdom, that all people, nations, and languages, should serve him: his dominion is an everlasting dominion, which shall not pass away, and his kingdom that which shall not be destroyed.—Dan. 7:14

> And the kingdom and dominion, and the greatness of the kingdom under the whole heaven, shall be given

to the people of the saints of the most High, whose kingdom is an everlasting kingdom, and all dominions shall serve and obey him.—Dan. 7:27

And if children, then heirs; heirs of God, and joint heirs with Christ; if so be that we suffer with him, that we may be also glorified together.—Rom. 8:17

Ephesus

Revelation 2

1 Unto the angel of the church of Ephesus write; These things saith he that holdeth the seven stars in his right hand, who walketh in the midst of the seven golden candlesticks.

THE CHURCH. Ephesus was once an important and magnificent city. It was the center of trade for a rich and beautiful country, and the seat of its government, learning, art, wealth, and religion. It was a place especially consecrated in the minds of the people by many myths and legends of gods and goddesses and by the presence of the temple which was one of the wonders of the world. This temple is said to have been 220 years in building. It was made of shiny marble, supported by 127 columns of Persian marble, each shaft being 60 feet long. The image of the goddess Diana held the central place in the temple, and from the throats of many thousands might be heard the cry, "Great is Diana of the Ephesians."

THE SPEAKER. To the church at Ephesus the speaker describes himself as "he that holdeth the seven stars in his right hand, who walketh in the midst of the seven golden candlesticks." Jesus is Lord and Master of the church. The ministers are His messengers. Jesus is the Faithful Witness. He does not flatter, but He mentions frankly the good points and just as frankly the bad points about each church. If the churches today would heed these letters that have been sent especially to them, they would save themselves much grief.

Revelation 2

2 I know thy works, and thy labour, and thy patience, and how thou canst not bear them which are evil: and thou hast tried them which say they are apostles, and are not, and hast found them liars:
3 And hast borne, and hast patience, and for my name's sake hast laboured, and hast not fainted.

PRAISE. Ephesus was a working church. Some of the greatest workers of the day were members of that church. The results of its labors could be seen throughout Asia Minor.

The word *patience* means "steadfastness." The church at Ephesus held true to the faith. It did not lower its standards of belief or practice for policy's sake. It not only kept unbelief out of the church, but it also kept out unbelievers. Those who made a false profession to gain membership were tested and shown up to be liars. It insisted upon an honest confession of faith without mental reservation on the part of its members and ministry.

Jesus commends this church because it took care of the doctrinal standards of its pulpit. It allowed no one to occupy it who was not loyal to Christ and the gospel. This church had greatly profited by the injunctions of the Apostle Paul: "Take heed therefore unto yourselves, and to all the flock, over the which the Holy Ghost hath made you overseers, to feed the church of God, which he hath purchased with his own blood. For I know this, that after my departing shall grievous wolves enter in among you, not sparing the flock."—Acts. 20: 28, 29.

Revelation 2

4 Nevertheless I have somewhat against thee, because thou hast left thy first love.
5 Remember therefore from whence thou art fallen, and repent, and do the first works; or else I will come unto thee quickly, and will remove thy candlestick out of his place, except thou repent.

REPROOF. "Nevertheless I have somewhat against thee, because thou hast left thy first love." The word "somewhat," which was inserted by the translators, may seem to soften the censure. Such, however, was not the case. It means "I have something serious against you." This is the place where most churches begin to weaken. This weakness cannot be seen from the outside until it arrives at an advanced stage; at first only Christ can see it.

This church retains its faith without wavering. It does the same things it always did. It is still faithful in service, but the motive is changing. In the beginning everything that was done was done purely out of love for Christ. Christ was the motive. The gospel was the driving power. The great program of Christ for the salvation of souls and the spread of the gospel was the source of inspiration, the driving force, that made its members labor until they were exhausted, and to bear great burdens on their hearts for the salvation of souls.

But with an increasing membership and a growing responsibility, organization was necessary. There is a great danger in organization, in societies with special memberships and demanding special loyalty to the society. The work they do may be exactly the same to all outward appearances, but the incentive may be loyalty to the organization, a desire to see it grow and prosper.

At first everything is Christ; then gradually the *church* begins to take on importance and church work begins to take the place of Christian labor. At first this condition is so slight as to be imperceptible, but its tendency is always to increase until church work has entirely supplanted Christian labor. Church work is that which is done for the church rather than for Christ. We are the church. Most of the labor and most of the money expended in church work is for ourselves. Beautiful windows, comfortable seats, elaborate music, eloquent preaching, new hymnbooks, well-equipped kitchens and dining rooms, etc., are all for our own enjoyment. Therefore, it is easy for our motives to shift from love of Christ to love of the church. Then we become the center of our own affections. This is a serious situation, and the church that allows it is in danger of losing its place among the candlesticks.

Although this church was faithfully serving Christ, He knew that if the motive changed it would not be very long before the work would change and the church would become engaged in all kinds of temporal activities. The real work of the gospel would suffer.

Temporal activities and reforms may be entered into by those who do not love Christ. There is no longer any opportunity for separation or for testing or for steadfastness. There may be a great sense of loyalty built up, but it must be remembered that loyalty to the church is not always loyalty to Christ. When we love the church, we love ourselves. The first love is Christ. The second love is the church. Christ here warns the church of the danger of leaving her first love.

Revelation 2

6 But this thou hast, that thou hatest the deeds of the Nicolaitans, which I also hate.

THE NICOLAITANS. There is not known to have been any sect of Nicolaitans. It was evidently the name applied to the new movement within the church. *Nico* is the Greek word for conquer. *Laitanes* is the word from which we get our word laity. The word, therefore, means "conquerors of the laity." It is the beginning of priesthood or the ecclesiastical control of individual churches. When a church leaves its first love, it begins to turn its attention to ecclesiastical power and influence. When its leaders talk about "church loyalty," they are actually demanding loyalty to themselves while they are leading the people away from the Bible. The movements of the churches to enhance their political power and social prestige by union, federation, and worldly alliances are the deeds of the Nicolaitans. It is the effort of the church to restore by its own method what it has lost by forsaking God's method.

Smyrna

Revelation 2

8 And unto the angel of the church in Smyrna write; These things saith the first and the last, which was dead, and is alive;

9 I know thy works, and tribulation, and poverty, (but thou art rich) and I know the blasphemy of them which say they are Jews, and are not, but are the synagogue of Satan.

10 Fear none of those things which thou shalt suffer: behold, the devil shall cast some of you into prison, that ye may be tried; and ye shall have tribulation ten days: be thou faithful unto death, and I will give thee a crown of life.

Churches as a whole have fared as well or better than the average person. They have had the respect of the community and sometimes have been supported by the government, but there have been times when the church has faced hardships, tribulation, persecution, and poverty. Christians in some countries have had to be faithful unto death. For these churches there is a candlestick brightly burning. They have a candle standing for them in the candelabra. What is said to the Smyrna Church is said to all persecuted churches.

It was poor but the Judge said, "Thou art rich." This is in sharp contrast with the Laodicean Church which said, "I am rich," and the Judge said, "Thou art poor."

There are two churches that have no reproof—Smyrna and Philadelphia. As far as the record is concerned, they are perfect churches. Each of these churches has this same element—those who say they are Jews and are not. This is not the fault of the church, and the church is not blamed for their presence. The church is not even told to get rid of them. The Judge does not criticize the church, but attacks the hypocrites themselves. The only time these so-called Jews appear is in the otherwise perfect churches, and they appear in both of them even though they represent churches many centuries apart.

Who are these who say they are Jews and are not? And what is the synagogue of Satan? To the Philadelphia Church, the Judge says, "Behold, I will make them of the synagogue of Satan." Why would they say they are Jews if they are not? And even if they did, what difference would it make?

In a Christian church an argument over whether or not a person is a Jew would make very little sense. Evidently something else is meant by the expression. This is a prophecy. Words have to be found to make mention of things and situations which did not exist in the first churches. New situations came with changing conditions. The complexion, if not the very nature, of the church changed. Churches today are vastly different from those of as little as 200 years ago.

Even the word "church" has a different meaning now than it did in Bible times. Then the church was a group of Christians, although the name Christian was not universally used. Christianity was called "The Way" and Christians were "The Called." The word "church" referring to a denomination or a group of churches having a common headquarters or leadership was unknown. Buildings were never called churches; there was no building program.

Yet if we are to have a prophecy, we have to take these new things into consideration and words have to be found. When a church becomes a denomination or convention, it has certain doctrinal and ethical standards. These standards eventually are challenged by wolves in sheep's clothing. Not all who say they are Baptists are Baptists. Not all who claim membership in the Methodist Church are real Methodists. Traitors creep in. How could such a situation be expressed before there were church names? Only by some such way as "those who say they are Jews and are not."—Rev. 2:9.

Why are they called the synagogue of Satan? This is Satan's doing, and that is why the church is not reproved or condemned as it is for some other things. A similar situation is illustrated in the parable of the tares. It was Satan who sowed the tares among the wheat. It was no one's fault; the Lord said nothing could be done about it. "Let them grow together until the harvest." Tares are not something that just naturally happen; they are deliberately planted. They are of the synagogue of Satan.

Only two of the seven churches are so plagued. Satan sows tares only where there is wheat. Churches leaving their first love, churches filled with Nicolaitans and Balaamites, churches dominated by Jezebel, churches completely apostate, have no need of tares. Satan has other, more direct ways with these churches. Only perfect churches are tormented by tares.

Tares are counterfeit wheat. The point of the parable is that the tares look so much like the wheat they cannot be separated before the harvest. These counterfeit Christians say they are Jews and are not, but are of the planting of Satan.

Pergamos

Revelation 2

12 And to the angel of the church in Pergamos write; These things saith he which hath the sharp sword with two edges;

13 I know thy works, and where thou dwellest, even where Satan's seat is: and thou holdest fast my name, and hast not denied my faith, even those days wherein

Antipas was my faithful martyr, who was slain among you, where Satan dwelleth.

All of the letters present problems, but none more than the one to Pergamos, "where Satan's seat [*thronos*—throne] is." The *Pulpit Commentary* says: "The throne of Satan has perplexed commentators." Of course there were satanic institutions in Pergamos, but no more than in other cities. It is not just that Satan has a throne in Pergamos, but that he has a throne at all is startling, and when that throne is in an earthly city, and its presence there makes things difficult for the church, it is no wonder that commentators are perplexed.

We come now to one of the mysteries of the church, the mystery of Satan's church, the only church that claims temporal power, has a potentate sitting on a throne, and is crowned with a triple crown. From the beginning, Satan's chief aspiration has been to be God. That, in fact, was the cause of his fall. So Satan very early developed a form of worship. All idolatrous systems in the world come out of Satan's attempt to displace God as the Supreme Being.

Satan offered Christ all the kingdoms of the world; the condition was that Christ should fall down and worship Satan. This overpowering ambition will be temporarily realized when he causes all the world to worship him. When Satan reigns as the god of this world, it will be on a throne.

The first elaborate satanic religious system was developed in Babylon. There was little opportunity or necessity for further development or religious activity until Christianity was founded. This called for prompt action on the part of Satan, for Satan must also have a church. But Satan's conception of a church was somewhat different from Christ's. It involved temporal power, a throne.

One would think that it would be impossible for Satan to pick up ancient Babylonian idolatry bodily and superimpose it on the new Spirit-filled church, yet that is exactly what Satan tried to do, and with some success. Jesus was born in poverty and spent His first hours in a manger. He never possessed a house, a field, or a surplus of money. The founders of Christianity were simple men; there was no outward show of authority or power, no peculiar dress to indicate special piety.

All religious pomp and ceremony, all ritualistic forms, motions of the arms, robes, miters, incense, crucifixes, images, thrones, processions, holy water, priests, popes, shrines, relics, charms, superstitions—all came from Satan's religion, originating in Babylon. Romanism is Babylonian idolatry changed only enough to accommodate it to Christian conceptions, and the central feature is a throne. Romanism is Satan enthroned.

If there is a throne, there must be a city—a capital. The Christian Church did not have a capital or central government and was not supposed to have one. The reason is simple: when the church has a governing body, it is necessary for Satan to get control of only a few people at the top, and he has the whole church. Nearly all the world evangelization that has been done in the past 2,000 years has been done by a multitude of different churches. A united church becomes corrupt almost instantly. Satan's first onslaught against Christ was to unify the churches and establish a governing body. The Holy Spirit was replaced by a throne.

In the beginning Satan's throne was in Babylon. Now it was to be set up in Rome. Why, then, was Pergamos designated as the city where Satan's throne is? Satan's church came gradually. It began with deeds, then developed into doctrines. The letter to Ephesus mentions the deeds of the Nicolaitans; in Pergamos they become doctrines. It reaches its complete form in Thyatira. It was because of these doctrines, which had their beginning in Pergamos, that the wicked woman Jezebel corrupted the church of Thyatira.

There is no mention of Antipas in history or tradition. He stands as a type. Here Christ is giving recognition to the thousands of martyrs and those who were faithful in the face of martyrdom. Rome has been a killer of Christians and will be again. It will undoubtedly be Antichrist's instrument in the persecution of the Tribulation Saints.

THE DOCTRINE OF BALAAM

Two items are marked up against this church.

Revelation 2

14 But I have a few things against thee, because thou hast there them that hold the doctrine of Balaam, who taught Balac to cast a stumblingblock before the children of Israel, to eat things sacrificed unto idols, and to commit fornication.

15 So hast thou also them that hold the doctrine of the Nicolaitans, which thing I hate.

16 Repent; or else I will come unto thee quickly, and will fight against them with the sword of my mouth.

Balaam was the only Gentile prophet; he was the only prophet to mention the star in connection with the coming of Christ. "I shall see him, but not now: I shall behold him, but not nigh; there shall come a star out of Jacob, and a sceptre shall rise out of Israel."—Numbers 24:17. The only Gentiles to visit Christ at His birth were those who followed the star. Balaam was a great prophet. He knew God. He must have been noted in his day for the King of Moab to put so much confidence in him. His prophecy contains in essence the message of the later prophets.

God is not a man, that he should lie; neither the son of man, that he should repent: hath he said, and shall he not do it? or hath he spoken, and shall he not make it good? Behold, I have received commandment to bless: and he hath blessed; and I cannot reverse it. He hath not beheld iniquity in Jacob, neither hath he seen perverseness in Israel: the Lord his God is with him, and the shout of a king is among them. God brought them out of Egypt; he hath as it were the strength of an unicorn. Surely there is no enchantment against Jacob, neither is there any divination against Israel: according to this time it shall be said of Jacob and of Israel, What hath God wrought!—Num. 23:19-23

There is nothing here that would discredit Balaam. He followed God's instructions in everything he did and spoke only the word of God. He was to be paid for his work only if he cursed Israel, but he "blessed them altogether." This is as far as the Old Testament story goes. (But see Numbers 31:16.) [1] It is in the New Testament that we read of "the error of Balaam" (Jude 11), [2] "the way of Balaam" (II Pet. 2:15), [3] and the "doctrine of Balaam" (Rev. 2:14). We gather that, although Balaam refused to curse Israel, he stayed on and advised the king of the Moabites how to corrupt Israel by what we call today "infiltration."

BALAAM'S DOCTRINE consisted of two items: (1) To eat things sacrificed to idols; (2) To commit fornication. Translated into terms of the church it would amount to making, using, and worshipping idols, and contamination with the world, or a mixing of the world and the church. Fornication in a spiritual sense is for a church to demand and receive special favors from government. It is sometimes called a union of church and state. It is a basic doctrine of the Romish Church. (See Rev. 17.)

It seems strange that a Christian church should have any use for images and charms; these were the trappings of Babylonian idolatry. Here is revealed the germ of the whole Romish system. It had not yet developed into a complete working organization. There were still no bishops, car-

---

1. "Behold, these caused the children of Israel, through the counsel of Balaam, to commit trespass against the Lord in the matter of Peor, and there was a plague among the congregation of the Lord" (Num. 31:16).
2. "Woe unto them! for they have gone in the way of Cain, and ran greedily after the error of Balaam for reward, and perished in the gainsaying of Core" (Jude 11).
3. "Which have forsaken the right way, and are gone astray, following the way of Balaam the son of Bosor, who loved the wages of unrighteousness" (II Pet. 2:15).

dinals, dioceses, popes, or any of the inventions that came later.

If the Pergamos Church had heeded this letter, it could have stopped this perversion at the start. Instead, it was allowed to run into the Thyatira Church, where it became organized and dominated the whole church.

Thyatira

Revelation 2

18 And unto the angel of the church in Thyatira write; These things saith the Son of God, who hath his eyes like unto a flame of fire, and his feet are like fine brass;

19 I know thy works, and charity, and service, and faith, and thy patience, and thy works; and the last to be more than the first.

20 Notwithstanding I have a few things against thee, because thou sufferest that woman Jezebel, which calleth herself a prophetess, to teach and to seduce my servants to commit fornication, and to eat things sacrificed unto idols.

THE SON OF GOD. "These things saith the Son of God." This is the only place in Revelation that Christ is called the Son of God. In the first chapter He is the Son of man. His most used name is the Lamb, but to a church that makes so much of the Virgin Mary, He appears as the Son of God.

THE WOMAN JEZEBEL. Thyatira does not represent the Church of Rome in this letter. That church is Jezebel, the self-styled prophetess. She is the one that puts into practice the evil doctrines of Pergamos, "to teach and seduce my servants to commit fornication, and to eat things sacrificed unto idols."

A woman, symbolically, is a church, but there were other church groups that were not connected with the Romish system, and there were people in the Catholic Church who did not follow the evil ways of the woman. Martin Luther, for instance, was one of those in the Thyatira Church who was not corrupted by the woman. We must make a distinction between the innocent people in the church and the hierarchy. Sometimes people are saved in spite of their church.

A somewhat similar situation is presented in the parable of the leaven. It is the woman who put the leaven into the meal. Church teaching is corrupted, not by outsiders, but by the church itself. It is not the church members, but the church leaders that do the damage. They hold official positions; they control church policy. The woman represents the organization whose leaders continually insert false teaching into the Sunday school literature and preacher's courses of study.

The same is true of the Thyatira Church. There is in the church an element, firmly seated on the throne, which corrupts the whole church. The Romish Church likes to contend that it is the mother church and the Protestants are her harlot daughters. The Romish Church is always calling us back to the fold. This teaching fools some people.

The Bible conception is somewhat different. In this letter the church hierarchy does not represent the whole church but is a festering growth that must be removed. The Protestant Church did not separate itself from the mother church, but instead it cast out the wicked woman. Protestantism, not Rome, is in the line of succession. The line goes from Pergamos to Thyatira to Sardis. Jezebel is dropped. She becomes the harlot woman of the 17th chapter. She is not a part of the church; she is Satan's church; she is Satan's answer to Christ's church. She began in Babylon, she continued Babylonian idolatry, and she will in the end return to Babylon. There her true nature will be revealed.

Revelation 2

21 And I gave her space to repent of her fornication; and she repented not.

22 Behold, I will cast her into a bed, and them that commit adultery with her into great tribulation, except they repent of their deeds.

23 And I will kill her children with death; and all the churches shall know that I am he which searcheth the reins and hearts: and I will give unto every one of you according to your works.

24 But unto you I say, and unto the rest in Thyatira, as many as have not this doctrine, and which have not known the depths of Satan, as they speak; I will put upon you none other burden.

25 But that which ye have already hold fast till I come.

The fact that these churches are types of the churches in different periods of their history does not prevent them from having a literal fulfillment at some specific time. Just as there will be a church corresponding to that of the Laodicean and another to the Church of Philadelphia at the time of the Rapture, there could also be churches like Thyatira and all the others.

Nothing that we have said exhausts the meaning of these letters. A large amount of information has been packed into a small space. We have the original churches, we have the churches as types, we could also have a picture of the church of the last days. These seven letters could depict seven kinds of churches that will come into being as a result of a great upheaval in the religious world at about the time that prophecy begins to be fulfilled in a new and marvelous way. This Thyatira Church will have its day just before the Rapture, not then as a type, but as a literal fulfillment.

Jesus said, "I will put upon you none other burden. But that which ye have already hold fast till I come." It is hard to see how Jesus could say that to the Thyatira Church back there in Asia. They would not be told to hold on for two thousand years.

Jesus said that the situation was bad, but there was nothing they could do about it because the time was too short. All they could be expected to do was to hold on till His return. Such a statement could be made only to a church in the very last days before the Rapture.

We may see some great changes in the make-up of the church in the last days of this age. These will not be ordinary days and our usual modes of thinking will not apply. A world crisis will change everything, including the churches, and out of it may come all seven of these churches in their final form, which will be a perfect and literal fulfillment of these letters. The one exception may be the Smyrna Church, which is the only church that looks forward to death rather than to the coming of Christ. Smyrna could represent the church of the Tribulation Saints.

These are things we cannot foresee now because the changes will be so great, but these letters contain elements that require something more than has ever happened for their perfect fulfillment.

The Thyatira Church was told to look for the coming of Christ, at which time the evil elements would pass into the great tribulation. Then are described some of the features of that tribulation.

Chapter Three

THE SEVEN CHURCHES
(Continued)

Sardis

Revelation 3

1 And unto the angel of the church in Sardis write; These things saith he that hath the seven Spirits of God, and the seven stars; I know thy works, that thou livest, and art dead.

2 Be watchful, and strengthen the things which remain, that are ready to die: for I have not found thy works perfect before God.

3 Remember therefore how thou hast received and heard, and hold fast, and repent. If therefore thou shalt not watch, I will come on thee as a thief, and thou shalt not know what hour I will come upon thee.

4 Thou hast a few names even in Sardis which have not defiled their garments; and they shall walk with me in white: for they are worthy.

Sardis was a mighty church with a great name. It shook off Jezebel but retained many of her forms and trappings. Its reform was not perfect. Ceremonies, liturgy, ecclesiastical attire, candles, altars, processions, soft music—anything that produces a synthetic spiritual atmosphere is a substitute for, and therefore a replacement of, the Holy Spirit. These things stem from the Roman Catholic Church, not the apostolic church. They hark back to Babylon, not Pentecost.

The Judge said, "Thou art dead." This practice of putting make-believe in place of genuine spiritual experience is always a deadening thing. There is very little to be approved in such a church even though it has a good name. It stands high in the esteem of the world. It has a large number of professing Christians but comparatively few spiritual Christians.

Such a church would naturally not be interested in the prophetic Scriptures or in such things as the Rapture or anything that is spiritually discerned. The Rapture will overtake this church as a thief in the night. Actually it ranks only slightly better than the Laodicean Church.

We noted that to the church that makes so much of Mary, Christ appeared as the Son of God, a name not used in the first chapter. Now again we have a departure from the first chapter, also for an obvious reason. To the church that has replaced the Holy Spirit with forms and trinkets, the Lord comes as one having the seven Spirits of God, "the seven Spirits being the Holy Spirit in His sevenfold activity."—*Pulpit Commentary.*

Philadelphia

Revelation 3

7 And to the angel of the church in Philadelphia write; These things saith he that is holy, he that is true, he that hath the key of David, he that openeth, and no man shutteth; and shutteth, and no man openeth;

8 I know thy works: behold, I have set before thee an open door, and no man can shut it; for thou hast a little strength, and hast kept my word, and hast not denied my name.

9 Behold, I will make them of the synagogue of Satan, which say they are Jews, and are not, but do lie; behold, I will make them to come and worship before thy feet, and to know that I have loved thee.

This is the only active church that has no reproof. It stands out as the greatest and best of the churches. It is first of all a truly Spirit-filled church; next, it is an active missionary church, and it has successfully withstood all attempts of Satan to corrupt its doctrine. It has none of the faults of the previous churches. This is the only church in the entire list that could go out and evangelize the world. It is the only church that could carry the gospel unadulterated to the ends of the earth. These letters do not recognize denominations as such.

The individual churches and denominations may change. They come and go or even pass into the Laodicean state; the Philadelphia Church goes right on. New churches take the place of those that change their beliefs and practices, so there is always a Philadelphia Church. Toward the end, the shift from Philadelphia to Laodicea becomes more apparent, but there is always a church that is true to the faith.

Departure from the faith on the part of the church is a characteristic of the last days; that is what produces the Laodicean Church. This letter is addressed to those churches that are faithful. This gives point to the designation Christ gives himself: "He that is holy, he that is true."

The only reference to the first chapter here is the *key* which He holds. In the first chapter it is called the keys of death and the grave. Here it is called the key of David. There is a reference in Isaiah (22:22)[1] to the key to the house of David. Although the wording is similar, there is no other point of contact. The reference in Isaiah is to something entirely different. It has to do with a situation which will face Israel at some period during the return. No explanation is made of it.

The only clue we have is in the first chapter where it is said to be a key to death and the grave. This could also well be called the key of David because of his many references to death, the Resurrection, and the everlasting kingdom. ("I shall be satisfied when I awake with thy likeness"— Ps. 17: 15.)

---

1. "And the key of the house of David will I lay upon his shoulder; so he shall open,. and none shall shut; and he shall shut, and none shall open" (Isa. 22:22).

The similarity of the statements, "He that openeth and no man shutteth," and "Behold, I have set before thee an open door," has suggested that the key is one that opens opportunities for evangelism. This may be only accidental. It seems to me that if God could, by turning a key, open the doors of the world to evangelism, He would not have waited until the nineteenth century to do it.

Also, if fields are suddenly closed and the missionaries killed or expelled, this is not because God has turned a key; rather, it is the spirit of Satan or the spirit of nationalism that closes mission fields.

The opening and closing that requires the use of a key is that of death and the grave. When God opens the graves at the Resurrection, none can close them; when He closes them in judgment, none can open them. This letter, more than any of the others, looks to the Resurrection. The Philadelphia Church is the one that is kept out of the tribulation by the Rapture.

To open the graves requires a key and the ability to use it. Jesus has the key of death and the grave. He can open; He can close. Our security lies in the fact that He is holy and true.

This church is commended for keeping His Word and not denying His name. This suggests that there are churches that are not faithful to His Word. We have a name for it: modernism. The letter clearly indicates that there is to be a division among the churches. Those belonging to Philadelphia are those who have kept the faith. The others will be accounted for in the next letter.

Again we encounter those who say they are Jews and are not. (See the letter to Smyrna.) These are tares, the planting of Satan. The church is not held responsible for their presence, for they are counterfeits. The church is not told to get rid of them. They are judged as a separate group and consigned to their own place. They belong to Satan's church.

Revelation 3

10 Because thou hast kept the word of my patience, I also will keep thee from the hour of temptation, which shall come upon all the world, to try them that dwell upon the earth.

THE TRIBULATION. The Greek *peirasmos* is the usual word for temptation, but here the definite article is added: "out of the hour of *the* temptation," referring to a special hour, or brief time of trouble that is coming on the entire inhabited earth, for that is the meaning of *world* here. "The hour of trial seems to be that which Christ had foretold should precede His coming, especially the triumph of Antichrist. Hence, the declaration in the next verse."—*Pulpit Commentary*.

Revelation 3

11 Behold, I come quickly: hold that fast which thou hast, that no man take thy crown.

Quickly describes the manner, not the time, of His coming. The tribulation and the judgment that follows will be the most destructive and terrible thing ever to happen to mankind. The Philadelphia Church will exist right up to the very moment of the start of the calamity that will come upon the world as a thief, but the Philadelphia Church will not go into that time of trouble. Christ will come quickly, suddenly, and deliver the church. The Rapture is a rescue. God's people will be delivered (a word which means *rescued* in Daniel 12:1). This sudden deliverance is more fully described further on in Revelation. (See chapters 4 and 12.)

"That no man take thy crown" does not mean "that no man take your crown away from you," but rather, "that no man get the crown that should have been given to you." In other words, BE READY.

And take heed to yourselves, lest at any time your hearts be overcharged with surfeiting, and drunkenness, and cares of this life, and so that day come upon you unawares. For as a snare shall it come on all them that dwell on the face of the whole earth. Watch ye therefore, and pray always, that ye may be accounted worthy to escape all these things that shall come to pass, and to stand before the Son of man.—Luke 21:34–36

Laodicea

Revelation 3

14 And unto the angel of the church of the Laodiceans write; These things saith the Amen, the faithful and true witness, the beginning of the creation of God.

THE CHURCH OF THE LAODICEANS. This is usually changed to "the church in Laodicea" to make it harmonize with the other letters, but there may be a reason for calling it the church of the Laodiceans. These letters are remarkably accurate, even to the last detail, in describing the characteristics of the times. This is the final church and represents the church of the last days of church history on earth.

Two previous churches were plagued by the Nicolaitans—priest control of the laity. This is the church of the people where the pew controls the pulpit. It is a popular church, and unpopular truth is simply not mentioned. Preachers preach to the grandstands, the main object being to fill the church. Pastors are graded according to their ability to draw a crowd and to raise money. The church wants good mixers, not true witnesses. It is the church of the *Laodiceans*.

It is remarkable how the description of Christ always fits the peculiar circumstance of each church. To the church that has ceased to witness to the truth, the Lord comes as the faithful and true witness. Some churches are almost as successful in keeping their people in ignorance as are the Roman Catholics.

THE AMEN. This is the only place that *Amen* is used as a proper name. It means "the true one." In John's Gospel it is translated "verily, verily." In Isaiah 65: 16 "the God of truth" is literally "the God of Amen."

To an age of skepticism, unbelief, discarding of creeds; to a church that no longer holds the Bible inspired and is in open rebellion against the plain teachings of Jesus concerning things to come—to this age and to this church Jesus comes as the Amen.

Revelation 3

15 I know thy works, that thou art neither cold nor hot: I would thou wert cold or hot.
16 So then because thou art lukewarm, and neither cold nor hot, I will spue thee out of my mouth.

LUKEWARM. Cold water is good. Hot water is good. But lukewarm water is sickening. This describes the feeling of nausea that comes when the Judge contemplates this church. "I will spue thee out of my mouth." This church is finally and completely rejected as a church, and the appeal is no longer to the church but to the individual. "Behold, I stand at the door, and knock: if *any man* . . . open the door, I will come in."—Rev. 3: 20.

Here is a so-called Christian church with Christ on the outside—a church that does not believe in Christ. It is more honorable to be an outright atheist than to be an unbelieving church member. Jesus' complaint against the Pharisees was due to their hypocrisy (Matt. 23: 25).[1] Modernism is hypocrisy running rampant. It uses Scriptural terminology, Christian ceremonies, spiritual hymns, and buildings dedicated to the worship of Christ, for the expression and propagation of rank unbelief.

---

1. "Woe unto you, scribes and Pharisees, hypocrites! for ye make clean the outside of the cup and of the platter, but within they are full of extortion and excess" (Matt. 23:25).

Revelation 3

17 Because thou sayest, I am rich, and increased with goods, and have need of nothing; and knowest not that thou art wretched, and miserable, and poor, and blind, and naked:
18 I counsel thee to buy of me gold tried in the fire, that thou mayest be rich; and white raiment, that thou mayest be clothed, and that the shame of thy nakedness do not appear; and anoint thine eyes with eyesalve, that thou mayest see.
19 As many as I love, I rebuke and chasten: be zealous therefore, and repent.

A RICH CHURCH, YET POOR. The tendency today is toward unification and consolidation. The result is costly churches, completely equipped with everything imaginable for comfort and convenience, all the paraphernalia for ritualistic service, and provision for the social and recreational life of the whole community. They "have need of nothing." This church does not realize its own miserable condition. It is rich—that is true—but the wealth is all in this world's goods. It has no treasure in heaven. It is blind. It glories in its intellect and its higher educational advantages. It spends millions upon educational institutions, yet it knows little or nothing of the Word of God and God's plan for the ages.

IT IS NAKED. Having its own righteousness it has no part in the righteousness of Christ. Isaiah said, "All our righteousnesses are as filthy rags."—Isa. 64: 6. That is a fit description of the kind of righteousness that modernism is producing. II Peter 2: 18–22[1] is a telling exposure of this kind of righteousness.

---

1. "For when they speak great swelling words of vanity, they allure through the lusts of the flesh, through much wantonness, those that were clean escaped from them who live in error. While they promise them liberty, they themselves are the servants of corruption: for of whom a man is overcome, of the same is he brought in bondage. For if after they have escaped the pollutions of the world through the knowledge of the Lord and Saviour Jesus Christ, they are again entangled therein, and overcome, the latter end is worse with them than the beginning. For it had been better for them not to have known the way of righteousness, than, after they have known it, to turn from the holy commandment delivered unto them. But it is happened unto them according to the true proverb, The dog is turned to his own vomit again; and the sow that was washed to her wallowing in the mire" (II Pet. 2:18–22).

The falling away from the faith on the part of the church in the last days of this age is known as apostasy. Modernism is another name for apostasy. This is not a falling away from the church, but a falling away from the faith on the part of the church; a falling away from its belief in the inspiration of the Bible, the Deity and virgin birth of Christ, the bodily resurrection of Christ and the saints, the vicarious suffering of Christ, the second coming of Christ, and the other plain teachings of the Word of God.

Apostasy will result in the worship of a man.

Let no man deceive you by any means: for that day shall not come, except there come a falling away first, and that man of sin be revealed, the son of perdition; who opposeth and exalteth himself above all that is called God, or that is worshipped; so that he as God sitteth in the temple of God, shewing himself that he is God.—II Thess. 2:3, 4

The type of church that predominates in the last days of this age is to be rejected as a church, but it has in it many fine people who are not themselves apostates. Actual apostasy is confined almost entirely to the leaders who, like Judas, have betrayed their Lord for a price. The price is usually greater popularity, a bigger church, more influence in the denomination.

The people are deceived, led astray, because they trust their leaders. Most of them could just as easily have been led into the truth. This is the church that will be strongest when the Rapture comes. This is the church that will enter the tribulation that follows. It will be rebuked by being left behind when the saved are caught up, but many of its members will be saved.

Revelation 3

20 Behold, I stand at the door, and knock: if any man hear my voice, and open the door, I will come in to him, and will sup with him, and he with me.

Jesus pictures himself as standing at the door and knocking. You do not knock at the door of a church. You knock at the door of a home. Christ may not enter the Laodicean Church. Modernism saves no souls. But Christ loves the sincere but misguided people in that church. The church is rejected, but there is a final appeal to the people themselves to open their hearts and their homes to the Lord. The Laodicean Church will be destroyed by Antichrist, but many of its members will become martyrs for Christ.

It is important that we understand this Laodicean period of church history. The transition may be gradual. We do not suddenly go from one to the other. There may be many churches like the Laodicean long before the Laodicean period comes in its fullness. Also, the greatest days of the Philadelphia Church may come toward its close.

There is no miracle in the Bible more sensational than prophecy when it is being fulfilled. Some of the most remarkable prophecies are to come toward the end of the age which should give the Philadelphia Church a grand opportunity to interest people in the Bible. This is what the angel referred to when he told Daniel, "Many shall run to and fro, and knowledge shall be increased." To run to and fro could mean to become interested in, to investigate. The angel told Daniel that these things would be sealed, or hidden, until the time of fulfillment; then they would become known. This should be a great day for the church.

The same conditions will also breed false religions. Jesus recognized this when He said, "Take heed that ye be not deceived; for many shall come in my name, saying, I am [Christ]; and the time draweth near: go ye not therefore after them."—Luke 21:8.

False teachers know what to preach. The fact that they say "the time draweth near" indicates that they are basing their appeal on fulfilled prophecy. The only indication of this in the letters is the reference to those who say they are Jews and are not, but are of the synagogue of Satan. The number of false teachers will increase greatly toward the end.

Most of the prophecies to be fulfilled as the age draws to a close have no connection with the church and therefore do not appear in these letters. Some of them are political and have to do with the formation of the nations into the pattern set for the last days. The key is *world dominion*: a world crisis, a world man, a world city, then world prosperity and wealth, the exaltation of man.

Other prophecies concern the Jews and Palestine. These would not be found in Revelation because Revelation deals only with the church and those things that directly involve the saints. They are sensational in their fulfillment, so much so that they should spark a revival in the church. The second coming of Christ will be a familiar topic.

Then a reaction will set in. With a new found peace and prosperity, the world will settle down to enjoying itself, as it did in the days of Noah. "There shall come in the last days scoffers, walking after their own lusts, and saying, Where is the promise of his coming? for since the fathers fell asleep, all things continue as they were from the beginning of the creation."—II Pet. 3:3, 4.

It is then that the Laodicean period will be in full swing.

Chapter Four

SAINTS IN HEAVEN

Third Room

HEAVEN

Saints Organized to
Administer God's
Judgments Contained
in the Seven-Sealed
Book

FROM THE RAPTURE TO
THE RETURN OF CHRIST

Chapters 4—11

The history of the church on earth has now been brought to a close; the scene changes to heaven. It is at this point that many commentators go astray. They fail to recognize the fact that we have here the story of what will take place in heaven after the Resurrection. This is the first time that a reporter has written his story from heaven. John sees things happening on the earth and records them, but it is as one in heaven looking down.

Prophets in the past had at times stood on the earth and looked into heaven, but never before had a prophet gone into heaven and looked down upon the earth. Because this is the first time such a thing has happened, we have difficulty adjusting our thinking to it. There are no symbols in this section, but there are words which sound like symbols because of the difficulties involved in trying to express heavenly things in earthly words. Imagination helps but it is not enough; these things are spiritually discerned.

TRIBULATION AND JUDGMENT

SAINTS ORGANIZED IN HEAVEN — Chapters 4 to 11

FIRST SIX SEALS	**SEVENTH SEAL**		
FOUR HORSEMEN	SEVEN TRUMPETS — VIALS		
The Great Tribulation	1. EARTH	5. KINGDOM of the BEAST	7. AIR
The First Resurrection	2. SEA	6. EUPHRATES	
	3. RIVERS		
SAINTS KILLED BY ANTICHRIST	4. SUN, MOON		
		Two Witnesses	

Rapture (left side) — Return of Christ (right side)

ARMAGEDDON

Tribulation 3 ½ years	6 Seals 3 ½ yrs.	Two Witnesses 3 ½ yrs.

REIGN   OF   THE   BEAST

This section has two main divisions which may be designated by two words: *Tribulation* and *Judgment*.

Notice that the time covered is from the Rapture to the Return of Christ, the chapters are 4 through 11, and the scene is heaven. Everything that happens on the earth is a result of something that happens in heaven.

In this section you are continually passing from cause to effect. The cause is in heaven; the effect is on the earth.

The Trumpet Call
Revelation 4

1 After this I looked, and, behold, a door was opened in heaven: and the first voice which I heard was as it were of a trumpet talking with me; which said, Come up hither, and I will shew thee things which must be hereafter.

2 And immediately I was in the spirit: and, behold, a throne was set in heaven, and one sat on the throne.

HEREAFTER. "After these things" is after the seven churches or the time covered by the seven churches.

> For the Lord himself shall descend from heaven with a shout, with the voice of the archangel, and with the trump of God: and the dead in Christ shall rise first: then we which are alive and remain shall be caught up together with them in the clouds, to meet the Lord in the air: so shall we ever be with the Lord.—I Thess. 4:16, 17

The Resurrection is the first of a series of events that will bring this age to an end and usher in the Kingdom of God. Jesus said these days would be as the days of Noah. That was a time of judgment. God destroyed the earth by a flood, but Noah and his family entered the open door into the ark and God closed the door. Then the ark was raised above the earth on the waters of the flood, and when the judgment was over, the ark settled down again upon dry land. Thus it will be in that day when God judges the earth by fire, pestilence, and plague. The faithful will be taken up from the earth and will escape that time of trouble. After it is over, they will return to the earth with Christ.

The word *resurrection* refers to the dead who will be raised. (Only the dead in Christ will be glorified at that time.) The living Christians will not die. The saved who are living at the time of the Resurrection will never die. Jesus said to Martha: "I am the resurrection, and the life: he that believeth in me, though he were dead, yet shall he live: and whosoever liveth [in that day] and believeth in me shall never die."—John 11: 25, 26. This translation of the living saints together with the Resurrection is called the Rapture.

Sometimes the Rapture is referred to as the Second Coming of Christ. It is the coming of Christ for His church, but it is not until a few years later that He actually comes to the earth with His saints. The part we are now studying is

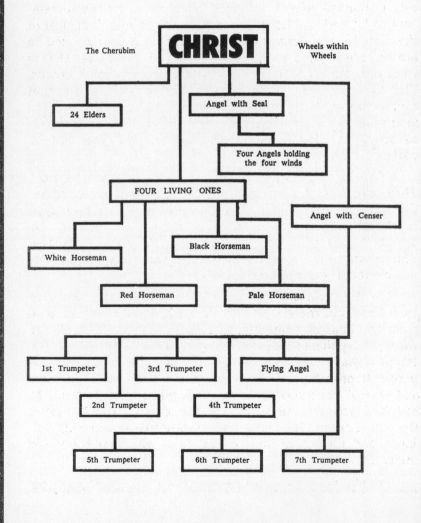

ORGANIZATION OF HEAVEN FOR THE
REDEMPTION OF THE EARTH

The Cherubim

CHRIST

Wheels within
Wheels

24 Elders

Angel with Seal

Four Angels holding
the four winds

FOUR LIVING ONES

Angel with Censer

White Horseman

Black Horseman

Red Horseman

Pale Horseman

1st Trumpeter

3rd Trumpeter

Flying Angel

2nd Trumpeter

4th Trumpeter

5th Trumpeter

6th Trumpeter

7th Trumpeter

the scene that we will behold and the experiences we will pass through immediately after the Rapture.

We have now entered the section of Revelation that is designated in the first chapter as *things that shall be hereafter*—after the church has run its course, after the trumpet call is sounded, after the church has given up its saved members to be with the Lord. The experience of John is typical of the Church, the Bride of Christ. He saw a door opened in heaven. He heard a voice as the sound of a trumpet. That is what the saints will hear when the resurrection morn breaks. The voice said, "Come up hither." That is the invitation that causes the saints to mount up with wings as eagles; it is the invitation to the marriage supper of the Lamb. John responded, as will the church. He saw what the saints will see and experience in that day.

Two kinds of churches will be involved in the Rapture. These are typically set forth in the previous chapter under the heads of Philadelphia and Laodicea. The Laodicean type of church will be left behind. It will not hear the call. The threat, "I will spue thee out of my mouth," will be realized. This refers to the church as a whole. There may be individual members who will hear the call.

To the Philadelphia type of church it is said, "Because thou hast kept the word of my patience, I also will keep thee from the hour of temptation, which shall come upon all the world, to try them that dwell upon the earth."—Rev. 3:10. The Rapture may come in a period of peace and apparent prosperity. It probably will, for it is when "they shall say, Peace and safety" that sudden destruction will come (I Thess. 5:3).[1] It is from this sudden destruction that the Rapture saves the true Church. The peace and prosperity will suddenly collapse, and the strong arm of Antichrist will bring the world under Satanic rule.

---

1. "For when they shall say, Peace and safety; then sudden destruction cometh upon them, as travail upon a woman with child; and they shall not escape" (I Thess. 5:3).

While these momentous events are happening upon the earth, activity begins in heaven. The arrival of the saints is the signal for a new movement in heaven. In chapters 4 through 11 we will study the development of the heavenly movement for the redemption of the earth. The scene is laid in heaven; the actors are saints, redeemed from the earth. The church does not change its work when it goes to heaven; rather it completes it. The work of the church is the redemption of the world.

We have now reached the consummation of this great work. From this point on, the work of redemption centers in heaven because that is where the saints are. We will see what will take place in heaven while the devil is preparing for his last stand upon the earth.

The activities of the saints in heaven during this period will have direct results upon the earth. But always the viewpoint is that of heaven looking down upon the earth. As we study these scenes, remember that this is what we will actually experience in that day.

The Throne of God

Revelation 4

3 And he that sat was to look upon like a jasper and a sardine stone: and there was a rainbow round about the throne, in sight like unto an emerald.

4 And round about the throne were four and twenty seats: and upon the seats I saw four and twenty elders sitting, clothed in white raiment; and they had on their heads crowns of gold.

5 And out of the throne proceeded lightnings and thunderings and voices: and there were seven lamps of fire burning before the throne, which are the seven Spirits of God.

This throne is set for a certain time and purpose. John saw it as it was being set up. Daniel saw the same scene.

I beheld till the thrones were cast down [put in place], and the Ancient of Days did sit, whose garment was white as snow, and the hair of his head like the pure wool: His throne was like the fiery flame, and his wheels as burning fire. A fiery stream issued and came forth from before him: thousand thousands ministered unto him, and ten thousand times ten thousand stood before him: the judgment was set, and the books were opened.—Dan. 7:9, 10

AND HE THAT SAT WAS TO LOOK UPON LIKE A JASPER AND A SARDINE STONE. There is no attempt to name, much less to describe, absolute Deity. John could see only the beauty and brilliancy. In the next chapter God is seen holding a little book in His right hand.

THE RAINBOW is the seal of God's promise that He never again will destroy all mankind as He did in the flood (Gen. 8:21, 22; 9:8–17). When God made this everlasting covenant with mankind and sealed it with the rainbow, He did not do it with the mental reservation that although He would not again destroy all flesh with water, He would destroy it with something worse—fire. For God said, "Neither will I again smite any more every thing living, as I have done. While the earth remaineth, seedtime and harvest, and cold and heat, and summer and winter, and day and night shall not cease."—Gen. 8:21, 22.

The rainbow is the token of this promise. The promise is for all time and to all generations. The earth is to be redeemed. That which is redeemed is not destroyed. There are two ways of purging: by fire and by blood. People may be purged by blood, but the earth must be purged by fire. The nations that refuse the blood must pass through the fire. This is the day of the Lord.

But the day of the Lord will come as a thief in the night; in the which the heavens shall pass away with a great noise, and the elements shall melt with fervent heat, the earth also and the works that are therein shall be burned up.—II Pet. 3:10

And the heaven departed as a scroll when it is rolled together.—Rev. 6:14

And men were scorched with great heat.—Rev. 16:9

And the third part of trees was burnt up, and all green grass was burnt up.—Rev. 8:7

And there fell a great star from heaven, burning as it were a lamp.—Rev. 8:10

Every one of the seven last plagues carries fire. The earth is literally on fire, but the fire does not come to all parts of the earth at the same time. People live through it. The nations are still here when it is all over. God will keep His promise. Many will die it is true, but God will not again destroy all mankind or every living thing. The rainbow is round about the throne.

ELDERS. On earth God's people are divided into churches. In heaven churches lose their identity. The saints are divided into new groups. Their work has not ended, only the methods have changed, and a new element has been added. The present work of the church does not include judgment. This is the day of grace, but judgment is coming and the saints are the agents in judgment, just as they are in grace.

The work which the saints must do after the Rapture is greater than that which they face now. Organization is necessary. The saints will be organized, probably according to their ability and qualifications. These groups of saints are called by names which at first seem strange to us. We must remember that John was in heaven. Nothing that he saw has ever been seen on earth, so there are no earthly words to describe it. Paul was once caught up into heaven and saw things which he said were impossible to utter.

John has to use words of earth to tell of heavenly things. These words are not adequate, but they are all we have. First, there are the elders; they sit upon thrones. Their number is 24. This is a representative number. These 24 elders

represent saints of both the Old and New Testament times—
a very great number—just as the 12 patriarchs and the 12
apostles represent the saints of both dispensations. This
number is used in the same way of the Holy City to indicate
the saved of the Old and New Testament times. The 12 gates
and the 12 foundation stones are named for the 12 tribes and
the 12 apostles. It indicates that the Holy City is the abiding
place of all the saved (Rev. 21: 12–14).

Saints in heaven may be identified by their clothing,
work, and position. Their clothing is white (Rev. 19: 8;
3: 5). They wear crowns (Rev. 2: 10; 3: 11). They sit on
thrones (Rev. 3: 21; 2: 26, 27; Matt. 19: 28). Their work involves redemption, which includes the preaching of the gospel and the administration of the judgments and the plagues.
Later it will include the reconstruction of all things during
the reign of Christ.

Other groups of saints in this heavenly army are called
living ones (beasts), horsemen, and angels. They all represent saints organized for the great work at hand. "Do ye not
know that the saints shall judge the world?"—I Cor. 6: 2.

> Let the saints be joyful in glory:
> Let them sing aloud upon their beds.
> Let the high praises of God be in their mouth,
> And a two-edged sword in their hand;
> To execute vengeance upon the heathen,
> And punishments upon the people;
> To bind their kings with chains,
> And their nobles with fetters of iron;
> To execute upon them the judgment written:
> **This honour have all his saints.**—Ps. 149:5–9

There is a division of work. We will be made rulers over
many things according to our faithfulness over few things.
The elders, living ones, and horsemen do not represent individuals, but groups, divisions of labor and responsibility,
from the highest to the lowest. There are wheels within

wheels until they reach the earth. The living ones lead all heaven in praising God and are next under Christ in authority in carrying out the program of redemption. Living ones, elders, horsemen, and others—all redeemed ones—"execute the judgments written" in the seven-sealed book that is about to be opened.

LIGHTNINGS, VOICES, AND THUNDERS. The rainbow was evidence of mercy and grace. The lightnings, voices, and thunders are evidences of judgment and wrath. When God was about to visit Egypt's sins upon her, He sent thunder, hail, and fire which ran along upon the ground, and Pharaoh said, "Entreat the Lord that there be no more voices of God."— Ex. 9:28.

The rainbow was seen before the lightnings. Grace always precedes judgment. There are two kinds of judgment sent forth in this day of the Lord. First comes judgment mixed with grace. War, famine, pestilence, falling stars will cause even the great men of the earth to run for cover; but they will be accompanied by the preaching of the gospel, and millions will be saved. That, in fact, is the purpose of this judgment.

Next comes wrath poured out without mixture: pure, punitive, purging judgment. During this second period of judgment and plagues no one is said to be saved, but the earth will be cleansed. The purpose of the second part of the judgment is to cleanse the earth of the effects of sin. When sin came, God cursed the ground for man's sake. That curse will some day be lifted, but first the results of sin must be destroyed. The earth must be purged. This is the meaning of the lightnings, thunders, and voices.

THE SEVEN SPIRITS OF GOD. The seven lamps of fire are the seven Spirits of God. These are not candles on candlesticks, but torches born aloft, indicating preparation for battle. When Gideon went forth against the Midianites, his three hundred men took each a burning torch in his left hand and a trumpet in his right, and they cried, "The sword of the Lord and of Gideon."

When Jesus came to earth the first time, it was to usher in the Dispensation of Grace. The Holy Spirit was seen descending upon Him like a dove. The second time He comes, He will make war with His enemies and destroy those that destroy the earth. No longer does the Holy Spirit appear as a dove, but as flaming torches prepared for battle. (See Psalm 18:7–16.)

These seven torches are not symbols of the Holy Spirit. We are not dealing now with symbols, but with literal heavenly things. The dove which John saw was not a symbol of the Holy Spirit, but a manifestation of the Holy Spirit. It was the form the Holy Spirit took to make himself known. It represented the character of the work He would do. These seven torches are likewise a manifestation of the Holy Spirit, indicating the nature of the work He is about to do.

The Four Living Ones

Revelation 4

6 And before the throne there was a sea of glass like unto crystal: and in the midst of the throne, and round about the throne, were four beasts full of eyes before and behind.

7 And the first beast was like a lion, and the second beast like a calf, and the third beast had a face as a man, and the fourth beast was like a flying eagle.

8 And the four beasts had each of them six wings about him; and they were full of eyes within: and they rest not day and night, saying, Holy, holy, holy, Lord God Almighty, which was, and is, and is to come.

The translators called them "beasts," probably because of their appearance, but they are similar to the cherubim of Ezekiel. The scene and the circumstances are also similar.

These living ones are likened to a lion, a calf, a man, and an eagle in flight.

Again John is using earthly words to express heavenly things. We should understand these animal characteristics in the same way we understand the meaning of Lamb and Lion when applied to Christ. He is called the Lamb a number of times in Revelation. We do not picture Christ in our minds as looking like a lamb or even acting like one. He is called a Lamb because, like the sacrificial lamb, He died for the people.

Jesus may also be likened to a calf or ox because He was the servant of both God and man. He washed the disciples' feet. Jesus is likened to a man because He took on himself the form of sinful flesh. He is like a flying eagle because the heavenly places are His habitation. He came down from heaven and went back to heaven.

These four living ones do not represent Christ, however. They represent saints. They worship Christ, but "when we see him we shall be like him, for we shall see him as he is."— I John 3:2.

Four is an important number in redemption. It is the number of the earth. When four is in evidence, God is dealing with the earth.

Redemption is God's program of all ages. During this age, the process of redemption is occupied with the preaching of the gospel for the saving of individual souls. At the time of the Rapture, the process of redemption will reach another stage, that of consummation. God will then be dealing with the earth in a more direct and potent way. The gospel must be presented to every kindred, tongue, people, and nation, accompanied by severe judgments. This is the work of Christ and the saints. The saints will be organized into an army. The highest officers are represented by the living ones.

Another group of saints will carry out the orders sent down by the living ones. They are called horsemen. Still other groups are seen as angels or messengers. The angels have their trumpets and vials full of the seven last plagues. These are also saints (Rev. 21: 9; 22: 8, 9).

The created angels are ministering spirits for the saints, but the saints alone are God's administrators in the process of preaching the gospel and judging the world.

These are not symbolic. We are not dealing now with symbols. The throne of God is real and literal. The elders are real and literal. Heavenly things are not symbolized. They sometimes sound like symbols to us because we have to use earthly words to express heavenly things. When we get to heaven we will not see an earthly lamb or lion or calf or flying eagle. Then we will have new bodies, new eyes, and new experiences, and we will see these living ones having a nature and character expressed by the prophet in these inadequate earthly words.

WORSHIP IN HEAVEN. Before every great event of this grand consummation of redemption, there is a worship service in heaven, led by the saints.

Chapter Five

THE SEVEN-SEALED BOOK

Revelation 5

1 And I saw in the right hand of him that sat on the throne a book written within and on the backside, sealed with seven seals.

2 And I saw a strong angel proclaiming with a loud voice, Who is worthy to open the book, and to loose the seals thereof?

3 And no man in heaven, nor in earth, neither under the earth, was able to open the book, neither to look thereon.

4 And I wept much, because no man was found worthy to open and to read the book, neither to look thereon.

REDEMPTION OF THE EARTH

After the reunion in heaven and the organization of the saints for the work at hand, all eyes are fixed upon Him that sits upon the throne. He holds in His right hand a little book or scroll. It has writing inside and out and is sealed with seven seals. The business of breaking these seals is the most important work in all of God's creation at the time.

The scene is in heaven. The time is immediately after the Rapture. The actors are Christ and the saints, with the created angels looking on and rejoicing.

A strong angel proclaimed throughout heaven, "Who is worthy to open the book and to loose the seals?" John wept because no man was found worthy to take the book and break its seals. This is the final scene in the process of redemption that began as soon as man sinned. Genesis tells of the beginning of redemption, and Revelation deals with the consummation of redemption. Christ started this work of redemption, the church continued it, now Christ and the church will finish it.

To understand the full scope of redemption, we must realize what was lost by sin, for redemption is the restoration of all that was lost through sin. This may be considered under three heads.

1. *Man lost his soul.* "For in the day that thou eatest thereof thou shalt surely die."—Gen. 2: 17. "The soul that sinneth, it shall die."—Ezek. 18: 4.

2. *Man lost his body.* He could no longer eat of the tree of life, and he began to get old. "For dust thou art, and to dust shalt thou return."—Gen. 3: 19.

3. *Man lost the earth.* He lost dominion over the earth. It produced a living for him only by hard labor. It developed weeds and pests, disease and plagues. It passed into the control of Satan (Gen. 3: 17–19) .[1]

If the result of sin is threefold, then redemption must be threefold. Redemption is not complete until all that was lost by sin has been restored. When we think of redemption, our minds naturally go back to the cross. But that was only the beginning, Redemption is a process that began with the cross, is continued by the preaching of the gospel, and will be brought to its consummation in the Day of the Lord.

---

1. "And unto Adam he said, Because thou hast hearkened unto the voice of thy wife, and hast eaten of the tree, of which I commanded thee, saying, Thou shalt not eat of it: cursed is the ground for thy sake; in sorrow shalt thou eat of it all the days of thy life; thorns also and thistles shall it bring forth to thee; and thou shalt eat the herb of the field; in the sweat of thy face shalt thou eat bread, till thou return unto the ground; for out of it wast thou taken: for dust thou art, and unto dust shalt thou return" (Gen. 3:17–19).

Three main events in redemption are:

1. *Conversion,* the saving of the soul.

2. *Resurrection,* the redemption of the body.

3. *The Second Coming of Christ,* the redemption of the earth.

The first two have taken place and the third is in preparation. This third phase of redemption concerns the earth and those who are on the earth after the Rapture. The devil is in possession of the earth and is reigning in the person of Antichrist. He will oppose every step in the process of redemption, from the Rapture, when he is repulsed by Michael, to the coming of Christ, when he will marshal the armies of the world to battle.

John's weeping shows how serious the situation would be if no one could be found worthy to open the book. John was not weeping because he had been denied a knowledge of the contents of the book. The book is never said to be read. It was not for the purpose of reading the book that the seals were to be broken. In fact, John probably knew the nature and contents of the book. Ezekiel was given a similar vision in which the contents of the book were revealed: "And when I looked, behold, an hand was sent unto me; and, lo, a roll of a book was therein; and he spread it before me; and it was written within and without: and there was written therein lamentations, and mourning, and woe."   Ezek. 2:9, 10. Ezekiel was told to eat the book and it was in his mouth as honey for sweetness; but he carried out the instruction "in bitterness" (Ezek. 3:3, 14).[1]

In the same way John was told to eat the little book after the seals had been broken, and it was in his mouth as sweet as honey but it made his belly bitter (Rev. 10:8–10).

---

1. "And he said unto me, Son of man, cause thy belly to eat, and fill thy bowels with this roll that I give thee. Then did I eat it; and it was in my mouth as honey for sweetness.... So the spirit lifted me up, and took me away, and I went in bitterness, in the heat of my spirit; but the hand of the Lord was strong upon me" (Ezek. 3:3, 14).

As these seven seals are broken, they produce upon the earth lamentations and mourning and woe.

The word "redemption" comes down to us from an Old Testament custom. When the children of Israel possessed the Promised Land, certain provisions were made to keep the land evenly distributed among the people. It could be sold or otherwise disposed of, but the bill of sale was of the nature of a lease, which would expire automatically in the year of Jubilee, and the land would revert to its original owner.

If a man lost his property or sold it, thus disinheriting his children, any kinsman could buy back the land at any time by paying the purchase price. Then the land could be restored to its rightful owners. This process was known as redemption, and the man who bought it back was the redeemer. Later the land would actually pass into the hands of the heirs, and they would move onto it and possess it. This was called the "redemption of the purchased possession."

When a kinsman thus redeemed the property, an instrument of writing was drawn up. On the inside were written the specifications, terms of sale, and the like. On the back were the signatures and witnesses. This deed was rolled up and sealed. The sealed book was delivered to the original owner or to the heir. The heir could at his convenience break the seals, and with the opened book as his authority, take possession of the land by force if necessary. Such a transaction is recorded in Jeremiah 32:6–15.

Jesus is the heir of all things, but the devil is in possession. In the last days Satan will reign supremely in this world. He has no right here. The land has been bought back. The redemption price has been paid. The evidence thereof is in the right hand of Him that sits upon the throne.

But the devil, the "lawless one," knows no law. He not only refuses to leave, but he is fortifying himself and preparing to resist eviction. Therefore it will be necessary to break the seals and proceed with the authority of the open book.

But who is to break the seals? Who dares attempt the eviction of Satan? Who has a chain that can bind him? All heaven is thrown into a state of consternation. They have not forgotten the great war in heaven when Satan attempted to prevent the Resurrection, and when Michael and all his angels, the greatest force in all the universe, succeeded only in driving Satan down to the earth and strengthening his position in the world.

This picture is portrayed in vivid detail in the 41st chapter of Job. Michael and his angels are not equal to this emergency. "Behold, the hope of him is in vain: shall not one be cast down even at the sight of him? Lay thine hand upon him, remember the battle, do no more. None is so fierce that dare stir him up: who then is able to stand before me?" "Who is worthy to open the book, and to loose the seals thereof?"

No wonder John wept at such a scene as this. Heaven never underestimates the power of Satan. Only the uninformed on earth do that.

THE REDEMPTION OF THE PURCHASED POSSESSION

> In whom ye also trusted, after that ye heard the word of truth, the gospel of your salvation: in whom also after that ye believed, ye were sealed with that Holy Spirit of promise, which is the earnest of our inheritance until the redemption of the purchased possession.—Eph. 1:13, 14

An inheritance is property; so is a purchased possession. However, there is a difference between an inherited possession and a purchased possession. It may represent the same property, but the difference is in the kind of ownership. This language is taken from the Old Testament and had to do with the laws concerning the land.

> The land shall not be sold for ever: for the land is
> mine; for ye are strangers and sojourners with me. And
> in all the land of your possession ye shall grant a redemp-
> tion for the land. If thy brother be waxen poor, and hath
> sold away some of his possession, and if any of his kin
> come to redeem it, then shall he redeem that which his
> brother sold.—Lev. 25:23–25

To redeem is to buy back something that has been lost
to the rightful heir. A purchased possession, therefore, was
not a permanent possession, but was always subject to redemption. One who held a purchased possession could not
settle down with peace of mind knowing that he had provided a home for himself and his family. He never knew
what minute some kinsman of the former owner would produce the price of redemption, which amounted to rent for
the time he would have had the land until the year of jubilee,
when it would automatically return to the original heir (Lev.
25: 27, 28).[1]

A purchased possession, then, was only a temporary
possession, never secure. Only an inherited possession was
a secure possession. The process of restoring land to its rightful heir was called redemption, and the kinsman who restored
it was the redeemer. This was all typical of the great redemption of the earth.

The fact that the earth must be redeemed supposes that
it has been lost. When Jesus said the meek shall inherit the
earth, He was admitting that the meek do not now possess
the earth.

The earth is now a purchased possession. The court-
houses record the names of the temporary possessors, not
the permanent owners of the land. Some of the land may
have been inherited from relatives, but it is still a purchased

---

1. "Then let him count the years of the sale thereof, and restore the overplus unto
the man to whom he sold it; that he may return unto his possession. But if he be not
able to restore it to him, then that which is sold shall remain in the hand of him that
hath bought it until the year of jubilee; and in the jubilee it shall go out, and he shall
return unto his possession" (Lev. 25:27, 28).

possession, for "the earth is the Lord's and the fulness thereof."

The saints are heirs, joint-heirs with Christ. We do not receive our inheritance when we are saved. The earth is not yet redeemed, but we receive the Holy Spirit, the assurance of God's promise of our inheritance, until the redemption of the purchased possession.

The redemption of the earth is the main subject of Revelation. There, Jesus is usually called by His redemptive name—the Lamb. The notable exception is when He comes in power to reign.

It should be noted that redemption and regeneration are different phases of one process. They always go together, and the whole process may be known as redemption.

All the action of Revelation stems from the breaking of the seals of the book that originally is held in the right hand of God. The breaking of the seals sets in motion the most violent forces ever to strike this earth. This violence will stem from three directions:

From the heavens. Frightening words are used to express it. "The heavens departed as a scroll when it is rolled together." "The stars of heaven fell to the earth." It would seem that the earth will pass through the path of an exploding star. Great rocks, white with heat, will strike the earth with a tremendous roar. The withering heat will melt everything for hundreds of miles. The earth will shake and tremble under the impact.

From the earth. Peace will be taken from the earth. The nations will be angry. Wars will break out everywhere— nation against nation, and kingdom against kingdom. The earth will be in turmoil.

From the prison house of evil spirits. Evil spirits, relics of past and forgotten ages, taking on terrifying forms, will be turned loose by the millions. This is the worst of all the plagues and is preceded by the warning cry: "Woe, woe, woe to the inhabiters of the earth."

It is impossible to exaggerate the terror of these plagues. Men will seek death, and death will flee from them. Yet these are not callous judgments sent by a capricious God because He is angry at somebody. Every judgment has a purpose. Every one is necessary to accomplish the tremendous task of regeneration. All the results of sin must be destroyed. They have reached deep into the earth and into the human race.

How easy it seems now to be saved! What a simple matter to escape all of these things! But it was not easy for God. It was done at tremendous cost. It is easy for us only because Jesus paid the price for us. When God begins to redeem the world by purging it of all the results of sin, the world will begin to understand a little of what it cost Christ to offer free salvation to all who would accept.

Death is an enemy that must be destroyed, "and there shall be no more death." Before death can be destroyed, the causes of death must be wiped out, together with all the effects and results of sin. God must have a world and a human race like He would have had if sin had never been known.

Only God knows the depths to which sin has penetrated the original perfect creation. It must all be purged. Every one of the seven last plagues is aimed at a definite mark; every one has a specific purpose. If one were omitted, then there would be some portion left uncleansed. The Millennium is the remaking of a perfect world. The purging comes first, then the restoration. The redemption of the purchased possession is an undertaking of first magnitude, even for God.

Although redemption is a process running over many years, there are some special high points. A large number of events dot the proceedings. Two of these high points were made the subjects of prophecy at the very beginning. "I will put enmity between thee and the woman, and between thy seed and her seed; it shall bruise thy head, and thou shalt bruise his heel."—Gen. 3: 15.

Here is a prediction of the crucifixion which seemed to be a victory for Satan, and a prediction of the return of Christ, which event marks the end of Satan's power. Between these two climactic events which happen on the earth, there is one of equal interest which takes place in heaven.

The redemption of the purchased possession has a legal side; redemption is, in fact, a legal process. The kinsman or redeemer who was able and willing to pay the price of redemption would, after having paid the price, take the sealed book from the rightful owner and break the seals. The open book was his right to evict the usurper and repossess the land. Breaking the seals was equivalent to burning the mortgage.

The case recorded by Jeremiah differs from this procedure somewhat because of circumstances. Land was purchased by Jeremiah for himself. The heir was Hanameel, but the land did not go back to him. It was still a purchased possession, subject to future redemption. Therefore Jeremiah says, "So I took the evidence of the purchase, both that which was sealed according to the law and custom, and that which was open."—Jer. 32: 11.

In this case both documents were buried because the redemption would not be for a long time. "Thus saith the Lord of hosts, the God of Israel, Take these evidences, this evidence of the purchase, both which is sealed, and this evidence which is open; and put them in an earthen vessel, that they may continue many days. For thus saith the Lord of hosts, the God of Israel; Houses and fields and vineyards shall be possessed again in this land."—Jer. 32: 14, 15.

This looks forward to a future redemption when the deed will be found, its seals broken, and the land possessed by its rightful heirs. The sealed book meant that the land was subject to redemption and would some day be redeemed.

In the case of the purchased possession, the earth, the legal process is a heavenly procedure. It has nothing to do with the people on the earth. It is, therefore, left for Revelation to record it. The legal transaction must take place after the price has been paid and before the actual possession is effected. That is, it must take place between the first and second comings of Christ.

It is only natural that the heirs should be present in such a ceremony. It would be expected that the ceremony in which the saints are so vitally concerned would wait for the resurrection of the saints and the great gathering together in heaven. This is, of course, when it happens—right after the catching up of the saints. There they are from every kindred, tongue, people, and nation, all the redeemed from all time (Rev. 5: 9).

After a most impressive preliminary worship service, all interest is centered in a book or scroll, sealed with seven seals and held in the right hand of Him that sits upon the throne.

Never in all the history of the earth from Genesis on has Satan been in more complete possession of the earth. Jesus called him the prince of this world, and he will become king indeed. When the saints are removed from the earth and the Holy Spirit is taken out of the way of iniquity, allowing it free course; when the man of sin is revealed and all the world worships him; when only those may buy or sell legally who have his mark—then it may be said that Satan is in complete possession of the earth. *But it is a purchased possession.*

Satan has always had a claim to this world ever since Adam sold out and thus disinherited all his seed, but the claim is that of a usurper. He did not come by it honestly; it was

not an inheritance. From the beginning, it was only a purchased possession.

And now, when Satan seems to be for the first time in
complete possession, there appears in the right hand of Him
that sits on the throne in heaven a sealed book, the title deed
to the earth. It is sealed. That means that the property has
passed out of the hands of the rightful owner and is subject
to redemption—providing a kinsman can be found who is
able and willing to pay the price, or who has already paid
the price and is now qualified to break the seals.

THE LION OF THE TRIBE OF JUDAH

Revelation 5

**5 And one of the elders saith unto me, Weep not:
behold, the Lion of the tribe of Juda, the Root of David,
hath prevailed to open the book, and to loose the seven
seals thereof.**

**6 And I beheld, and, lo, in the midst of the throne
and of the four beasts, and in the midst of the elders
stood a Lamb as it had been slain, having seven horns
and seven eyes, which are the seven Spirits of God sent
forth into all the earth.**

John was looking for some great, spectacular force that
could match that of Satan. The elder said, "Behold the Lion."
When John looked for the Lion, he saw instead a Lamb that
had been slain, now alive and ready for action. The Lamb of
God never has lost a battle with Satan. He prevailed in the
wilderness, in the garden, on the cross, and in the tomb. He
has gone up leading captivity captive. As the Lamb slain, He
paid the redemption price. As the Lion of the tribe of Judah,
He will take possession. The breaking of the seals is the preparation for taking the purchased possession by force.

After the seals are all broken, the papers are served,
which is the legal act of taking possession. This is recorded
in the tenth chapter. Actual possession occurs at the coming
of Christ, recorded in the 19th chapter.

THE LAMB SLAIN. From this point on, Christ is usually called the Lamb. It is His redemption name. How could a person look like a lion and a lamb at the same time? Here we have a good illustration of heavenly language as opposed to the language of earth. On earth, personal appearance does not necessarily reflect the nature or character of the individual; in a sense, clothes make the man. In heaven, appearance does reflect character. A robe of righteousness may be worn only by a righteous person. When John the Baptist first saw Jesus, he said, "Behold the Lamb of God." Jesus is the Lamb slain. When He first appears near the throne surrounded by all the saints of all the ages, it will be as one who has paid the price of redemption. John the seer saw in Christ exactly what John the Baptist saw—the Redeemer, the Lamb slain. But to redeem the world requires more than sacrifice; it takes power. Satan must be evicted. Jesus is more than a Lamb; He is also a Lion. When He comes again to possess the earth, He is not called the Lamb, but the "KING OF KINGS, AND LORD OF LORDS."

All this is revealed in the name and description of Jesus when He appears before the throne to begin the work for which He gave His life.

SEVEN HORNS, SEVEN EYES. Seven always means totality—all power, all knowledge. "All power is given unto me in heaven and in earth." The seven eyes are explained; they are the seven Spirits of God, the Holy Spirit in His fullness. This is not a symbol like the seven horns of the beast. As a symbol, a horn is a nation. In heaven a horn refers to power or strength. Hannah sang, "Mine horn is exalted."—I Sam. 2: 1.

These two characters are found in one verse in II Chron. 16: 9: "For the eyes of the Lord run to and fro throughout the whole earth, to shew himself strong in the behalf of them whose heart is perfect toward him."

Revelation 5

7 And he came and took the book out of the right hand of him that sat upon the throne.

This act will go unnoticed on the earth, although it will not be long before its consequences will be felt. In heaven, however, it is the climax of a long history. No one knows how long ago God planned for the day when He would break the seals of that book and begin the last chapter in the redemption of the earth. Revelation speaks of names written in the book of life before the foundation of the world.

The Living ones, and Elders, and all the hosts of angels, are filled with adoring wonder and joy, as if another fiat had gone forth from God for a new creation. *"And when He took the book,"* there went a thrill through the universal heart of living things. *"The four Living ones, and the twenty-four Elders fell down before the Lamb."*

A song, which was never sung before, broke from their lips. John hears the lofty anthem rolling sublimely through heaven: THOU ART WORTHY TO TAKE THE BOOK, AND TO OPEN THE SEALS OF IT; *for You were slain, and redeemed us to God by your blood, out of every tribe and tongue and people, and nation, and You have made us unto our God, kings and Priests, and we shall reign on the earth."*

It must have been a great day in the experience of the angels when God made something grow whose seed was in itself, thus opening up a whole new vista of change and progress. Heaven gets excited over things that God does.

The coming of Jesus into the world as a babe was a cause for rejoicing among the heavenly host, and, although we are not told, probably His return to heaven was the signal for a universe-wide celebration. The Resurrection is a very special event for heaven, even more than for the earth, because it is heaven that will receive the saints, and it is heaven that will get rid of Satan when he is cast down to the earth. This event, especially the defeat of Satan by the forces of Michael, will cause great rejoicing in heaven.

> Therefore rejoice, ye heavens, and ye that dwell in them. Woe to the inhabiters of the earth and of the sea! for the devil is come down unto you, having great wrath, because he knoweth that he hath but a short time.—Rev. 12:12

But no event in the long story of the earth is as far reaching in its consequences as the one so simply stated: "And he came and took the book out of the right hand of him that sat upon the throne."

In order to qualify for this honor, He had first to suffer the agonies of the Garden and the shame of the cross, with all the unknown suffering of bearing the sins of the world. He had to be the Lamb slain. This could not be accomplished by anyone less than God, because He also had to have all power. Even that was not enough; the problems encountered in purging and perfecting the earth and the human race are almost beyond solution. Sin has left a deep scar; Satan has been thorough. Only God would have the wisdom to solve the human problem. The Lamb must have the seven Spirits of God.

Only in Jesus, our kinsman, do all these things exist. He alone is both Lion and Lamb. He alone is able to approach the throne and take the book from the right hand of God. He alone can break its seals. He alone can redeem the purchased possession. He alone can evict Satan.

This act is the signal for the greatest outburst of rejoicing in heaven since that day in the long past when the morning stars sang together and the sons of God shouted for joy.

Revelation 5
8 And when he had taken the book, the four beasts and four and twenty elders fell down before the Lamb,

having every one of them harps, and golden vials full of odours, which are the prayers of saints.

9 And they sung a new song, saying, Thou art worthy to take the book, and to open the seals thereof: for thou wast slain, and hast redeemed us to God by thy blood out of every kindred, and tongue, and people, and nation;

10 And hast made us unto our God kings and priests: and we shall reign on the earth.

THE PRAYERS OF THE SAINTS. This is the time of answered prayer. All the prayers of the saints of all ages might be summed up in the words, "Thy kingdom come, Thy will be done on earth." No prayer is lost, no real prayer forgotten. Some day the prayers of the saints will be presented before the Lord as sweet odours. God will make good every promise in His Word.

"And hast redeemed us to God by thy blood . . . and made us unto our God kings and priests." The American Standard Version has changed this to read: "And didst purchase unto God with thy blood men of every tribe, . . . and madest them to be unto our God a kingdom and priests." There is not sufficient reason for this change. It seems to have been made to favor those who do not believe in a future reign of Christ on the earth with His saints. One of the ancient manuscripts, the *Codex Alexandrinus,* omits the word "us." All the other manuscripts contain it. The weight of evidence is in favor of the King James Version. The *Pulpit Commentary* admits that "the reading *us* is supported by various manuscripts and similarly the first person is used in verse 10 [and *we* shall reign on the earth]" and adds, *"thou didst purchase us at the price of thy blood* would perhaps give the sense more correctly; for such is the force of the words, *in thy blood."*

We have a rule by which we can determine the correct rendering of this verse. Whenever Christ is mentioned throughout the book of Revelation, some reference is made to the first chapter. Christ is mentioned here as the Lamb

and the Lion who takes the book from the hand of God preparatory to opening the seals. The response of the saints is
in harmony with this action of Christ. The reference is to
the first chapter and the fifth and sixth verses, where both
the lamb and lion characters of Christ are in view. It reads:
"And from Jesus Christ, who is the faithful witness, and the
first begotten of the dead, and the prince of the kings of the
earth. Unto him that loved us, and washed us from our sins
in his own blood, and hath made us kings and priests unto
God and his Father." These are almost the same words as
we find in the fifth chapter. The American Standard Version
translates this verse: "Unto him that loveth us, and loosed us
from our sins by his blood; and he made us to be a kingdom,
to be priests unto his God and Father." The American Standard
Version is, therefore, inconsistent in its translation of these
identical statements, while the Authorized Version is correct.

THE NEW SONG. Long before daylight we were on the
road traveling to the Billy Sunday Tabernacle, fifty miles
away. At every main crossroad other cars joined the proces-
sion. There was to be a morning Thanksgiving service. We
arrived in time to get a front seat in the middle aisle. The
tabernacle seated 15,000 people. In a few minutes it was full,
and they sent for Mr. Sunday.

While we were waiting, someone near the front in one
corner began to sing. Others nearby took up the strain, and
the song rolled back and back across that immense throng
until it reached the farthest corner of the tabernacle. The
very walls seemed to shake as those fifteen thousand people
sang, "This is my story, this is my song, praising my Saviour
all the day long."

So I imagine it will be in that day when all the saved of
earth and all the hosts of heaven, stretching out into measure-
less space, watch with wonder and amazement as the Lamb
approaches and takes the book from the right hand of Him
that sits upon the throne. And then spontaneously a song

breaks out among the elders and living ones near the throne; others take it up and it rolls out and out into space until all creation vibrates with praises to God.

No wonder the earth will quake, the mountains move out of their places, and islands of the sea disappear. No wonder the stars of heaven will fall to the earth as a fig tree drops her green figs when she is shaken by a mighty wind. No wonder brave men will hide in the rocks and in the caves for fear in the great day of God Almighty.

This is called a new song, but there seems to be nothing new in it, nothing that the saints have not been singing through the years. This is not a song that will be learned after they get to heaven. It is a familiar song, one that they all know, which bursts forth spontaneously in the ecstacy of the moment.

It is, however, a new song in heaven. It is the first time that a song of redemption has ever been sung in heaven. Angels cannot sing the song of redemption because Christ never died for them. This song has all the elements of a familiar gospel chorus: "Thou wast slain and hast redeemed us to God by thy blood out of every kingdom and tongue and people and nation."

> And when, in scenes of glory,
> I sing the new, new song,
> 'Twill be the old, old story,
> That I have loved so long.

It is only after the redemption song has died away that the created angels raise their voices in praise to God. This closes the worship in heaven preparatory to the opening of the seals and the resultant distress on earth.

Revelation 5

13 And every creature which is in heaven, and on the earth, and under the earth, and such as are in the sea, and all that are in them, heard I saying, Blessing, and

**honour, and glory, and power, be unto him that sitteth
upon the throne, and unto the Lamb for ever and ever.**

There is a truth expressed in this verse that is not very
well understood because it is something we cannot see. There
is an unseen world of spirit beings. They are just as real as
we are, and they have actual bodies, but their bodies are not
made of dust or any earthly substance or anything that we
call physical.

When Moses and Elijah visited Jesus on the Mount of
Transfiguration, they made a miraculous appearance. When
they disappeared, they were probably no farther away. It was
their appearance, not their disappearance that required a
miracle.

After His resurrection, Jesus had a body. He said so:
"Handle me, and see; for a spirit hath not flesh and bones, as
ye see me have."—Luke 24:38.

There are disembodied spirits, but they are not in a hap-
py state. The loss of body was a punishment. The angels have
bodies; however, they cannot be seen by mortal eyes except
by miracle. Jesus, after His resurrection, could appear or disappear at will, pass through closed doors and ascend into
heaven. Physical things are not barriers to spiritual bodies.
The place we call heaven does not have to be far removed
from the earth; it could be very close. Angels could be all
around us. Some of the prophets recognized this.

When Elisha was surrounded by the armies of Syria, we
read:

> And when the servant of the man of God was risen
> early, and gone forth, behold, an host compassed the city
> both with horses and chariots. And his servant said
> unto him, Alas, my master! how shall we do? And he
> answered, Fear not: for they that be with us are more
> than they that be with them. And Elisha prayed, and said,
> Lord, I pray thee, open his eyes, that he may see. And
> the Lord opened the eyes of the young man; and he saw;

and, behold, the mountain was full of horses and chariots of fire round about Elisha.—II Kings 6:15–17

These hosts of angels did not come from some far distant place at the call of Elisha; they were there all the time. Jesus said He had legions of angels at His command.

As men explore what they call outer space, they have to arrive at new conceptions of distance, time, and size. Time stands still, size becomes unimportant, and distance is relative—if it exists at all. Such earthly things as time, temperature, and gravity are not factors in the world of beings that were made to inhabit the universe. These things—so new to scientists—are old truths in the Bible.

This throne of God standing on a sea of glass that John saw need not be any distance at all from the earth. So when all the angels and all the saints are gathered together, they extend out into space in all directions—down to the earth, under the earth, in the sea—everywhere.

Chapter Six

BREAKING THE SEALS

We have here a new chapter but not a new subject. Chapter divisions, while very convenient, sometimes separate a subject from its context. There should be no separation here. The scene is still around the throne. Jesus has taken the book and is about to begin breaking its seals. The seals are broken, one at a time; and as each seal is broken, something happens in heaven that usually has a result on the earth. In this section—the story of the tribulation and the Day of the Lord from the standpoint of heaven—we are always passing from cause to effect.

The cause is what takes place in heaven; the effect is felt on the earth. All action stems from the breaking of a seal. The key word is *administration*. The saints are going into action; they are the administrators of God's grace and judgment. Each seal brings the redemption of the earth one step nearer.

This is not mob violence. There is organization; each person has his work. There is reason and direction in every act. The elders and living ones do not represent individuals but groups. The saints are all there from every kindred, tongue, people, and nation. Now we encounter other groups of saints presided over by four horsemen. We have to put the horsemen in the same light as the elders and living ones, the Lion and Lamb. Again John is using earthly words to express heavenly scenes. They are called horsemen because they go forth from heaven to carry out the assignment revealed by the broken seal. Jesus breaks the seal; He is in charge of the whole program. The next one under Him gives the order. The next in line carries it out, until it reaches the earth. This is substantially what Ezekiel saw and described as wheels within wheels—in other words, organization to carry out a task.

The one thing we have to remember is that John was caught up in spirit into heaven and records what will happen there, so everything that is recorded in this section takes place in heaven. The earth is in view only if the heavenly act has a result on the earth.

IN WRATH REMEMBER MERCY. The sixth chapter of Revelation does not stand alone. A portion of the Olivet Discourse and a chapter of Habakkuk deal with the same events. Other prophets make reference to it. The prophets do not always view the scene from the standpoint of heaven. They supplement rather than duplicate each other; therefore, they add many important details.

The third chapter of Habakkuk is a prayer poem and uses the imagery of poetry. Habakkuk brings out vividly one feature that is important for us to understand: a peculiar mixture of wrath and mercy. This refers to a brief period immediately after the Rapture when the Tribulation Saints are being saved and persecuted. Revelation calls it the great tribulation.

(Please note: The word *tribulation* is often applied to the whole time between the Rapture and the Return of Christ. This is not Scriptural. Tribulation is not the name of a period of time—such as the Twentieth Century—but rather is an experience, especially of the saints. Persecution or tribulation may come any time. *In the world ye shall have tribulation.* Revelation distinguishes between the judgments of God on a wicked world and the persecution of saints by the forces of Antichrist. Only the latter is called tribulation. When the time of tribulation is over, the judgments of God—called the seven last plagues—start in earnest. The judgments of God are not tribulation in the Bible sense.)

TWO KINDS OF JUDGMENT

First Six Seals

Judgment mixed with grace
Purpose: To Save
The Great Tribulation

Multitudes saved

Joel 2:28–32
And it shall come to pass afterward, that I will pour out my spirit upon all flesh; and your sons and your daughters shall prophesy, your old men shall dream dreams, your young men shall see visions:

And also upon the servants and upon the handmaids in those days will I pour out my spirit.

And I will shew wonders in the heavens and in the earth, blood, and fire, and pillars of smoke.

The sun shall be turned into darkness, and the moon into blood, before the great and the terrible day of the Lord come.

And it shall come to pass, that whosoever shall call on the name of the Lord shall be delivered: for in mount Zion and in Jerusalem shall be deliverance, as the Lord hath

Seventh Seal
(Seven Trumpets)

Wrath without mixture
Purpose: To Purge
*The Great and Terrible Day
of the Lord*

No record of anyone being saved

Zeph. 1:14–18
The great day of the Lord is near, it is near, and hasteth greatly, even the voice of the day of the Lord: the mighty man shall cry there bitterly.

That day is a day of wrath, a day of trouble and distress, a day of wasteness and desolation, a day of darkness and gloominess, a day of clouds and thick darkness,

A day of the trumpet and alarm against the fenced cities, and against the high towers,

And I will bring distress upon men, that they shall walk like blind men, because they have sinned against the Lord: and their blood shall be poured out as dust, and their flesh as the dung.

Neither their silver nor their gold shall be able to deliver them in the day of the Lord's wrath; but the whole land shall

said, and in the remnant whom
the Lord shall call.

be devoured by the fire of his
jealousy: for he shall make
even a speedy riddance of all
them that dwell in the land.

There is only one petition in Habakkuk's prayer: "In
wrath remember mercy." He says, "I saw the tents of Cush-
an in affliction, and the curtains of Midian did tremble." This
is the poet's way of expressing what Jesus called the beginning of sorrows and Revelation calls the hour of temptation
that will try the whole world.

We must distinguish two kinds of judgment, or wrath,
in Revelation: first, a judgment whose purpose is salvation;
second, a judgment whose purpose is purging and punishment. First comes the judgment mixed with grace, then follows the wrath poured out "without mixture." The first
business at hand is the salvation of the Tribulation Saints.
That is the work of the four horsemen. Habakkuk puts it in
these words:

> Thou didst march through the land in indignation,
> thou didst thresh the heathen in anger. Thou wentest forth
> for the salvation of thy people, even for salvation with
> thine anointed."—Hab. 3:12, 13

(Parallel Scriptures: Zech. 6: 1; Matt. 22: 1–10; Matt. 24:
7–14)

The Four Horsemen

Revelation 6

**1 And I saw when the Lamb opened one of the
seals, and I heard, as it were the noise of thunder, one of
the four beasts saying, Come and see.**

The American Standard Version reads simply "come."
Both translations may be considered correct. The words "and
see" are in some of the ancient manuscripts. But the command
is not to John. He did not have to be told to pay attention. The

command is to the horseman. He is told to come (or go) and he goes forth conquering.

The Lamb directs the work; the four living ones, the four horsemen, the four angels, the seven angels, the elders, and the two witnesses carry on the work. We may not be able conclusively to identify all of these administrators; however, we know that the elders, the living ones, the two witnesses, and the seven angels are saints or groups of saints. They represent the various groups into which the saints are divided for this work of judgment. "He that overcometh, and keepeth my works unto the end, to him will I give power over the nations: and he shall rule them with a rod of iron; as the vessels of a potter shall they be broken to shivers." —Rev. 2:26, 27.

This is the day of judgment when the nations will be broken to shivers. The first six seals bring judgment mixed with grace. Thousands of people are saved. The gospel is preached to all the world—to every kindred, tongue, people, and nation, thus fulfilling the words of Jesus, "And this gospel of the kingdom shall be preached in all the world for a witness unto all nations; and then shall the end come." —Matt. 24:14.

The gospel will be preached, but not by anyone on the earth; that would be impossible after the restraining power of the Holy Spirit has been removed and Satan is in full control of the nations. The gospel must be preached from heaven, for that is where all the preachers are. From the earth these messengers will seem like angels flying through the air. In Revelation the messengers of the gospel are called angels. If we turn to the part of Revelation which tells about this, we read, "And I saw another angel fly in the midst of heaven, having the everlasting gospel to preach unto them that dwell on the earth, and to every nation, and kindred, and tongue, and people."

In this day of consummation of redemption, four things must be accomplished:

1. Everyone must hear the gospel.

2. The earth must be judged and purged.

3. Everything which cannot be redeemed must be destroyed.

4. There must be a reconstruction to make all things new.

We have now arrived at the first two of these: the preaching of the gospel to every nation and the beginning of sorrows. This is what Jesus referred to when He said:

> For nation shall rise against nation, and kingdom against kingdom: and there shall be famines, and pestilences, and earthquakes, in divers places. All these are the beginning of sorrows. Then shall they deliver you up to be afflicted, and shall kill you: and ye shall be hated of all nations for my name's sake. And then shall many be offended, and shall betray one another, and shall hate one another. And many false prophets shall rise, and shall deceive many. And because iniquity shall abound, the love of many shall wax cold. But he that shall endure unto the end, the same shall be saved. And this gospel of the kingdom shall be preached in all the world for a witness unto all nations; and then shall the end come.—Matt. 24:7–14

Notice the sequence of events: Christ takes the book from the right hand of God and breaks one of the seals; one of the four living ones issues an order to the first horseman: "Come," or as it would be better rendered in this case, "Go."

WHITE

Revelation 6

2 And I saw, and behold a white horse: and he that sat on him had a bow; and a crown was given unto him: and he went forth conquering, and to conquer.

THE WHITE HORSE. Notice that it is the *horse* that is white, red, black, or pale. The color applies to the horse, not the rider. It represents not the character of the rider but the nature of the work to be done. White connects with righteousness—always. Christ has white hair; the saints have white robes, God's great judgment throne is white. "They shall walk with me in white." White cannot by any stretch of the imagination be applied to Antichrist.

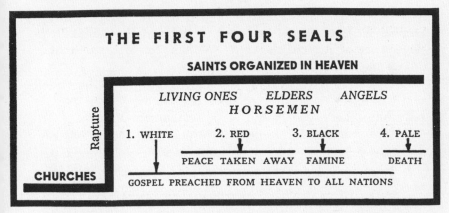

The white horseman causes the gospel to be preached to every kindred, tongue, people, and nation. It will be preached from heaven, but from the earth the messengers will seem like flying angels.

"He that sat on him had a bow." It has been said that he had a bow but no arrows, and therefore the man represents a counterfeit. But if we say a man carries a gun, we assume the gun to be loaded. The reference is to the third chapter of Habakkuk where this same scene is in view.

> Was the Lord displeased against the rivers? was thine anger against the rivers? was thy wrath against the sea? that thou didst ride upon thine horses and thy chariots of salvation? **Thy bow** was made quite naked, according to the oaths of the tribes, even thy word. —Hab. 3:8, 9

Notice the four questions, three referring to judgment and one to salvation. The bow represents the preaching of the Word accompanied by displeasure, anger, and wrath.

(When Christ comes with His saints, they will ride upon white horses, but at that time they will not carry bows. The day of preaching is past. The Word is then a sword proceeding from the mouth of Christ. He will do all the fighting in that day with the word of His mouth.)

"And a crown was given unto him." The Greek word is *stephanos*. It is always used of Christ and the saints. It is never used of Antichrist. Antichrist has "ten crowns," that is "diadema"—many crowns.

"He went forth, conquering and to conquer." The Greek word is *nikao*. It means "to have the victory." It is used in only one other place in the New Testament—Romans 8:37: "We are more than *conquerors* through him that loved us." The words "and to conquer" would suggest final victory.

I am well aware of the common interpretation of this verse, which claims this first horseman is a counterfeit, and the white, the bow, the crown, and the final victory should all be taken in reverse, as though they mean the opposite of what they usually mean in Scripture. There is nothing in the context to suggest that. He is sent forth by one of the four living ones. Are the living ones also counterfeit? When it says, "And the four living ones said, Amen. And the four and twenty elders fell down and worshipped him that liveth for ever and ever," is that also to be taken in reverse? Are they to represent false worshippers? Is all of Revelation to be read in reverse? What kind of interpretation are we being subjected to?

Nobody would see Antichrist coming out of heaven, commissioned by Christ, riding a white horse, carrying the Word, wearing a crown, and going forth to conquer, unless he had Antichrist in mind and was trying to find a place to fit him in. A straightforward interpretation, without some preconceived notion, would never find Antichrist in that verse. The inconsistency of such an interpretation is immediately apparent when you consider that there are four horsemen and only one Antichrist. To make the first horseman a man, the others such impersonal things as war, famine, and death, is so inconsistent as not to be worthy of our consideration. If the first one is a wicked man, then the others are men even more wicked. When you read the sixth chapter of Revelation, begin with the last verse of the fifth chapter and put the scene where it belongs—in heaven.

The number four is an important number in Bible numeration. It does not connect with Antichrist. His number is 6 or 666 (Rev. 13:18). Four represents God dealing with the earth. When Christ came to earth He was represented by four Gospels. The cherubim, whose number is four, are God's agents. They in turn send forth the four horsemen, also God's agents. The scene is in heaven, about the throne, where the Lamb is breaking the seals. Does Antichrist come out of heaven? Is he given a saintly crown and a bow (the Word of God), and is he sent forth by one of the living ones with a commission from the throne, to go forth conquering and to conquer?

It has been argued that Antichrist is a false Christ, and that he is pictured here in his assumed character instead of his true character, thus accounting for the white horse, the crown, the bow, and the victory. Such exegesis would put a question mark after every Bible description and make consistent interpretation almost impossible. Revelation is consistent in its use of numbers, symbols, and other highly descriptive words.

There is, moreover, no evidence that Antichrist will claim to be Messiah or that the Jews will ever receive him as such. He will confirm a treaty with many, as any foreign king might do. He is Antichrist, not because he imitates Christ, but because he *opposes* Christ. He will be a political ruler, a dictator over an empire. He may be a Gentile. At least he is to be a dictator over Gentile nations, and he will hate and persecute the Jews. The Gentile world will worship him, but the Jews never will worship him nor receive his mark. The Gentile world will also worship the dragon (devil) who gives him life. However, the world will not worship him because they think he is Christ returned. They will worship a superman, empowered by Satan. It is the climax of modernism, humanism, and pride.

RED

Revelation 6

3 And when he had opened the second seal, I heard the second beast say, Come [or Go] and see.

4 And there went out another horse that was red: and power was given to him that sat thereon to take peace from the earth, and that they should kill one another: and there was given unto him a great sword.

THE RED HORSE. In place of "come and see," read *come* or *go*. It is the same word that is translated "went" in the fourth verse. It should be read, "Go. And there went out," or "*Come*. And there came out." He takes peace from the earth. War is not mentioned but it is probably included. There is no peace anywhere. The Prince of Peace has been rejected. There will be perplexity of nations, the sea and the waves roaring, men's hearts failing them for fear of those things which are coming upon the earth, and "a man's foes shall be they of his own household." The betrayal of friends and relatives into the hands of Antichrist will be a common occurrence. No one will be safe. There will be no peace. Peace is a gift of God. It will be totally withdrawn from the world after the Rapture.

This connects with a large amount of Scripture. There will come a world crisis. "Ye shall hear of wars and rumours of wars."—Matt. 24:6. This is the beginning of the end and brings the Rapture very close. "When these things begin to come to pass, then look up and lift up your heads; for your redemption draweth nigh."—Luke 21:28.

However, the end (of the age) is not yet, Jesus said. There will follow a time of peace and prosperity. Great and wealthy cities will be built. Trade barriers will be broken down. Gold will be plentiful, and silver will be almost a base metal. For a detailed description of this wealth as represented by one city, see Revelation 18. This will be a false millennium inspired by Satan and put into operation by Antichrist. It is when they say "peace and safety" that sudden destruction comes upon them. The second horseman takes peace from the earth.

Peace could not be taken from the earth unless there were peace on the earth. The Rapture will come in a time of profound peace and world tranquility—the triumph of modernism (the Laodicean Church). It is this satanic peace that God will suddenly take from the earth. It is difficult to imagine what the world will be like when there is no peace anywhere. Cities have food for only a few days. With no peace among workers, no transportation could move. The most terrifying result of no peace would be famine, and that is exactly what happens.

BLACK

Revelation 6

5 And when he had opened the third seal, I heard the third beast say, Come and see. And I beheld, and lo a black horse; and he that sat on him had a pair of balances in his hand.

6 And I heard a voice in the midst of the four beasts say, A measure of wheat for a penny, and three measures of barley for a penny; and see thou hurt not the oil and the wine.

THE BLACK HORSE. The description is that of a food administrator. There is a careful measuring of food and medicine, indicating great scarcity and want. A measure is slightly more than a quart. A penny is a day's wage. Oil and wine must be carefully preserved for the sick and wounded.

It is not said that the rider on the black horse sends famine to the earth. Famine would be the natural result of universal war between nations and internal strife such as strikes and lockouts. There could be no commerce or trade if peace were taken from the earth. Jesus said, "Nation shall rise against nation, and kingdom against kingdom." The word for nation is *ethnos*: peoples, families, races. The whole world is in turmoil.

The work of the third horseman is to prevent the famine from wiping out mankind. This shows how terribly devastating is the absence of peace.

PALE

Revelation 6

7 And when he had opened the fourth seal, I heard the voice of the fourth beast say, Come and see.

8 And I looked, and behold a pale horse: and his name that sat on him was Death, and Hell followed with him. And power was given unto them over the fourth part of the earth, to kill with sword, and with hunger, and with death, and with the beasts of the earth.

THE PALE HORSE. We learn later that the total length of time during which these four horsemen operate is only three and one half years, so no one feature could last very long. Peace is also taken from the animal kingdom so that all animals become dangerous. This could result in a widespread destruction; however, it affects only a fourth part of the earth. We learn later that these operations have a single purpose: to give the saints some relief from the persecutions of Antichrist. So, we would expect that the part of the earth in which the horseman works is that controlled directly by Antichrist or is subject to the severest persecution.

Revelation 6

9 And when he had opened the fifth seal, I saw under the altar the souls of them that were slain for the word of God, and for the testimony which they held:

10 And they cried with a loud voice, saying, How long, O Lord, holy and true, dost thou not judge and avenge our blood on them that dwell on the earth?

11 And white robes were given unto every one of them; and it was said unto them, that they should rest yet for a little season, until their fellowservants also and their brethren, that should be killed as they were, should be fulfilled.

MARTYRS. We pass from cause to effect. The four horsemen have done their work. There is one more seal to be broken; then the final results will be in. The fifth seal does not have any result on the earth; rather, it shows the result of what has been happening on the earth. These people had been killed but had not yet been raised. They were waiting, somewhat impatiently, for the day of their resurrection. Their question reveals their identity.

They had been killed as martyrs; the killing was still going on. They were told that they would have to wait till all the rest of their number had also been killed; then they would all be raised at once. This happens in the next chapter.

This killing will be done by Antichrist. So far, Antichrist has not been mentioned in Revelation. The reason is that this is the story of heaven during this period. Antichrist does not come from heaven. He is of the earth and of Satan. He would naturally not appear in a history of heaven, but when the saints are killed and they are waiting their resurrection, their souls would be seen in heaven.

In the next section or "room," we have the same story from the viewpoint of the earth. Then Antichrist will appear and his story will be told in great detail. We will see the Resurrection and that part of the church that is left behind. We will see how Antichrist will persecute the saints, how the four horsemen will appear to the people on the earth, and many other details that would not appear in the heaven-side of the process.

These martyred saints were given white robes. They could not wear the robes before their resurrection. They were a foretaste, an object of anticipation like a girl's hope chest.

Sixth Seal

Revelation 6

12 And I beheld when he had opened the sixth seal, and, lo, there was a great earthquake; and the sun became black as sackcloth of hair, and the moon became as blood;

13 And the stars of heaven fell unto the earth, even as a fig tree casteth her untimely figs, when she is shaken of a mighty wind.

14 And the heaven departed as a scroll when it is rolled together; and every mountain and island were moved out of their places.

15 And the kings of the earth, and the great men, and the rich men, and the chief captains, and the mighty men, and every bondman, and every free man, hid themselves in the dens and in the rocks of the mountains;

16 And said to the mountains and rocks, Fall on us, and hide us from the face of him that sitteth on the throne, and from the wrath of the Lamb:

17 For the great day of his wrath is come; and who shall be able to stand?

THE SIXTH SEAL. This seal brings to a close the Dispensation of Grace. Every dispensation has ended in judgment, but the severest of all will come at the end of this dispensation. Compare this with Luke 21:25, 26.

And there shall be signs in the sun, and in the moon, and in the stars; and upon the earth distress of nations, with perplexity; the sea and the waves roaring; men's hearts failing them for fear, and for looking after those things which are coming on the earth: for the powers of heaven shall be shaken.

The Greek word for perplexity means "no way out." The nations can find no way out of their difficulties. The Greek word for distress means "a holding fast together." Conditions on the earth will cause the nations to huddle together while the signs in the heavens are driving them mad.

Of all the heavenly phenomena which have appalled mankind since creation, none has caused greater consternation than the appearance of fireballs hissing and thundering through the sky. Although the earth is continually bombarded by shooting stars, it is seldom that one actually reaches the ground. The study of meteorites is one of the youngest of sciences. On the nights of November 13 and 14, 1833, the earth was visited with great meteoric showers. The heavens were literally filled with falling stars. Again in November 1866, a similar shower occurred. These meteoric showers have come regularly at about thirty-year intervals for the past thousand years.

In 1900 and in 1933 the meteoric showers were not very severe. Scientists, however, may not have long to wait, for toward the end of the Great Tribulation, the heavens will shed stars like a tree dropping its fruit when it is shaken by a mighty wind. A star such as fell in Virginia thousands of years ago would kill all life and level every building for hundreds of miles around. The shock and heat would be felt as far as Ohio, and a tidal wave would flood the coast of Europe.

The building of bigger telescopes and satellites, the growing interest in heavenly bodies, in comets and falling stars, and the increased knowledge of what the powers of the heavens can do to the earth will only serve to intensify the horror of this calamity.

The rider on the white horse will superintend the preaching of the gospel during this time. It is no wonder that people are saved in large numbers. During the apostasy which prevails today, very few people are saved. Revivals are merely special meetings for church members. People are either bitter toward religion or have become indifferent church members, but the "latter rain" comes with these visitations from heaven, fulfilling the prophecy which Peter quoted, and was only partially fulfilled at Pentecost.

> And I will shew wonders in heaven above, and signs in the earth beneath; blood, and fire, and vapour of smoke: the sun shall be turned into darkness, and the moon into blood, before that great and notable day of the Lord come: and it shall come to pass, that whosoever shall call on the name of the Lord shall be saved.—Acts 2:19–21

The people on the earth, even the kings and the great men, are panic-stricken by the violent actions of the forces of nature. The earth has lost its stability and the heavens seem to have gone crazy. Satan is not able to control the world he claims to be master of.

Notice that the people realize where their trouble is coming from. They try to hide from the One who sits upon the throne and from the Lamb, saying, "The great day of his wrath is come."

Sometimes these plagues have been thought of as coming from Satan. This is not the case. They are directed against Satan and serve to defeat him in his purpose. They are sent from heaven as a direct administration of judgment whose primary purpose is redemption. They also hinder Satan's persecution of the saints. The Holy Spirit will no longer hinder Satan. Then, only the forces of nature as they are controlled from heaven may be used to hinder the efforts of Satan against the struggling church that still must survive for a short time.

These are not symbols as some expositors have supposed. Falling stars and earthquakes are not symbols of communism or any other passing fancy. There are no symbols in this section. If these are symbols, then one man's guess is as good as another's, and there have been plenty of guesses. Symbols follow strict rules of interpretation; they have positive meanings. All guesswork is eliminated. When Joel and Peter said "wonders in heaven and signs in the earth beneath; blood, and fire, and vapours of smoke," they meant just that.

Isaiah was not using symbols when he said:

> Fear, and the pit, and the snare, are upon thee, O inhabitant of the earth. And it shall come to pass, that he who fleeth from the noise of the fear shall fall into the pit; and he that cometh up out of the midst of the pit shall be taken in the snare: for the windows from on high are open, and the foundations of the earth do shake. The earth is utterly broken down, the earth is clean dissolved, the earth is moved exceedingly. The earth shall reel to and fro like a drunkard, and shall be removed like a cottage; and the transgression thereof shall be heavy upon it; and it shall fall, and not rise again. And it shall come to pass in that day, that the Lord shall punish the host of the high ones that are on high, and the kings of the earth upon the earth. And they shall be gathered together, as prisoners are gathered in the pit, and shall be shut up in the prison, and after many days shall they be visited. Then the moon shall be confounded, and the sun ashamed, when the Lord of hosts shall reign in mount Zion, and in Jerusalem, and before his ancients gloriously.—Isa. 24:17–23

This is the beginning of the fulfillment of II Peter 3: 10:

> But the day of the Lord shall come as a thief in the night; in the which the heavens shall pass away with a great noise, and the elements shall melt with fervent heat, the earth also and the works that are therein shall be burned up.

This is a part of the process of the redemption of the earth. There is no such thing as the end of the world. Where this expression occurs in the Bible, it should be translated "age." The word "world" is used to translate a number of Greek words, some of which refer to time or conditions, as, "This is a woman's world." That kind of world could come to an end. The created world will not come to an end.

> But Israel shall be saved in the Lord with an everlasting salvation: ye shall not be ashamed nor confounded world without end. For thus saith the Lord that created the heavens; God himself that formed the earth and made it; he hath established it, he created it not in vain, he formed it to be inhabited: I am the Lord; and there is none else.—Isa. 45:17, 18

> Unto him be glory in the church by Christ Jesus throughout all ages, world without end. Amen.—Eph. 3:21

Peter is careful to specify the exact time he is talking about. He says, "But the day of the Lord will come as a thief in the night; in the which the heavens shall pass away with a great noise, and the elements shall melt with fervent heat."— II Pet. 3: 10. The time is the day of the Lord. This expression is used throughout the Bible always with the same meaning. It refers to a period of time less than one generation in length when God will cleanse the earth of the effects of sin, and begin the development of a new world, also a new age. This, according to the promise, must be done without destroying the human race.

Jesus referred to this time in the Olivet Discourse. He said, "And except those days should be shortened there should no flesh be saved: but for the elect's sake those days shall be shortened."

That there will be people living here when the time of trouble is over is evident from the balance of the Discourse:

> Immediately after the tribulation of those days shall the sun be darkened, and the moon shall not give her

light, and the stars shall fall from heaven, and the powers of the heavens shall be shaken: and then shall appear the sign of the Son of man in heaven: and then shall all the tribes of the earth mourn, and they shall see the Son of man coming in the clouds of heaven with power and great glory.—Matt. 24:29, 30

All the tribes of the earth are still here after the tribulation of those days. If they are still here after that, then they will always be here, because Jesus said concerning that time: "For then shall be great tribulation, such as was not since the beginning of the world to this time, no nor ever shall be." —Matt. 24:21.

Jesus said there would be nations here after He returns. He said:

When the Son of man shall come in his glory, and all the holy angels with him, then shall he sit upon the throne of his glory: and before him shall be gathered all nations: and he shall separate them one from another, as a shepherd divideth his sheep from the goats.—Matt. 25:31, 32

Conditions on the earth after the day of the Lord are described in many places, for instance, Micah 4.

But in the last days it shall come to pass, that the mountain of the house of the Lord shall be established in the top of the mountains, and it shall be exalted above the hills; and people shall flow unto it. And many nations shall come, and say, Come, and let us go unto the mountain of the Lord, and to the house of the God of Jacob; and he will teach us of his ways, and we will walk in his paths: for the law shall go forth of Zion, and the word of the Lord from Jerusalem. And he shall judge among many people, and rebuke strong nations afar off; and they shall beat their swords into plowshares, and their spears into pruninghooks: nation shall not lift up a sword against nation, neither shall they learn war any more.—Mic. 4:1–3

During the Millennium people will live to be very old, although there will still be death. It is not till the end of the Millennium that death is conquered.

> For, behold, I create new heavens and a new earth: and the former shall not be remembered, nor come into mind. But be ye glad and rejoice for ever in that which I create: for, behold, I create Jerusalem a rejoicing, and her people a joy. And I will rejoice in Jerusalem, and joy in my people: and the voice of weeping shall be no more heard in her, nor the voice of crying. There shall be no more thence an infant of days, nor an old man that hath not filled his days: for the child shall die an hundred years old; but the sinner being a hundred years old shall be accursed. And they shall build houses, and inhabit them; and shall plant vineyards, and eat the fruit of them. They shall not build, and another inhabit; they shall not plant, and another eat: for as the days of a tree are the days of my people, and mine elect shall long enjoy the work of their hands. They shall not labour in vain, nor bring forth for trouble; for they are the seed of the blessed of the Lord, and their offspring with them. And it shall come to pass, that before they call, I will answer, and while they are yet speaking, I will hear. The wolf and the lamb shall feed together, and the lion shall eat straw like the bullock: and dust shall be the serpent's meat. They shall not hurt nor destroy in all my holy mountain, saith the Lord.—Isa. 65:17–25

There will also be a great increase in population during and after the Millennium.

> Thy people also shall be all righteous: they shall inherit the land for ever, the branch of my planting, the work of my hands, that I may be glorified. A little one shall become a thousand, and a small one a strong nation: I the Lord will hasten it in his time.—Isa. 60:21, 22

What then does Peter mean by saying that all these things shall be dissolved? First let me say that the English words in this passage are too strong to translate accurately the original. For instance, the word "dissolved" is used to translate Greek and Hebrew words meaning soften, solve, loose, and to become corrupted or wasted.

> For this they willingly are ignorant of, that by the word of God the heavens were of old, and the earth standing out of the water and in the water: whereby the world that then was, being overflowed with water, perished: but the heavens and the earth, which are now, by the same word are kept in store, reserved unto fire against the day of judgment and perdition of ungodly men. But, beloved, be not ignorant of this one thing, that one day is with the Lord as a thousand years, and a thousand years as one day. The Lord is not slack concerning his promise, as some men count slackness; but is longsuffering to us-ward, not willing that any should perish, but that all should come to repentance. But the day of the Lord will come as a thief in the night; in the which the heavens shall pass away with a great noise, and the elements shall melt with fervent heat, the earth also and the works that are therein shall be burned up. Seeing then that all these things shall be dissolved, what manner of persons ought ye to be in all holy conversation and godliness?—II Pet. 3:5–11

Peter's word for dissolved is also translated in other places: break, break up, destroy, loose, put off, unloose, melt. As an illustration, we have Matthew 21:2: "Go into the village over against you, and straightway ye shall find an ass tied, and a colt with her: *Loose* them, and bring them unto me."

The term "pass away" never means to be completely destroyed. We have friends and relatives who have passed away. We do not think of them as having been destroyed or thrown out of existence. There is nothing in the word "pass" or in the word "away" that suggests cessation of being. Our whole trouble with II Peter 3 is that we have read into it things that are not there.

New Testament writers obtained much of their information from the Old Testament. Verse 10 is evidently taken from Isaiah.

Come near, ye nations, to hear; and hearken, ye people: let the earth hear, and all that is therein; the world, and all things that come forth of it. For the indignation of the Lord is upon all nations, and his fury upon all their armies: he hath utterly destroyed them, he hath delivered them to the slaughter. Their slain also shall be cast out, and their stink shall come up out of their carcases, and the mountains shall be melted with their blood. And all the host of heaven shall be dissolved, and the heavens shall be rolled together as a scroll: and all their host shall fall down, as the leaf falleth off from the vine, and as a falling fig from the fig tree. For my sword shall be bathed in heaven: behold, it shall come down upon Idumea, and upon the people of my curse, to judgment.—Isa. 34:1-5

Notice also how Peter uses the word "perish." He says, "The world that then was, being overflowed with water, *perished*." It perished, but it was still here after the waters receded. The earth will perish again, but it will still be here after the time of trouble, and people will still be living here.

Robert Young, in his *Literal Translation of the Bible*, calls attention to the fact that in the Authorized Version the English word "destroy" is used to translate no less than forty-nine different Hebrew words. It is a very broad term. A boy could take an ax and destroy a piece of furniture with one blow. It could be repaired.

We must keep in mind God's program for this world. It is one of redemption. The earth is to be redeemed. The process of redemption involves cleansing. There are two purging agents: blood and fire. People may be purged by blood, the blood of Christ; but the physical earth must be purged by fire. Everything in II Peter may be found in Revelation, where God is cleansing the earth by fire. All the seven last plagues carry some kind of fire. The earth seems to be on fire. One-third of the trees and all the green grass are consumed. This fire does not strike all the world at the same time or with the same intensity. People live through it.

The Millennium is actually a time of reconstruction. Perfection will be attained only at the end. Then the new heaven and the new earth will be realized. It will take 1,000 years to perfect the earth. The final judgment takes out the last elements of evil; then "the tabernacle of God is with men, and he will dwell with them, and they shall be his people, and God himself shall be with them, and be their God."— Rev. 21:3.

The whole process is summed up in the words of Revelation 21:5: "Behold, I make all things new." Not all new things, but the old things made new—that is redemption.

Chapter Seven

TRIBULATION SAINTS

Revelation 7

1 And after these things I saw four angels standing on the four corners of the earth, holding the four winds of the earth, that the wind should not blow on the earth, nor on the sea, nor on any tree.

2 And I saw another angel ascending from the east, having the seal of the living God: and he cried with a loud voice to the four angels, to whom it was given to hurt the earth and the sea,

3 Saying, Hurt not the earth, neither the sea, nor the trees, till we have sealed the servants of our God in their foreheads.

FOUR ANGELS. In the midst of wrath, God remembers mercy. The rainbow has not been forgotten. The remaining judgments will be even more severe, so there must be protection provided for any of God's people who are to remain upon the earth. All the forces of nature which have been summoned to aid in this final cleansing of the earth are now held in check for a brief moment while certain preparations are being made. This in itself shows how awful the seven last plagues are which are about to come.

There is a divine principle illustrated here. At various times throughout the Bible, we encounter a form of judgment that is sent directly from God: the flood, the destruction of Sodom, the seven last plagues (trumpets and vials). These differ from disasters of natural origins. God promises no special protection from the natural workings of nature. When an earthquake strikes, it strikes all alike, whether good or bad; but when a special judgment, because of iniquity, is to be imposed by God himself, then God's people are first given protection. Thus the angel said to Lot, "Haste thee, escape thither; for I cannot do any thing till thou be come hither." God's people are always promised protection from God's judgments.

In harmony with this principle, God's people will be delivered before the tribulation starts. The Rapture must come before the tribulation because these tribulation judgments are not normal workings of nature, but direct visitations from God. The great men of the earth recognize this and say so. But there are people saved during these judgments. They must also be given protection, so they are sealed.

If they had been killed, of course they would not need this sealing, but if they are living at the end of the tribulation time, they will face the seven last plagues, which are much more terrible. They will be protected from the plagues by the seal. This is what Jesus meant, in part at least, when He said, "But he that shall endure unto the end, the same shall be saved."—Matt. 24: 13. That statement may include others not mentioned in Revelation.

Come, my people, enter thou into thy chambers, and shut thy doors about thee: hide thyself as it were for a little moment, until the indignation be overpast. For, behold, the Lord cometh out of his place to punish the inhabitants of the earth for their iniquity.—Isa. 26:20, 21

Revelation 7

4 And I heard the number of them which were sealed: and there were sealed an hundred and forty and four thousand of all the tribes of the children of Israel.

5 Of the tribe of Juda were sealed twelve thousand. Of the tribe of Reuben were sealed twelve thousand. Of the tribe of Gad were sealed twelve thousand.

6 Of the tribe of Aser were sealed twelve thousand. Of the tribe of Nepthalim were sealed twelve thousand. Of the tribe of Manasses were sealed twelve thousand.

7 Of the tribe of Simeon were sealed twelve thousand. Of the tribe of Levi were sealed twelve thousand. Of the tribe of Issachar were sealed twelve thousand.

8 Of the tribe of Zabulon were sealed twelve thousand. Of the tribe of Joseph were sealed twelve thousand. Of the tribe of Benjamin were sealed twelve thousand.

ISRAELITES SEALED. This is the first mention of the nation of Israel. A comparison with the parallel reference, Revelation 14: 1–5, shows that these Israelites have been saved. If they had been saved before the Rapture, they would have gone to heaven with the other saints. They must, therefore, have accepted Christ as their Saviour during the time that the gospel is preached from heaven. One might wonder why they were not killed the same as the Gentile believers. The reason is that they were Jews living in Palestine which will, for a time, be exempt from the persecutions of Antichrist. We know that Antichrist will attempt to appease the Jews, and therefore he will not persecute them during these first few years. Antichrist will later turn against the Jews, and there will be trouble in Palestine during a period of three and a half years before the return of Christ.

Not having been killed for their belief, they would not be in the company of Tribulation Saints that are raised from the dead. They are still on earth, so they are sealed (protected) against the plagues that are coming and against Antichrist and his threats.

Christ will return as King of the Jews. Two dispensations are coming to an end at the same time—the Jewish and the Christian. Both the Jews and the Christians look forward to the coming of Christ. The resumption of a time that might be called Jewish time makes possible the closing up of the old as well as the new dispensations.

God has always had a people upon the earth. Pentecost marked the beginning of a new age. The church took the place of the Jews in the program of redemption. After the Rapture there will still be a Gentile church made up of those saved after the Rapture. Satan will attempt to wipe them out. In a few years their number will be complete and they will be raised from the dead, thus completing the first Resurrection.

Therefore, this would be a time when God would have no representatives on the earth if the Jews did not come back into their former place as the chosen people. From Daniel we know this period is to last seven years. So the time from the sealing of the 144,000 to the advent of Christ is seven years.

There is no record that anyone is saved during the last seven years; in fact, it specifically states that in one instance no one repents (Rev. 16:9). These 144,000 are God's people on earth during this time; they will be here to welcome Christ when He comes.

Dr. Joseph A. Seiss says in *Lectures on the Apocalypse*: "All Jewish names are significant, and the meaning of those which here are given is not hard to trace. Juda means *confession* or *praise* of God; Reuben, *viewing the Son;* Gad, *a company;* Aser, *blessed;* Nepthalim, *a wrestler* or *striving with;* Manasses, *forgetfulness;* Simeon, *hearing and obeying;* Levi, *joining* or *cleaving to;* Issachar, *reward* or *what is given by way of reward;* Zebulun, *a home* or *dwelling-place;* Joseph, *added* or *an addition;* Benjamin, *a son of the right hand, a son of old age.* Now put these several things together in their order, and we have described to us: Confessors or praisers of God, looking upon the Son, a band of blessed ones, wrestling with forgetfulness, hearing and obeying the word, cleaving unto the reward of a shelter and home, an addition, sons of the day of God's right hand, begotten in the extremity of the age."

This certainly is very remarkable and cannot be taken as mere accident, particularly as the order of the names and some of the names themselves are changed from the enumerations of the twelve tribes found in other places. The same will also account for the omission of the names of Dan and Ephraim, and the substitution of the names of Levi and Joseph in their stead. Those names are not of the right import to describe these 144,000.

Dan means *judging* or *exercise of judicial prerogatives,* but these 144,000 are not judges and never become such.

Ephraim means *increase, growth by multiplication,* but these 144,000 are a fixed company, with none of the same class going before them, and none of the same class ever to come after them. The idea of increase or multiplication is altogether foreign to them. "They are virgins." These names are therefore unsuitable and are superseded by others better adapted to describe the parties to whom they are applied.

Ephraim is not actually omitted because the tribe of Joseph would be the same; only the name is changed. Dan is the only tribe not represented in the list. These tribes must be taken in somewhat the same sense as the United States. No attempt was ever made to keep the tribes separate. People could move from one tribe to another and intermarry, just as we cross state lines today. The tribes are geographical, not racial divisions.

Ezekiel tells where these tribal states will be located during the Millennium. Dan is the first one mentioned (Ezekiel 48:1). It lies north of Damascus, far up in Syria. At the time of the return of the Jews, Dan may be too far north to be included in Israel. It is only after the destruction of the enemies of Israel that the nation can occupy all the land originally given to it (Gen. 15:18).

Tribulation Saints

Revelation 7

9 After this I beheld, and, lo, a great multitude, which no man could number, of all nations, and kindreds, and people, and tongues, stood before the throne, and before the Lamb, clothed with white robes, and palms in their hands;

10 And cried with a loud voice, saying, Salvation to our God which sitteth upon the throne, and unto the Lamb.

11 And all the angels stood round about the throne, and about the elders and the four beasts, and fell before the throne on their faces, and worshipped God.

12 Saying, Amen: Blessing, and glory, and wisdom, and thanksgiving, and honour, and power, and might, be unto our God for ever and ever. Amen.

13 And one of the elders answered, saying unto me, What are these which are arrayed in white robes? and whence came they?

14 And I said unto him, Sir, thou knowest. And he said to me, These are they which came out of great tribulation, and have washed their robes, and made them white in the blood of the Lamb.

15 Therefore are they before the throne of God, and serve him day and night in his temple: and he that sitteth on the throne shall dwell among them.

16 They shall hunger no more, neither thirst any more; neither shall the sun light on them, nor any heat.

17 For the Lamb which is in the midst of the throne shall feed them, and shall lead them unto living fountains of waters: and God shall wipe away all tears from their eyes.

THE TRIBULATION SAINTS. The preaching of the gospel, directed by the rider upon the white horse and assisted by the other horsemen, will result in the conversion of a multitude from all nations. They are saved after the Rapture during the Great Tribulation and are immediately persecuted and killed by Antichrist. They are all raised from the dead at one time and appear in heaven as a separate group, arriving late. This completes the Resurrection of the saints, called the *first resurrection* (Rev. 20:4, 5). It also marks the end of the Dispensation of Grace.

THE METHOD OF PERSECUTION. Compare 13:12–17. "And he causeth all, both small and great, rich and poor, free and bond, to receive a mark in their right hand, or in their foreheads: and that no man might buy or sell save he that had the mark of the beast, or the number of his name."—Rev. 13:16, 17. Death will result from hunger, thirst, privation, and mental anguish due to loss of friends and home, "for a man's foes shall be they of his own household."—Matt. 10:36. Many a man will betray his loved ones in order to save his own life. But he that shall seek to save his life shall lose it. He that is willing to lose his life for Christ's sake shall find it. And "they shall hunger no more, neither thirst . . . and God shall wipe away all tears from their eyes."—Rev. 7:16, 17.

The Seven Last Plagues

So far the earth has been in view only as it was on the receiving end of heavenly administrations. We have read only of those things which happen as a result of the activities of the saints in heaven.

Many other things are taking place on the earth during this time, which we will discover when we read the next section and enter the room marked "EARTH." Then we will find that Satan has been cast down to the earth and has taken up his abode in the body of a man whom we sometimes call Antichrist. In Revelation he is called the beast.

The plagues that follow have a double purpose. They strike hard at Satan and his kingdom, both spiritual and material, and they serve to purge the earth. Cleansing is an essential part of redemption. Purging is a terrible experience.

We have been cleansed by the blood of Christ and so have escaped the terror because Christ did it for us.

The results of sin are heavy upon the earth. They must all be eliminated: the pests, the weeds, the works of man done in sin, all the causes of sickness, the desire to make war, and all other causes of distress.

The plagues are not sent haphazardly. They are directed and controlled in order that they may accomplish their purpose. Please take notice of this truth. The former judgments had as their primary purpose the saving of souls. Now that is past. The number of the redeemed is complete. They have all been raised from the dead. The first Resurrection has been completed, the day of grace is over, and we enter the time of wrath poured out without mixture.

Chapters 15 and 16 are parallel with 8 and 9. In those chapters we have the same series of events except that they are seen from the standpoint of the earth.

There is no difference between the trumpets and the vials except the viewpoint. From the mouthpiece end it seems like a trumpet blown; from the bell end it seems like a vial or bowl being poured out. It will be advantageous to consider these parallel passages together, inasmuch as details are sometimes added.

The rule is this: If it concerns heaven only, it is found only in the heaven section—chapters 4–11. If it concerns the earth only, it is found only in the earth section—chapters 12–16. If it concerns both heaven and earth, it is found in both sections. These two sections cover the same period of time exactly. They both begin with the Rapture; they both end with the Return of Christ. There is a difference in the method of presentation. The heaven section is chronological; every event is numbered. The earth section is topical, and sometimes symbols are used.

HARMONY OF REVELATION
Chapters 4–11 and 12–16

HEAVEN	EVENT	EARTH
4:1–3	Rapture	12:1–5
4:4–11	Saints in Heaven	
5:1–7	The Seven-Sealed Book	
5:8–14	Saints Sing the Redemption Song in Heaven	
	Satan Attempts to Prevent the Resurrection	12:3, 4
	War with Satan and His Angels	12:7, 8
	Satan Cast Down to Earth	12:9–12
	Satan Persecutes the Church Left Behind	12:13–17
	The Universal Power of the Beast	13:1–8
	The Satanic Trinity	13:11–18
6:1–8	The Four Horsemen — Gospel Preached by Agents from Heaven Amid Judgments and Plagues	14:6–20
6:9–11	Tribulation Saints Waiting Their Resurrection	
6:12–17	Earthquakes and Falling Stars Hinder Satan	12:15, 16
7:1–8	144,000 Saved Israelites Remain on Earth	14:1–5
7:9–17	All Tribulation Saints Raised	
8:1–5	Preparation for Seven Last Plagues	15:1–8
8:7	1st Trumpet Vial — The Earth	16:1, 2
8:8, 9	2nd Trumpet Vial — The Sea	16:3
8:10, 11	3rd Trumpet Vial — The Rivers	16:4–7
8:12, 13	4th Trumpet Vial — The Sun	16:8, 9
9:1–12	5th Trumpet Vial — The Seat of the Beast	16:10, 11
9:13–21	6th Trumpet Vial — The River Euphrates	16:12
10:1–11	Christ Takes Legal Possession of the Earth	
	Satan Counters by Marshalling His Forces	16:13–16
11:1–13	The Two Witnesses and Their Message	16:15
11:15–19	7th Trumpet Vial — The Return of Christ	16:17–21

When events are numbered, as the seven seals and the seven trumpets, the rule is this: When events are numbered, they take place in the order numbered. There are no "parenthetical chapters" in Revelation. Nothing is out of place; everything is in order.

Chapter Eight (with Sixteen)

TRUMPETS AND VIALS

Revelation 8

1 And when he had opened the seventh seal, there was silence in heaven about the space of half an hour.

This is the seventh and last seal. The book is now open. The full force of God's wrath is now to be poured out.

SILENCE IN HEAVEN. Prior to this time there has been anything but silence in heaven. The scene there might be described by such words as excitement, enthusiasm, rejoicing. First there was the reunion of long separated friends and relatives as a consequence of the Resurrection. Then there was the service of worship around the throne led by the four living ones and the four and twenty elders. Then was heard the song of redemption which reached out into space as far as there were created beings.

Following that came the intensive work of the four horsemen with the accompanying rejoicing in heaven whenever a soul was saved. The combined meeting of the 144,000 on Mount Zion and the choir of heaven filled the celestial spaces with music, and then came the grand climax when the resurrected Tribulation Saints arrived in heaven to join the throng of the redeemed.

But now suddenly there is silence. All music dies away. The seriousness of the moment is sufficient to hush all rejoicing. The seventh seal is the last one. The book is at last open. The climax of the ages has arrived. There will be no more delay. The Dispensation of Grace has been officially closed by the breaking of that last seal. The time of Jacob's trouble has come (Jer. 30: 7) .[1]

As a result of the opening of the seventh seal, the seven last plagues are sent to the earth, but first there must be preparation in the form of a service of worship.

Revelation 8

2 And I saw the seven angels which stood before God; and to them were given seven trumpets.

When the children of Israel crossed the Jordan and prepared to take the Promised Land, they found the key city to be Jericho, a walled city. Although they were armed and ready for battle, the city was taken with trumpets. Seven days they marched around the city, once each day. On the seventh day they marched around seven times and blew their trumpets. On the seventh time around, when the trumpets were blown, the walls fell down and the city was taken.

When God prepares to take the earth from Satan, seven seals are broken, but the seventh seal has seven trumpets. The trumpets are sounded, one at a time, and when the seventh trumpet sounds, the cities of the nations fall. The kingdom of God is established on the earth. Thus said the angel: "But in the days of the voice of the seventh angel, when he shall begin to sound, the mystery of God should be finished, as he hath declared to his servants the prophets."—Rev. 10: 7.

From the description, we may identify the angels. They are saints. The word *angel* means messenger, and in Revelation, is used of ministers, resurrected saints, and Christ, as well as of created angels. The saints may be identified by the description. They are clothed in linen pure and white, they

---

1. "Alas! for that day is great, so that none is like it: it is even the time of Jacob's trouble, but he shall be saved out of it" (Jer. 30:7).

are victorious over the beast, and they offer prayers of the saints to God as sweet incense. Moreover, we are specifically told that the saints will execute the judgments of God upon the earth. They wear golden girdles, garments which associate them with the work of the priesthood. We shall be kings and priests. As priests they offer up much incense with the prayers of the saints.

Seven angels appear and to each is given a trumpet or vial. As seen from heaven, it is a trumpet. The sounding of the trumpet, however, is not heard on the earth. To the people on the earth it appears as if a vial were poured out.

The same censer that carried the prayers of the saints to the throne of God brings calamity to the people on the earth. The same fire that burned the incense on the altar causes destruction in the world. Judgment is grace reversed. Fire, when properly used, is a blessing; when misused, it may destroy those whom it was meant to benefit.

The very elements in the nature of God that make grace possible, make sin, or the abuse of grace, disastrous. "For if the word spoken by angels was stedfast, and every transgression and disobedience received a just recompence of reward; how shall we escape, if we neglect so great salvation?" —Heb. 2:2, 3. The wrath of God is the grace of God working in reverse.

TRUMPET	VIAL
Revelation 8	Revelation 16
7 The first angel sounded, and there followed hail and fire mingled with blood, and they were cast upon the earth: and the third part of trees was burnt up, and all green grass was burnt up.	2 And the first went, and poured out his vial upon the earth; and there fell a noisome and grievous sore upon the men which had the mark of the beast, and upon them which worshipped his image.

FIRST: THE EARTH. All the plagues have the element of fire in them. It will seem that the whole world is on fire. The plagues are centered on Antichrist and his kingdom, but they reach to the ends of the earth.

Notice the progress of the plagues, first, on the earth, the land itself. The heat is intense; the earth itself is hot. This heat does not radiate from the sun but is the result of the hail mingled with fire which causes all the green grass to dry up and burn and a third of the trees to burn up. This plague covers the earth, but it does not cover all parts of the earth with the same intensity. The places where the influence of the beast is greatest will receive the greatest amount of fiery hail.

TRUMPET
Revelation 8

8 And the second angel sounded, and as it were a great mountain burning with fire was cast into the sea: and the third part of the sea became blood;

9 And the third part of the creatures which were in the sea, and had life, died; and the third part of the ships were destroyed.

VIAL
Revelation 16

3 And the second angel poured out his vial upon the sea; and it became as the blood of a dead man: and every living soul died in the sea.

SECOND: THE SEA. One-third of the animals in the sea die; one-third of the ships are destroyed; and all the people that seek refuge in the water because of the fire on the earth are caught in the fiery, bloody water and die.

Revelation 8

10 And the third angel sounded and there fell a great star from heaven, burning as it were a lamp, and it fell upon the third part of the rivers, and upon the fountains of waters;

Revelation 16

4 And the third angel poured out his vial upon the rivers and fountains of waters; and they became blood.

5 And I heard the angel of the waters say, Thou art righteous, O Lord, which art, and

11 And the name of the star is called Wormwood: and the third part of the waters became wormwood; and many men died of the waters, because they were made bitter.

wast, and shalt be, because thou hast judged thus.

6 For they have shed the blood of saints and prophets, and thou hast given them blood to drink; for they are worthy.

7 And I heard another out of the altar say, Even so, Lord God Almighty, true and righteous art thy judgments.

THIRD: THE RIVERS. The sources of pure water are contaminated and made bloody. Pure water becomes extremely scarce. The angel suggests that this is a fitting judgment for those who have shed the blood of saints and prophets. The wording in each case suggests that although the whole earth is the scene of these judgments, yet they rest most heavily upon the avowed enemies of God. That would naturally be the case, because these judgments are strictly punitive. The people have rejected the water of life; they have spurned the blood of Christ; they have spilled the blood of saints. Now their water supply is turned into poisonous blood.

Revelation 8

12 And the fourth angel sounded, and the third part of the sun was smitten, and the third part of the moon, and the third part of the stars; so as the third part of them was darkened, and the day shone not for a third part of it, and the night likewise.

Revelation 16

8 And the fourth angel poured out his vial upon the sun; and power was given unto him to scorch men with fire.

9 And men were scorched with great heat, and blasphemed the name of God, which hath power over these plagues: and they repented not to give him glory.

FOURTH: THE SUN. This is probably the most terrifying of the plagues so far, but it will not be the worst. It is merely the beginning, a mild prelude to the three woes that follow. The sun is darkened for one-third of the day. The idea here seems to be that there is darkness and extreme cold one-third of the day, and then suddenly the sun shines with a heat so intense that it actually scorches.

Revelation 8

13 And I beheld, and heard an angel flying through the midst of heaven, saying with a loud voice, Woe, woe, woe, to the inhabiters of the earth by reason of the other voices of the trumpet of the three angels, which are yet to sound!

The word *angel* in this verse is rendered *eagle* in most versions. It may well refer to saints. "They shall mount up with wings as eagles."—Isa. 40:31. "We find them spoken of also in the Saviour's great prophetic discourse in Matt. 24:26–28, where He admonishes His people not to trouble or disturb themselves to find Him in the day of His coming, and not to heed those who shall say, Behold, He is here, or there, 'for' says He, 'as the lightning cometh out of the east, and shineth even unto the west, so shall also the coming of the Son of man be; for wheresoever the carcase [slain body] is, there will the eagles be gathered together.' Here, as Hilary observes, 'He calls His saints eagles, soaring, as it were, to Him, the body, by a spiritual flight.' "—Seiss.

The flight of this eagle represents another activity of the saints during this time. This announcement divides the seven plagues into two parts: first four, then three. The last three are each known as a woe as well as a plague, showing that they are especially severe.

The first four are directed at inanimate objects of nature: the earth, the sea, the rivers, and the sun. They themselves inanimate forces: heat, blood, fire, wormwood, darkness.

The last three trumpets are directed toward people, especially the kingdom of the beast. These plagues are brought about by living beings. One swarm comes from the bottomless pit, one army comes from the river Euphrates, and one company comes from heaven. The living plagues are much more terrible than the inanimate ones. This is one reason for the pronouncement of the three woes. The fifth and sixth plagues destroy men, and the seventh destroys the works of man.

JUDGMENT WITH A PURPOSE

This is no ordinary judgment. It is not a calamity that comes as a result of natural causes or even as divine retribution on a wicked generation. It is the consummation of redemption. These judgments are a part of redemption. They are closely superintended by innumerable saints operating from heaven. Their purpose is the cleansing of the earth from the results of sin.

During the reign of Christ and the saints which is almost immediately to follow, the earth will be transformed into one grand paradise. The prophet says, "The desert will blossom as the rose." The rubbish has to be cleaned up and burned before the garden can be planted.

God cursed the ground for man's sake. This curse is about to be lifted. It cannot remain on the earth while Christ reigns. The results of the curse are weeds, pests, sickness-producing germs, flies, mosquitoes—everything that mars God's otherwise perfect creation.

Nothing will escape the fires of this judgment. They will cleanse every portion of the earth from the lowest depth to the rarest atmosphere. Every pest will be tracked down and killed. Every "giant" will meet his David. What science has been trying to do with only very limited success, and that after long and laborious attempts, the agents of God will do completely in seven years. This is a necessary part of the program of the redemption of the earth. "The meek shall inherit the earth," but it will be a cleansed, perfected, glorified

earth. The plagues will purge the good and destroy the bad
(Isa. 24:18–23).[1] The reign of Christ will restore all things.

---

1. "And it shall come to pass, that he who fleeth from the noise of the fear shall
fall into the pit; and he that cometh up out of the midst of the pit shall be taken in
the snare: for the windows from on high are open, and the foundations of the earth do
shake. The earth is utterly broken down, the earth is clean dissolved, the earth is moved
exceedingly. The earth shall reel to and fro like a drunkard, and shall be removed like
a cottage; and the transgression thereof shall be heavy upon it; and it shall fall, and not
rise again. And it shall come to pass in that day, that the Lord shall punish the host
of the high ones that are on high, and the kings of the earth upon the earth. And they
shall be gathered together, as prisoners are gathered in the pit, and shall be shut up
in the prison, and after many days shall they be visited. Then the moon shall be confounded, and the sun ashamed, when the Lord of hosts shall reign in mount Zion, and in
Jerusalem, and before his ancients gloriously" (Isa. 24:18–23).

Chapter Nine (with Sixteen)

TRUMPETS AND VIALS
(Continued)

TRUMPET
Revelation 9

1 And the fifth angel sounded, and I saw a star fall from heaven unto the earth: and to him was given the key of the bottomless pit.

2 And he opened the bottomless pit; and there arose a smoke out of the pit, as the smoke of a great furnace; and the sun and the air were darkened by reason of the smoke of the pit.

3 And there came out of the smoke locusts upon the earth: and unto them was given power, as the scorpions of the earth have power.

VIAL
Revelation 16

10 And the fifth angel poured out his vial upon the seat of the beast; and his kingdom was full of darkness; and they gnawed their tongues for pain,

11 And blasphemed the God of heaven because of their pains and their sores, and repented not of their deeds.

THE FIFTH PLAGUE. This plague is sent directly to the seat of the beast, that is, his kingdom and the center of his power. It reaches out over the earth. Probably no land is entirely free from the awful locusts, but the full force of the plague is felt in that part of the world directly ruled by Antichrist.

The fallen star (vs. 1). The word "fall" should be read "fallen." John did not see the star fall; he saw a star that had fallen from heaven. Any bright object falling from heaven is called a star, whether it is a meteor or angel. The meaning can be ascertained from the context. This star is an intelligent being, for things are distinctly ascribed to him. A key is given him. He takes the key and uses it for the unlocking of a door and lets forth from their prison the occupants of the abyss.

Satan is bent on letting loose against men all the evil powers at his command. He can do this only when he is allowed to, just as he could torment Job only when he was allowed to. This is the meaning of the giving and receiving the key to the bottomless pit. Because of the wickedness of the world, special powers are granted Satan. As people prefer the service of the devil, God allows them a full experience of his administrations.

The locusts are not earthly locusts. They are supernatural and infernal. They are a sort of infernal cherubim, in every respect the opposite of the living ones which are before the throne. The horse, the man, the lion, and the scorpion are combined in them. Their general appearance is like horses with battle armor. They have faces resembling the faces of men. Their backs and breasts are encased as if with iron plates, and their tails are the size and shape of a scorpion.

"These horrible creatures have a certain degree of intelligence. Commands are addressed to them. They are able to distinguish those who have the seal of the living God upon their foreheads. They have a king over them. This king is not Satan himself. Satan is, indeed, chief of all the powers of darkness, but he has princes under him, with their own particular commands. It is Satan who opens the door for the egress of these hosts from the pit; but their immediate king is one of Satan's angels—'the angel of the abyss.'

"This king has a descriptive name. It is given in Hebrew and in Greek, showing that this administration has to do with

Jews and Gentiles. Christ is named Jesus because He is the Saviour. This king is named Abaddon in Hebrew and Apollyon in Greek, because he is a destroyer—the opposite of saviour."—Seiss.

The pain from the sting of a scorpion, though not generally fatal, is perhaps the most intense that an animal can inflict upon the human body. The duration of this plague is five months. Death itself would be preferable to living in a world infested by such malignant demons from which there is no protection day or night. People will fervently desire to die and "shall seek death," but one of the features of this woe is that men cannot find death and cannot thus escape, for "death shall flee from them."

TRUMPET	VIAL
Revelation 9	Revelation 16

TRUMPET

Revelation 9

13 And the sixth angel sounded, and I heard a voice from the four horns of the golden altar which is before God,

14 Saying to the sixth angel which had the trumpet, Loose the four angels which are bound in the great river Euphrates.

15 And the four angels were loosed, which were prepared for an hour, and a day, and a month, and a year, for to slay the third part of men.

16 And the number of the army of the horsemen were two hundred thousand thousand: and I heard the number of them.

17 And thus I saw the horses in the vision, and them that sat on them, having

VIAL

Revelation 16

12 And the sixth angel poured out his vial upon the great river Euphrates; and the water thereof was dried up, that the way of the kings of the east might be prepared.

13 And I saw three unclean spirits like frogs come out of the mouth of the dragon, and out of the mouth of the beast, and out of the mouth of the false prophet.

14 For they are the spirits of devils, working miracles, which go forth unto the kings of the earth and of the whole world, to gather them to the battle of that great day of God Almighty.

15 Behold, I come as a thief. Blessed is he that watcheth, and keepeth his garments, lest he walk naked, and they see his

breastplates of fire, and of jacinth, and brimstone: and the heads were as the heads of lions; and out of their mouths issued fire and smoke and brimstone.

shame.

16 And he gathered them together into a place called in the Hebrew tongue Armageddon.

THE SIXTH PLAGUE comes out of the river Euphrates. It was in this locality that the powers of evil first made attempts against the human race. We do not know who these 200,000,000 evil spirits are, but we know that there are angels that "kept not their first estate," and are reserved in prison to be judged in the Day of the Lord. Compare Jude 6, 7; II Peter 2:4, 5; I Peter 3:18–20; Genesis 6:1–4; Joel 2:1–11.

Joel sees these evil spirits when they are turned loose on the world.

Blow ye the trumpet in Zion, and sound an alarm in my holy mountain: let all the inhabitants of the land tremble: for the day of the Lord cometh, for it is nigh at hand; a day of darkness and of gloominess, a day of clouds and of thick darkness, as the morning spread upon the mountains: a great people and a strong; there hath not been ever the like, neither shall be any more after it, even to the years of many generations. A fire devoureth before them; and behind them a flame burneth: the land is as the garden of Eden before them, and behind them a desolate wilderness; yea, and nothing shall escape them. The appearance of them is as the appearance of horses; and as horsemen, so shall they run. Like the noise of chariots on the tops of mountains shall they leap, like the noise of a flame of fire that devoureth the stubble, as a strong people set in battle array. Before their face the people shall be much pained: all faces shall gather blackness. They shall run like mighty men; they shall climb the wall like men of war; and they shall march every one on his ways, and they shall not break their ranks: neither shall one thrust another; they shall walk every one in his path: and when they fall upon the sword, they shall not be wounded. They shall run to and fro in the city; they shall run upon the wall, they shall climb up upon the houses; they shall enter in at the windows like a thief. The earth shall quake before them; the heavens shall tremble: the sun and the moon shall be dark, and the stars shall withdraw their shining: and the Lord shall utter his voice before his army: for his camp is very great: for he is strong that executeth his word: for the day of the Lord is great and very terrible; and who can abide it?—Joel 2:1–11

These spirits evidently once lived on the earth because they are imprisoned near the river Euphrates. They could hardly be of the Adamic race. All the dead are accounted for at the Great White Throne. These spirits belong to Satan's kingdom. There are angels that left their own environment to cohabit with people on the earth. They sinned just before the flood, we are told, and are imprisoned until the day of judgment.

> For if God spared not the angels that sinned, but cast them down to hell, and delivered them into chains of darkness, to be reserved unto judgment; and spared not the old world, but saved Noah the eighth person, a preacher of righteousness, bringing in the flood upon the world of the ungodly.—II Pet. 2:4, 5

The particular sin of these angels was going after strange flesh.

> And the angels which kept not their first estate, but left their own habitation, he hath reserved in everlasting chains under darkness unto the judgment of the great day. Even as Sodom and Gomorrah, and the cities about them in like manner, giving themselves over to fornication, and going after strange flesh, are set forth for an example, suffering the vengeance of eternal fire.—Jude 6, 7

The various versions vary the wording but not the meaning: "And angels—those who did not keep the position originally assigned to them, but deserted their own proper abode—He reserves in everlasting bonds, in darkness, in preparation for the judgment of the great day. So also Sodom and Gomorrah—and the neighboring towns in the same manner—having been guilty of gross fornication and having gone astray in pursuit of unnatural vice, are now before us as a specimen of the fire of the ages in the punishment which they are undergoing."

There are spirits in a special prison waiting judgment. They are not the ordinary run of human beings. They must be a very special group, somewhat different from the Adamic race in its purity, because they are treated as a group apart. We do not know the character of Noah's preaching or its purpose; it is quite apparent that no one was saved by it.

Peter also says that Jesus by the Spirit "went and preached unto the spirits in prison; which sometime were disobedient, when once the longsuffering of God waited in the days of Noah."—I Pet. 3: 19, 20.

Why this was necessary, we are not told, but it does show that this was a very special group which required something more than is given the sons of men. The preaching seems to have had no result, but it may have been necessary to satisfy legally the terms of God's justice.

In the past Satan has visited the earth as a serpent; he has infiltrated the earth with his angels; he has cooperated with men in building great monuments; he has possessed men's bodies; he has captured and controlled men's minds; he appeared without disguise and tempted Christ; he has counterfeited every miracle, sometimes rendering miracles useless; he has appeared as an angel of light and a minister of righteousness.

The last days are days of crises in Satan's kingdom. He is like a stag at bay—desperate. All his past exploits are as nothing compared to his final and all-out attempt to control and destroy mankind when the coming of Christ draws near.

The time referred to in these passages is so specific that it is not hard to locate the record.

And it came to pass, when men began to multiply on the face of the earth, and daughters were born unto them, that the sons of God saw the daughters of men that they were fair; and they took them wives of all they chose. And the Lord said, My spirit shall not always strive with man, for that he also is flesh: yet his days shall be an hundred and twenty years. There were giants in the earth in those days; and also after that, when the sons of God came in unto the daughters of men, and they bare children to them, the same became mighty men which were of old, men of renown.—Gen. 6:1–4

The usual explanation of this passage is that the sons of God refer to the godly line of Seth, while the daughters of men are the godless line of Cain. There is nothing in the record to lead us to this conclusion. The commentaries would have us believe that after 1500 years of voluntary separation, the men of one line suddenly discovered the women of another line.

During those 1500 years from Adam to the flood, life expectancy was many hundreds of years. The population of the earth could easily have been as big as it is today. Certainly there were many millions of inhabitants. The idea that the two lines of Seth and Cain remained separate all this time is a little hard to believe. There were no laws against intermarriage.

If there was a godly line, why were they not saved in the ark? Again, if they were godly, why did they do such ungodly things? And why did God wipe them off the earth? There is no such thing as a godly line. Men are not reckoned godly because they descended from a righteous forefather. These sons of God filled the earth with violence.

This was no ordinary affair. Marriages had been going on since creation, but this was different. This was a special kind of union that would have corrupted the human race. It was an unnatural union that brought forth a strange new race called *nephilim* (erroneously translated giants). This race had to be destroyed.

The Hebrew is *nephilim*. It means "fallen ones" (Young).

There is in the Bible no such teaching as the universal fatherhood of God. Men are not called sons of God because they belong to a certain group or line of descent. You cannot be unrighteous and godly at the same time. None of the sons of Seth except Noah and his family were found righteous.

On the other hand, "sons of God" in the Bible has a very special meaning. It always refers to directly created beings. In that sense, Adam and Eve were sons of God; their descendants were not. The angels are sons of God because each one was directly created. This would include Satan, who was Lucifer, the anointed cherub.

In Job we read: "Now there was a day when the sons of God came to present themselves before the Lord, and Satan came also among them."—Job 1:6.

God challenged Satan, not concerning his right to be among the sons of God, but concerning what he had been doing.

In the New Testament, son of God has the same meaning. A person is a son of God only if he is a new creature in Christ. We are not sons of God because we belong to a certain church, but because there has been a definite, creative act performed in us.

> But as many as received him, to them gave he power to become the sons of God, even to them that believe on his name.—John 1:12

So the idea that all the male descendants of Seth were sons of God simply because they could, rather dubiously, trace their ancestry back to Seth, is foreign to all Bible teaching.

In this case Moffatt's translation gives the correct rendering: "Now when men began to multiply over all the world and had daughters born to them, the angels noticed that the daughters of men were beautiful, and they married any one of them that they chose. . . . It was in these days that the Nephilim giants arose on earth, as well as afterwards whenever angels had intercourse with the daughters of men and had children born to them; these were the heroes who were famous in the days of old."—Gen. 6:1, 2, 4.

This is almost identical with the record in the book of Enoch. Enoch is not one of the inspired books, but it is very old and it shows how the ancient scholars understood these words.

Not all evil spirits are in prison, as are these 200,000,000. There were legions of demons on the loose in Christ's day, and missionaries today have many experiences with them. J. A. Seiss, in his book *The Apocalypse,* shares these insights on the demon world during God's Judgment Day. To tell exactly who these seducing spirits are, and how they manage their infernal mission, may not be in our power. It is not necessary to have that kind of definite knowledge. But this is not the only place where their agency and successes are mentioned.

Paul says the Spirit speaks expressly that in the latter times seducing and teaching spirits shall manifest themselves, deceiving mankind with their lies (I Timothy 4:1-2). They are "demon spirits" sent forth by the dragon trinity. They are the ungodly elect agents to awaken the world in an attempt to abolish God Almighty's purpose on the earth. They are froglike in that they come forth out of the dark quagmires of the universe. They set the armies of the whole earth stirring up evil commotions."

They seek the final crushing of the atoning Lamb and His power. Revelation chapters 9 and 16 make it clear that these evil spirits have been locked up. The necessity of this is evident by the vicious way they react when they are loosed. This is probably the worst of all the plagues and gives point to the warning of the angel: "Woe, woe, woe, to the inhabiters of the earth by reason of the other voices of the trumpet of the three angels, which are yet to sound!"—Rev. 8: 13.

THE HOUR, DAY, MONTH, AND YEAR. The American Standard Version is better: "prepared for *the* hour." This could mean that they are prepared for this exact time, or more likely it means that they are prepared to operate on the earth for a year, month, day, and hour. It is the length of time they remain at large.

It is noticeable that no length of time is set for events before the Rapture, but after the Rapture times are freely given. The Rapture is the only secret event. The time of the coming of Christ is not secret after the Rapture. Satan knows exactly when to marshal the armies around Jerusalem. Christ will overtake the world as a thief, not because the time is not revealed, but because the world pays no attention to the Word of God, if indeed, it is possible to find a copy of the Bible.

> Behold, the days come, saith the Lord God, that I will send a famine in the land, not a famine of bread, nor a thirst for water, but of hearing the words of the Lord: and they shall wander from sea to sea, and from the north even to the east, they shall run to and fro to seek the word of the Lord, and shall not find it.— Amos 8:11, 12

FOUR ANGELS. These would be fallen angels, angels that left their first estate. Their number is four, yet their armies number two hundred million. Four is used the same way as in the 5th and 6th chapters. There were four living ones, but they represented a great company of saints. The same was true of the four horsemen. Four is the world number: the whole world is in view. This is in contrast with the fifth trumpet, which was limited to the kingdom of the beast; this one covers the whole world.

Revelation 9

18 By these three was the third part of men killed, by the fire, and by the smoke, and by the brimstone, which issued out of their mouths.

19 For their power is in their mouth, and in their tails: for their tails were like unto serpents, and had heads, and with them they do hurt.

20 And the rest of the men which were not killed by these plagues yet repented not of the works of their hands, that they should not worship devils, and idols of gold, and silver, and brass, and stone, and of wood: which neither can see, nor hear, nor walk:

21 Neither repented they of their murders, nor of their sorceries, nor of their fornication, nor of their thefts.

THIRD PART OF MEN KILLED. These extremely destructive plagues are always limited to a portion of the people of the earth or to a portion of the earth such as the kingdom of the beast. A certain number of people always live through them. Still a plague that kills one-third of the population of the earth is unprecedented. This is the time of trouble such as never was since there was a nation (Daniel 12:1). See Joel 1.

NO REPENTANCE. The day of grace is over; this is judgment. There is no record of anyone being saved during this period. There will be a witness to Israel which will cause many to glorify God. No more is said concerning these people. The full effect will not be manifest until after the coming of Christ. The evils of the day are listed; the remarkable feature is the return of idolatry, the making of idols to worship. This is not surprising when we consider that the Romish Church with all its worship of images will be Antichrist's church and probably will be his agent in the persecution of the Tribulation Saints. These judgments are severe, but the sins that bring them on would be much more destructive if allowed to continue. The great moral sin is fornication, the same sin that brought in the flood.

Chapter Ten

CHRIST TAKES POSSESSION

Revelation 10

1 And I saw another mighty angel come down from heaven, clothed with a cloud: and a rainbow was upon his head, and his face was as it were the sun, and his feet as pillars of fire:

2 And he had in his hand a little book open: and he set his right foot upon the sea, and his left foot on the earth.

THE LITTLE BOOK OPEN. This is the same little book or scroll that first appeared in the right hand of God. When we first saw it, it was sealed. Now the last seal has been broken; six of the seven trumpets have sounded. The last one, yet to sound, will bring us to the end of this day of trouble. The seventh trumpet ushers in the Millennium.

Christ is called a mighty angel. Throughout Revelation heavenly beings, whether Christ, the saints, or created angels, are called angels. They may be identified by their description. This description follows the rule that when Christ is mentioned, some portion of the first chapter is repeated. There is added the rainbow which was round about the throne. The rainbow is the sign of God's purpose to redeem, not destroy the world and the human race.

The first step is nearly over. The book is opened and it is time now to take possession of the earth. Breaking the seals was a legal process; the one who broke the seals had the right to possess the property. He set His right foot on the sea and His left foot on the earth. This is an act of possession.

Jesus has not yet actually returned. This is a spiritual act, seen only by heaven and possibly Satan, because he reacts to it. It is like taking legal possession in a lawyer's office before actually going to the property and taking physical possession. Now that all preliminary steps have been taken, Jesus will come and take over the rulership of the earth. This is the outcome of the seventh trumpet (11:15).

Revelation 10

3 And cried with a loud voice, as when a lion roareth: and when he had cried, seven thunders uttered their voices.

4 And when the seven thunders had uttered their voices, I was about to write: and I heard a voice from heaven saying unto me, Seal up those things which the seven thunders uttered, and write them not.

SEVEN THUNDERS. If the words of the seven thunders were not to be recorded, why did they speak at all? Was it simply for John's benefit? I think not. John saw what was going to happen. When the time comes the seven thunders will shout; their voices will be heard. What they say will be known. It is simply not to be made known in advance.

Most secrets, like the time of the Rapture, are kept from Satan rather than the saints or the angels. If the saints or the angels knew it, Satan could find it out. As far as Satan is concerned, this is war, an invasion of his domain. It is an invasion of the earth from outer space. The whole world will unite at Armageddon against the forces from space. Satan will certainly attempt to belittle the heavenly host. He will probably call them "the Martians" or some other such derisive term. In a war there are top secrets. The voices of the seven thunders were classified.

Revelation 10

5 And the angel which I saw stand upon the sea and upon the earth lifted up his hand to heaven,

6 And sware by him that liveth for ever and ever, who created heaven, and the things that therein are, and the earth, and the things that therein are, and the sea, and the things which are therein, that there should be time no longer:

7 But in the days of the voice of the seventh angel, when he shall begin to sound, the mystery of God should be finished, as he hath declared to his servants the prophets.

TIME NO LONGER. This is sometimes rendered "There shall be no more delay." That is undoubtedly the meaning, but the word is *chronos*—time. Our idiom would be, "The time is up." This proves the correctness of our structure of Revelation, which makes chapters 12 to 16, and again 17 and 18, parallel as to time, taking the same series of events from different standpoints. This means that the entire period from the Rapture to the Millennium is covered by the seals and trumpets, and that the seventh trumpet, like the seventh vial, brings us to the end of the time of trouble. If we had to put chapters 12 to 18 after the seventh trumpet, it could not be said at this period that the time is up. The angel explains the meaning.

THE MYSTERY OF GOD. A mystery is a revealed secret. It may still be a secret after it is revealed. The whole future program of God was revealed to the prophets. "Surely the Lord will do nothing, but he revealeth his secret unto his servants the prophets."—Amos 3: 7. Revealed secrets are not always understood. Some of God's secrets, although revealed, are carefully guarded. "The wise shall understand."—Dan. 12: 10.

In Isaiah there are flash visions of the Millennium and after, but by far the greater part of prophecy converges on the Day of the Lord which reaches its climax with the coming of Christ. This will be finished when the seventh angel sounds.

Revelation 10

8 And the voice which I heard from heaven spake unto me again, and said, Go and take the little book which is open in the hand of the angel which standeth upon the sea and upon the earth.

9 And I went unto the angel, and said unto him, Give me the little book. And he said unto me, Take it, and eat it up; and it shall make thy belly bitter, but it shall be in thy mouth sweet as honey.

10 And I took the little book out of the angel's hand, and ate it up; and it was in my mouth sweet as honey; and as soon as I had eaten it, my belly was bitter.

11 And he said unto me., Thou must prophesy again before many peoples, and nations, and tongues, and kings.

THE LITTLE BOOK. This poses some problems, but they should not be taken lightly. This little book has been the center of attention through the whole proceedings; all action has stemmed from it. Now the action is about over; the book is open. With the authority of the open book, the earth has been reclaimed. The book is then given to John. We think of John as being on the isle of Patmos, seeing action which will take place some 2,000 years afterwards. How then can John take part in the action?

Types are usually associated with the Old Testament, with the fulfillment coming in the New Testament. Revelation is the one New Testament book that makes use of types. Because they are unsuspected, they may not be recognized. The seven churches are types of seven kinds of churches that come later. John is also a type. When he enters into the action, he does so as a type of the church—the whole body of the redeemed.

This little book could not have been given to the elders or the living ones, because they represent only groups among the redeemed, not the whole body. John is a type of the saved when he is caught up into heaven. It is a type of the Rapture. Again he becomes a type when he eats the little book.

The little book is the title deed to the earth. It becomes John's absolute possession. The meek shall inherit the earth. Dominion was originally given to man. Through sin it passed into the possession of Satan, and Satan became the prince of this world. Dominion will be restored to man when the saints inherit the earth. This is what Paul evidently referred to when he wrote:

> In whom also we have obtained an inheritance, being predestinated according to the purpose of him who worketh all things after the counsel of his own will: That we should be the praise of his glory, who first trusted in Christ. In whom ye also trusted, after that ye heard the word of truth, the gospel of your salvation: in whom also after that ye believed, ye were sealed with that Holy Spirit of promise, which is the earnest of our inheritance until the redemption of the purchased possession, unto the praise of his glory.—Eph. 1:11–14

This is a sweet contemplation. It will be wonderful to inherit the earth. Many a man has dreamed of conquering the world, but the saints will inherit it.

However, there is a hard, a bitter side. Who would want the earth as it is now? It must be purged, cleansed, and redeemed. This is not a pleasant undertaking. There is much hard work to do before our dreams may all come true.

Sending forth those plagues is a bitter experience even for those who are out of danger. There is rejoicing in heaven over one sinner that repents, but during the tribulation that joy will soon be turned into terrible suspense and anguish as the saved sinner begins to suffer the persecutions of Antichrist. When these Tribulation Saints get to heaven, God will wipe away all tears from their eyes. Why the tears? Martyrs are not given to shedding tears. It could not be the physical suffering of these martyrs that would produce tears that only God could wipe away.

There are other experiences worse than hunger and thirst or even death. In those days guilty knowledge will be punished the same as a guilty act. Professing Christians must be reported to the authorities under penalty of death. Mother will betray daughter and a son his father. "The love of many shall wax cold," and "a man's foes shall be they of his own household." Jesus did not become the Redeemer of the world without terrific sacrifice, and the saints will not become the possessors of the world without some bitter experiences in connection with its restoration.

THOU MUST PROPHESY AGAIN. The key to this passage is found in the words, "before [concerning] many peoples, and nations and tongues and kings." The fourteenth chapter tells of messengers from heaven having the everlasting gospel to preach to every nation, kindred, tongue, and people. This is parallel to the sixth chapter and the work of the rider on the white horse. The tribulation saints are a great multitude "of all nations, and kindreds, and people, and tongues." The preachers are the resurrected saints. They fly in the midst of heaven.

As a type of all the saints, John must prophesy again. Prophesying is more than preaching, even as the prophets were more than preachers. It includes all the various phases of redemption. The gospel in the tribulation period is the work of all the horsemen. The prophesying is not only to these peoples but also concerning them.

Chapter Eleven

THE TWO WITNESSES

Revelation 11

1 And there was given me a reed like unto a rod: and the angel stood, saying, Rise, and measure the temple of God, and the altar, and them that worship therein.

2 But the court which is without the temple leave out, and measure it not; for it is given unto the Gentiles: and the holy city shall they tread under foot forty and two months.

REED LIKE UNTO A ROD. John was given a reed which looked like a rod. A reed is an instrument of measurement, a yardstick. A rod is an instrument of punishment. This was at once a measuring and a judgment. It follows that when property is possessed or redeemed, there must be a survey and an inventory. Then there will be a general cleaning up.

In the previous chapter, the Lord took legal possession of the earth; now there is a measuring and a cleansing. This work has been in process ever since the Rapture but with special attention to the Gentile nations, the beast, and his kingdom. So far Palestine has not been mentioned. The kingdom of Antichrist will not include Palestine until the last three and a half years before the return of Christ.

Now we have one chapter given over to the Jews, although they are not mentioned by name. Even Jerusalem is referred to without naming it. Revelation is about the church, not the Jews, but they must be included here because it is a part of the work of the saints to measure and judge even the Jews. This is the day of Jacob's trouble.

> For thus saith the Lord; We have heard a voice of trembling, of fear, and not of peace. Ask ye now, and see whether a man doth travail with child? wherefore do I see every man with his hand on his loins, as a woman in travail, and all faces are turned into paleness? Alas! for that day is great, so that none is like it: it is even the time of Jacob's trouble; but he shall be saved out of it.—Jer. 30:5–7

FORTY AND TWO MONTHS. Three and one-half years is the length of time Antichrist will attempt to force the Jews to worship him. Jesus referred to this when He said: "And they shall fall by the edge of the sword, and shall be led away captive into all nations: and Jerusalem shall be trodden down of the Gentiles, until the times of the Gentiles be fulfilled."—Luke 21:24.

This is not the total length of the reign of Antichrist. That is not given here or elsewhere. It is the length of time Antichrist and his Gentile hordes will attempt to possess Palestine.

Daniel, speaking of Antichrist, says: "He shall confirm the covenant with many for one week [seven years]: and in the midst of the week [after three and one half years] he shall cause the sacrifice and the oblation to cease, and for the overspreading of abominations he shall make it desolate."—Dan. 9:27. This is what Jesus referred to when He warned the Jews that when they saw the abomination of desolation, spoken of by Daniel the prophet, standing in the holy place, they should flee from the city of Jerusalem.

Revelation 11

3 And I will give power unto my two witnesses, and they shall prophesy a thousand two hundred and

threescore days, clothed in sackcloth.
4 These are the two olive trees, and the two
candlesticks standing before the God of the earth.

THE TWO WITNESSES. The scene is still in heaven. The angel who had the little book is still talking to John and telling him what is going to happen on the earth as a result of this measuring. The two witnesses are evidently to be sent down from heaven, for they have supernatural power; and when their testimony is complete, they return to heaven. The time of their prophesying coincides with the time that the Gentiles are persecuting the Jews in Palestine. A thousand two hundred and three score days is forty-two months, or three and one-half years.

The question will arise: Who are these two witnesses? They are not named but it is almost certain that one of them is Elijah, fulfilling the prophecy of Malachi 4: 5, 6: "Behold, I will send you Elijah the prophet before the coming of the great and dreadful day of the Lord: and he shall turn the heart of the fathers to the children, and the heart of the children to their fathers, lest I come and smite the earth with a curse."

There may be some question as to the identity of the other witness. Some think it might be Enoch, as Enoch and Elijah are the two men who never died. John was told that these two witnesses are the two olive trees and the two candlesticks standing before the God of the earth. When the women came to the sepulchre on the resurrection morn and found the stone rolled away and the sepulchre empty, we were told that two men stood by them in shining garments and reminded them of the words of Jesus that He must be crucified and the third day rise again. They were God's witnesses to the resurrection.

At the time of the ascension of Jesus, "while they looked stedfastly toward heaven as he went up, behold, two men stood by them in white apparel," and witnessed to the second coming of Christ.

On the Mount of Transfiguration there appeared two men who talked with Jesus concerning that which He would accomplish. Here they are named. They are Moses and Elijah. They might well be the two candlesticks standing before the God of the earth, for Moses represents those who die and will be raised again, while Elijah represents those who will never die but will be caught up at the Rapture.

Revelation 11

5 And if any man will hurt them, fire proceedeth out of their mouth, and devoureth their enemies: and if any man will hurt them, he must in this manner be killed.

6 These have power to shut heaven, that it rain not in the days of their prophecy: and have power over waters to turn them to blood, and to smite the earth with all plagues, as often as they will.

THE TESTIMONY. John is not told what the two witnesses say, but in the parallel account, the earth history, their testimony is heard: "Behold, I come as a thief. Blessed is he that watcheth, and keepeth his garments, lest he walk naked, and they see his shame."—Rev. 16: 15. This is the testimony to Israel: "Prepare ye the way of the Lord." It is also a prophecy against Antichrist.

The plagues with which they smite the earth will restrain Antichrist in his malignant attack on the Jews. No rain for three and one-half years will cause untold hardship throughout Antichrist's kingdom. This is not the first time that Elijah has done this. James 5: 17 says that "he [Elijah] prayed earnestly that it might not rain: and it rained not upon the earth for a space of three years and six months."

Moses demonstrated the power of God by sending plagues on Egypt. The works of these two witnesses will continually remind the Jews of Moses and Elijah, yet their experiences will run parallel to those of Jesus in many ways. Here we have, on one hand, all the power that the Jews would expect in their Messiah combined with the testimony and atoning work of Jesus.

Revelation 11

7 And when they shall have finished their testimony, the beast that ascendeth out of the bottomless pit shall make war against them, and shall overcome them, and kill them.

8 And their dead bodies shall lie in the street of the great city, which spiritually is called Sodom and Egypt, where also our Lord was crucified.

9 And they of the people and kindreds and tongues and nations shall see their dead bodies three days and an half, and shall not suffer their dead bodies to be put in graves.

10 And they that dwell upon the earth shall rejoice over them, and make merry, and shall send gifts one to another; because these two prophets tormented them that dwelt on the earth.

11 And after three days and an half the Spirit of life from God entered into them, and they stood upon their feet; and great fear fell upon them which saw them.

12 And they heard a great voice from heaven saying unto them, Come up hither. And they ascended up to heaven in a cloud; and their enemies beheld them.

DEATH, RESURRECTION, ASCENSION. It is not so much what the two witnesses say as what they do that makes an impact upon the Jews. The Jews would willingly accept Christ as their Messiah if He should come and deliver them from their enemies, but that is not enough. They must also see in Him the one whom they rejected and caused to be crucified. They must "look upon him whom they pierced."—John 19: 37.

These two witnesses actually re-enact the life, death, resurrection, and ascension of Jesus. Their ministry is three and one-half years in length, the same as that of Jesus. We are not told the manner of their death but crucifixion is suggested. "Where *also* our Lord was crucified."

The bodies of the two witnesses will not be buried. Antichrist will not make the same mistake that Pilate made in allowing the body to be buried in such a way that it might be stolen or otherwise disappear. This time the bodies will be left in the street for everyone to see. No one can say that their bodies were stolen by friends to make possible a resurrection story.

At the report of the death of the two witnesses a strange thing happens. People all over the world begin to make merry and send presents one to another. This is a remarkable prophecy. There naturally will be no celebration of Christmas during the reign of Antichrist. The Christmas habit, however, is of long standing and deep seated. At the first provocation it breaks out afresh, and they make merry and send presents. This prophecy could not have been fulfilled in John's day. In three and one-half days the news of the death of the two witnesses travels around the world, a holiday is declared, and presents are purchased and sent. This requires fast communication and travel.

TELEVISION. Aside from the armies of Antichrist which are trying to take possession of Palestine, Jerusalem is a Jewish city at this time. If people of all nations are going to see those dead bodies in the streets of Jerusalem, they must do it by some kind of television.

The resurrection and ascension of the two witnesses will make a profound impression upon the Jews. No longer can they deny the death, resurrection, and ascension of Jesus. So the two witnesses will accomplish their main purpose by their death, the same as Jesus did.

Revelation 11

13 And the same hour was there a great earthquake, and the tenth part of the city fell, and in the earthquake were slain of men seven thousand: and the remnant were affrighted, and gave glory to the God of heaven.

14 The second woe is past; and, behold, the third woe cometh quickly.

A GREAT EARTHQUAKE. Earthquakes attended the death and resurrection of Jesus, but we read of no death occasioned by them. Those were days of mercy and grace; these are days of judgment. Seven thousand are killed by this earthquake. The rest are terrified and give glory to God. This evidently refers to the Jews as they are being prepared to receive their King. Under Jewish control, the city of Jerusalem becomes so wicked that it will be likened to Sodom and Egypt. They will go back there in unbelief. Not until Christ reigns will Jerusalem and its people become holy.

This brings to an end the second woe which began with the sixth trumpet (Rev. 9:13). That which is to follow constitutes the third woe and follows directly upon the ascension of the two witnesses. The third woe brings us to the return of Christ when He takes His great power and reigns. It is evident, therefore, that the three and one-half years during which these two witnesses prophesy are the last three and one-half years before the return of Christ.

Seventh Plague

TRUMPET	VIAL
Revelation 11	Revelation 16

15 And the seventh angel sounded; and there were great voices in heaven, saying, The kingdoms of this world are become the kingdoms of our Lord, and of his Christ; and he shall reign for ever and ever.

16 And the four and twenty elders, which sat before God on their seats, fell upon their faces, and worshipped God,

17 Saying, We give thee thanks, O Lord God Almighty, which art, and wast, and art to come; because thou hast tak-

17 And the seventh angel poured out his vial into the air; and there came a great voice out of the temple of heaven, from the throne, saying, It is done.

18 And there were voices, and thunders, and lightnings; and there was a great earthquake, such as was not since men were upon the earth, so mighty an earthquake, and so great.

19 And the great city was divided into three parts, and

en to thee thy great power, and hast reigned.

18 And the nations were angry, and thy wrath is come, and the time of the dead, that they should be judged, and that thou shouldest give reward unto thy servants the prophets, and to the saints, and them that fear thy name, small and great; and shouldest destroy them which destroy the earth.

19 And the temple of God was opened in heaven, and there was seen in his temple the ark of his testament: and there were lightnings, and voices, and thunderings, and an earthquake, and great hail.

the cities of the nations fell: and great Babylon came in remembrance before God, to give unto her the cup of the wine of the fierceness of his wrath.

20 And every island fled away, and the mountains were not found.

21 And there fell upon men a great hail out of heaven, every stone about the weight of a talent: and men blasphemed God because of the plague of the hail; for the plague thereof was exceeding great.

Before every great event there is a service of worship in heaven conducted by the saints, the elders, and the living ones taking the lead. This time they praise God because He has taken His great power and has reigned. This is spoken of as already an accomplished fact, agreeing with the words of the angel who said that when the seventh trumpet sounds there would be no more delay.

THE NATIONS WERE ANGRY AND THY WRATH IS COME. This is a reference to the gathering of the nations at Armageddon in anger against the Lord to prevent Christ from taking over the earth.

The judgment of the dead is still future, but it is linked with the rewards of the righteous. The reign of Christ guarantees that the dead will be judged, the saints will be rewarded, and those who destroy the earth will be destroyed. This is announced now, but the whole process may require as much as a thousand years, for it is not until the end of the thousand-year reign of Christ that all the wicked on the earth are destroyed.

DESTROY THEM THAT DESTROY THE EARTH. This is a remarkable statement. Satan is the destroyer, but never has he attempted to destroy the earth. Men have destroyed cities, but even to threaten the whole earth has been beyond human might. Only now, after the invention of the atom bomb, rockets, and satellites, has it been possible for man to destroy the earth. This is the first time that Satan has had men with the capacity and willingness to destroy the earth. It will not happen because God will act first.

THE ARK OF THE COVENANT. There is a temple in heaven, but it is not the temple of Solomon which was upon the earth. There is an ark in heaven, but it is not the ark which was in the temple of Solomon. Both the temple and the ark were made according to patterns provided by God. These were patterns of the heavenly temple and ark. The ark of the covenant was the only furniture in the temple that looked forward specifically to the second coming of Christ.

Although the ark contained the mercy seat upon which the blood was sprinkled and therefore looked forward to the atonement of Christ, it also was the symbol of victory and possession of the land. This part of the symbolism of the ark will be fulfilled when Christ comes again.

The original ark of the covenant, which led the Israelites to victory, seems to have disappeared from the temple in the days of Solomon. It was not in the temple at the time of the crucifixion of Christ when the veil was rent in twain, thus bringing to an end, by fulfillment, the symbolism of the temple furniture. It was probably by divine design that the ark was not there, because its symbolism will not be completely fulfilled until the return of Christ.

It is, therefore, possible that the ark of the covenant will reappear and again demonstrate to the world the power of God to restore Palestine to the Jews and the Jews to Palestine.

THE FINAL EARTHQUAKE will be the greatest ever experienced since creation. The earth itself will reel like a drunkard, so that the mountains will move out of their places and into the sea; new islands, if not new continents, will appear, and the whole topography of the earth will be changed.

It would seem that the works of man, done in sin, must all be destroyed. What is left after this mighty earthquake will be destroyed by hail, every stone weighing about a talent. A talent is sixty-five pounds. This brings to an end the purging and the destruction necessary to do away with the results of sin, and brings us to the time when the reconstruction of the earth may begin. This reconstruction will be according to a perfect plan and be supervised by Christ and the saints.

TWO ACCOUNTS OF THE SAME EVENT. These two records—the seventh trumpet and the seventh vial—give us a good example of the two histories of this period. It is quite evident that they both refer to the same thing—the coming of the kingdom of God. The trumpet record views the scene from heaven. There are the twenty-four elders and the worship in heaven that would not be seen from the earth. The temple of God is opened and the heavenly ark of the covenant is seen.

The vial record tells the same story but from the standpoint of the earth. There we encounter the thunders, lightnings, Jerusalem divided into three parts, the cities of the nations falling, and Babylon destroyed. Also we see in more vivid detail the results of the final earthquake and hail.

This brings to an end the story of that whole period between the Rapture and the return of Christ. We have seen what will happen in heaven after the Rapture and the effect it has on the earth. Next we will look at the earth during this time and see what will happen here between the Rapture and the return of Christ. In this story Antichrist dominates the scene.

THE TIME ELEMENT

The heaven history is chronological. Events are numbered. They all take place in the order numbered. Some length of times are given: three and a half years; and a year, month, and day.

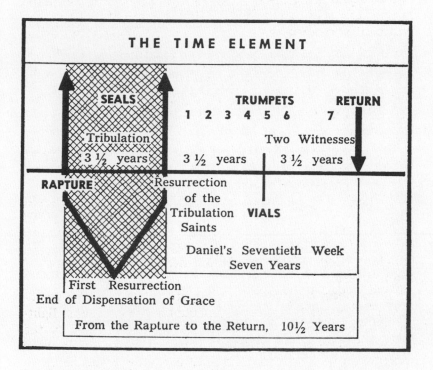

The earth history that is to follow is topical. Events are topical. They are arranged according to subject. The general order is the same, as may be seen from the harmony of the two sections. Two series of events may be happening at the same time, or one series may start before another ends, so a topical arrangement may not be wholly chronological. The topics are these:

The Tribulation

FIRST 3½ YEARS AFTER THE RAPTURE

1. The Rapture and the part of the church left behind (12)
2. How Antichrist persecutes the Tribulation Saints (13)
3. The 144,000 on Mount Zion (14: 1–5)
4. How the gospel is preached during the tribulation (14: 6–20)

This first 3½ years is called the great tribulation (7: 14), literally, the tribulation, the great one. There may be other times of great tribulation. This is the one in which the saints are involved, so it is the only one noted in Revelation.

SEVEN YEARS FOLLOWING THE TRIBULATION

5. Preparations for the seven last plagues (15)
6. The seven last plagues (16)
7. Preparations for Armageddon (16: 13–16)

Topics 5–7 cover the period known as Daniel's seventieth week.

We have become so accustomed to thinking that there are just seven years between the Rapture and the Return that it is hard to break the spell. Somebody jumped to a conclusion and everybody else followed along. Seven years does not give us enough time. One 3½-year period comes at the beginning and the other at the end of the whole period. In between there is one plague lasting a year, a month, and a day; and five other plagues.

If we extend the dispensation of grace for 3½ years after the Rapture, we eliminate all difficulties.

First, we are no longer forced to mix grace and law by having the Tribulation Saints come out of Daniel's seventieth week. We bring the Dispensation of Grace to an end before we start the balance of the Dispensation of Law. This makes sense.

Second: We give everything enough time to happen.

Third: We follow precisely the order of events given in Revelation.

Fourth: We put the first Resurrection where it belongs, at the end of the Dispensation of Grace. The Tribulation Saints are included in the first Resurrection (Rev. 20:4, 5). The Rapture and the resurrection of the Tribulation Saints, taken together, are the first Resurrection. This would have to be so because we read, "Blessed and holy is he that hath part in the first resurrection: on such the second death hath no power."—Rev. 20:6. This is certainly true of the martyrs of the tribulation. "For the Lamb which is in the midst of the throne shall feed them, and shall lead them unto living fountains of waters."—Rev. 7:17. The natural place to end the Dispensation of Grace would be at the completion of the first Resurrection. This also solves the problem of how people can be saved after the Rapture.

WILL THE CHURCH GO THROUGH THE TRIBULATION?

The Rapture must come before the tribulation; however, there will be saints on earth during the tribulation. They may be accounted for by the work of the four horsemen. So it may be said that there will be a church during the tribulation. In that sense, the church will go through the tribulation. Conditions will be so much different that it may not be recognized as a church. There could be no church services or preaching as we know it today. Satan will be in full command, and the complete annihilation of the church will be the first order of business. The church will be what we call underground.

208

Editor's Note:

A Proposition: The second trumpet referred to in Revelation 8:8–9 compared with the second bowl in Revelation 16:3, are identical judgments.

The question is: Are the judgments called the seven trumpets and the seven bowls ("vials" in the old King James Version) two views of the same event? There is unusual harmony between them. If you look at the descriptions, you will find that they both follow the same sequence: the earth, the sea, the great star falls, the darkening of the sun and the moon, the demons from the abyss, the Euphrates and the great army, and last, the great earthquake and Jesus' coming. Are there any conflicts? Yes. Let me point out one of them:

- NKJV Revelation 8:8–9: *"The second angel sounded . . . **and a third of the living creatures (ktisma) in the sea died,** and a third of the ships were destroyed."*
- NKJV Revelation 16:3: *"Then the second angel poured out his bowl on the sea, and it became blood as of a dead man; **and every living creature in the sea died."***

This difference of *"a third of"* in Revelation 8 and the phrase *"every living creature"* of Revelation 16 causes many scholars to say that these two judgments are separate events.

However, the old King James Version favors the word *souls* in Revelation 16:3 rather than the word *creatures*. *"Every living soul (psuche) died in the sea."* This is also the word used in Young's Literal Translation of Revelation 16:3: *"Every living soul died in the sea."*

In the book of Revelation we read about this second judgment in chapter 8, verse 9: It says that *"a third of the living creatures died,"* and in chapter 16, verse 3 that *"every living soul died."*

What we propose is that these two judgments are not at two different times; rather, they describe the very same judgment. It tells us two facts: that a third of the creatures of the sea died, but that all the human souls on the ships died. In the new Testament the Greek word for "soul" is used over fifty times and almost always refers to people not sea-creatures.

—HJB

Chapter Twelve

THE RAPTURE

Fourth Room
EARTH
Tribulation Saints Persecuted by Antichrist
Preparation for Armageddon
FROM THE RAPTURE TO THE RETURN OF CHRIST
Chapters 12–16

Having finished the story of the saints in heaven from the Rapture to the Return, John now retraces his steps to the room marked *church*. He leaves this room by another door and enters the room marked *earth*, and sees what will happen on earth during this same period. This is not the whole story of the earth during this time but only those things that concern the saints.

Such grand procedures as the return of the Jews and the kingdom of David are not in the scope of this narrative because they do not concern the church directly. Although as an organization the church cannot last more than 3½ years after the Rapture, there will always be Christians here. The 144,000 and any of the Tribulation Saints that are not killed by Antichrist are here all the way through. Jesus spoke of "these my brethren" who will be here when He comes again.

What will be the makeup of the church after the Rapture? There are some, like the wicked servant, who said, "My Lord delayeth his coming." Jesus consigned him to his place among the hypocrites, but there are others. One wonders what becomes of those represented by the five foolish virgins. The Lord said to them "I know you not." That has an ominous sound, but the fact remains that they were believers, even in the Lord's return.

They absented themselves at the wrong time, but still it was for a worthy purpose. They went to get oil. When they came back, we must assume they had the oil, but it was too late. They were not "wicked servants"; they must still be considered a part of the church organization—considerably wiser. In every other instance where Jesus discusses the separation of the saved and lost at the Resurrection, He consigns the lost to their place of punishment: furnace of fire, outer darkness, among the hypocrites.

In the case of the foolish virgins, such statements are missing. They are not condemned, merely left out. They represent a vast number of church members who are not antagonistic to Christ; there would certainly be a great revival among them after the Rapture.

This is not a "second chance." That refers to another chance after death. Many people are given more than one chance while they are living. So even though all those who are "Christ's at his coming" are caught up, there would still be a church on earth, and this church would have a seed, new converts.

The Rapture

We come now to the study of the details of the Resurrection. So far in Revelation the Resurrection has not been mentioned. There is a suggestion of it in the fourth chapter, where John was caught up in spirit into heaven and saw things that shall be hereafter. John saw the saints in heaven, so we assume the Resurrection to have taken place.

We would expect, however, that a book which calls itself "The Revelation of Jesus Christ," and which gives in great detail the events of the Day of the Lord, would not omit the details of the Resurrection. Jesus included it very definitely in His summary. Moreover, Revelation would be unintelligible without a conception of the Resurrection. It is not only a part of the Day of the Lord; it is one of the two main features of that day.

There must, therefore, be some good reason for its omission in the fourth chapter. The reason is that the details are given in this parallel chapter. In point of time, the 12th chapter begins at exactly the same place as the 4th, the difference being that in the 12th, John remains on the earth to see the rise of Antichrist and the other events of the Day of the Lord from the standpoint of the earth.

We should approach this lesson having in mind the Bible teaching concerning the Resurrection. This may be found in the following verses:

> I tell you, in that night there shall be two men in one bed; the one shall be taken, and the other shall be left. Two women shall be grinding together; the one shall be taken, and the other left. Two men shall be in the field; the one shall be taken, and the other left.—Luke 17: 34–36

This shows how the Resurrection will affect those that are alive. The saved will be taken, the others left.

> For the Lord himself shall descend from heaven with a shout, with the voice of the archangel, and with the trump of God: and the dead in Christ shall rise first: then we which are alive and remain shall be caught up together with them in the clouds, to meet the Lord in the air: and so shall we ever be with the Lord.— I Thess. 4:16, 17

This tells the manner of the Resurrection. There will be a shout, a voice, and a trumpet call. The saved dead shall rise first; afterwards those who are living will be caught up with them. Notice the term "caught up" as expressive of the manner of our going. Notice also there is the voice of the archangel. Michael is the archangel. He has a definite work to do in connection with the Resurrection.

> And at that time shall Michael stand up, the great prince which standeth for the children of thy people: and there shall be a time of trouble, such as never was since there was a nation even to that same time: and at that time thy people shall be delivered, every one that shall be found written in the book. And many of them that sleep in the dust of the earth shall awake, some to everlasting life, and some to shame and everlasting contempt. And they that be wise shall shine as the brightness of the firmament; and they that turn many to righteousness as the stars for ever and ever.—Dan. 12:1–3

Here we have the reason for the Rapture. It is to save God's people from a time of trouble such as never was since there was a nation upon the earth. This is a strong statement when we consider the wars and calamities that have come at various times upon the earth. This time is known as "the" tribulation and the seven last plagues. It will not be only the worst trouble that the world has ever experienced, but it will be different in nature. It is not only trouble that is the result of the failures of men in self-government, such as war and famine and the spread of disease and pests—these things are included—but there is much more besides. This is a time of judgment which, like the flood, is a direct visitation of God's wrath.

Add to this the fact that Satan himself is to be judged upon this earth after having reigned here in person for a time, during which he will bring evil to a state of harvest, and you will begin to see why Daniel would say that this was to be a time of trouble such as never was since there was a nation upon the earth. The Rapture will take place before this time of trouble begins for the same reason that Noah entered the ark before the flood came and Lot and his family were taken out of Sodom before the fire came.

Daniel says that Michael shall stand up. That does not mean that Michael is sitting down; it means that he suddenly goes into action. There is a great opposition to be overcome. The devil, the great destroyer, will fight with all his tremendous power to retain the bodies of the dead. Never have two such opposing forces met in decisive battle as when Michael at the head of God's armies stands up in defense of the children of God. This same idea is carried out in Daniel's words "at that time thy people shall be delivered." The Hebrew *netsal* means to "snatch away, to rescue." It corresponds exactly with the New Testament expression "caught up." In both cases it implies that we are to be rescued out of great danger.

Revelation 12

1 And there appeared a great wonder in heaven; a woman clothed with the sun, and the moon under her feet, and upon her head a crown of twelve stars.

A GREAT WONDER. The American Standard Version has *sign* in place of *wonder*. The corresponding verb is used in 1:1: "And he sent and signified it by his angel unto his servant John." It is used again in 15:1: "And I saw another sign in heaven." Although symbols are used at times in this section, the word *sign* is not meant to express that fact. It does not mean symbol; it means a great or wonderful revelation. The King James *wonder* expresses the thought. "In heaven" here means in the sky. The woman would have to be in the sky if she is standing on the moon. The scene is transferred to the earth as soon as the child is born.

THE WOMAN. A woman in Scripture, in its broadest sense when used symbolically, always represents a church; this would include the saints of the Old Testament. (A wicked woman is an evil or false church.)

This woman represents the visible church. A visible church includes all its members. There is an invisible church which consists only of the saved. Not all church members are saved. People join the church for various reasons.

This woman is the symbol of the church of the 2nd and 3rd chapters. There the word *church* means the visible church. There even Thyatira and Laodicea are considered churches. Only in the day of separation will the true church be revealed. The church holds her place among the candlesticks only because of the faithful ones within her.

CLOTHED WITH THE SUN. To be clothed with the sun is to be clothed with light. Light is the garment of God. He is light. The church is the custodian of that light: "Ye are the light of the world." If there is any truth, the church has it; if there is any knowledge that can survive the grave, the church has it. All the light shed upon life's problems and mysteries by the Holy Spirit is hers. She is clothed with the sun.

THE MOON UNDER HER FEET. She is victorious in her position. The moon, the symbol of darkness and error, is under her feet.

"As the sun is king of the day, so the moon is empress of the night and hence a fit picture of the kingdom of darkness. And so to be clothed with one is to be a glorious light-bearer to the world; so to tread the moon under foot is the image of victory over the powers of darkness."—Dr. Joseph A. Seiss.

A CROWN OF TWELVE STARS. The crown is a sign of royalty. "But ye are a chosen generation, a royal priesthood, an holy nation, a peculiar people [literally, 'a purchased people']; that ye should shew forth the praises of him who hath

called you out of darkness into his marvelous light."—I Pet.
2: 9.

Twelve could refer to either the Old or New Testament
saints. At the time she is seen here the Rapture is about to
take place. The woman represents the church as it exists at
the time of the Rapture.

Revelation 12

**2 And she being with child cried, travailing in birth,
and pained to be delivered.**

**3 And there appeared another wonder in heaven;
and behold a great red dragon, having seven heads and
ten horns, and seven crowns upon his heads.**

**4 And his tail drew the third part of the stars of
heaven, and did cast them to the earth: and the dragon
stood before the woman which was ready to be delivered,
for to devour her child as soon as it was born.**

**5 And she brought forth a man child, who was to
rule all nations with a rod of iron: and her child was
caught up unto God, and to his throne.**

THE MAN-CHILD. If the woman is a symbol, then the
child is also a symbol. Logically, if the woman represents a
large body of people, the visible church, then the child represents a smaller body of people which comes out of the larger
body. The child is the invisible church. There is to be a birth, a
sudden separation.

This is a picture of the Rapture. The child is "caught up"
into heaven. The church that is left must face Antichrist.

Here we have three symbols: a woman, a child, and a
dragon. The meaning of one is told in this chapter, the meaning of the second is given in another, and the third may be
understood from these two. Let us proceed from the known
to the unknown. The 9th verse tells the meaning of the dragon. It represents the devil. The stars which follow him are
his angels (verse 7).

We are told who the child is: "Who was to rule all nations with a rod of iron." This expression is used in the Bible
to refer both to Christ and the saints. In Revelation it refers
specifically to the saints.

In each of the seven letters there is a promise to him
that overcomes. These overcomers are the ones that will be
"caught up" at the Rapture. These promises do not apply ex-
clusively to the church addressed, but taken together, they
constitute a sevenfold promise applying to all the saved. One
of these promises reads:

> And he that overcometh, and keepeth my works
> unto the end, to him will I give power over the nations:
> and he shall rule them with a rod of iron; as the vessels
> of a potter shall they be broken to shivers: even as I
> received of my Father.—Rev. 2:26, 27

We have been studying how the saints would sit upon
thrones after the Rapture and be judges of the earth. Over
and over again we are told that they are to be the kings and
priests and will reign upon the earth. This child represents
those who rule the nations. The story of the woman and the
child is interrupted to tell of the dragon which stands ready
to devour the child as soon as it is born.

Upon birth, the child is immediately "caught up" into
heaven to escape the dragon. This is accomplished with the
aid of Michael and his angels who engage the forces of evil
in a battle. It would seem that all the resources of heaven
are required to accomplish the successful birth of the child.
The resurrection of all the saved dead and the translation of
all the living saints is a tremendous undertaking in which
great forces of heaven are engaged.

It has been thought by some that this woman represents
Israel and the man-child, Christ. This is an impossible interpretation, for it would make a symbolic woman give birth
to a literal child. That would be a monstrosity. Moreover, it
cannot be said that Christ was "caught up" into heaven to

escape the devil. Jesus was not "caught up" into heaven at birth but remained upon the earth for thirty years or more. He suffered death at the hands of Satan's forces, and when He went to heaven, He was not "caught up" but ascended slowly, deliberately, victoriously. Jesus ascended by His own power; the saints will be caught up by the power of God. This man-child did not ascend. He was "caught up." The symbol could not possibly apply to Christ.

The Bible does not use symbols to prophesy past events. Symbols are for the purpose of foretelling future events.

Some have objected that we must not go back to the Rapture at this point. Then they go back to the birth of Christ to find the fulfillment of the prophecy. Nothing happened to Israel after the birth of Christ to correspond with the experience of this woman that brought forth the man-child. If the 5th verse refers to the ascension of Christ, then we must put two thousand years between verses 5 and 6. But there is nothing here to indicate any such lapse of time. The story of the child is interrupted to tell of the attempt of Satan to devour the child as soon as it was born. This indicates that the fall of Satan out of heaven down to the earth comes at the same time as the birth of the child and is a part of the story. The casting of Satan out of heaven down to the earth results in the persecution of the saints by Antichrist, a condition which prevails immediately after the Rapture. The man-child is born just before the tribulation. Paul uses the same symbol in Thessalonians:

> For when they shall say, Peace and safety; then sudden destruction cometh upon them, as travail upon a woman with child; and they shall not escape.—I Thess. 5:3

TRAVAILING IN BIRTH. This symbolism is not new to the Bible. There is a similar symbol in the Old Testament. It is concerning Israel. The conditions are entirely different, but there are points of similarity. Ezekiel describes the revival

of Israel as a resurrection of dry bones. They will come from
the whole world—a nation born in a day.

> Then he said unto me, Son of man, these bones
> are the whole house of Israel: behold, they say, Our bones
> are dried, and our hope is lost: we are cut off for our
> parts. Therefore prophesy and say unto them, Thus saith
> the Lord God; Behold, O my people, I will open your
> graves, and cause you to come up out of your graves,
> and bring you into the land of Israel. And ye shall know
> that I am the Lord, when I have opened your graves, O
> my people, and brought you up out of your graves, and
> shall put my spirit in you, and ye shall live, and I shall
> place you in your own land: then shall ye know that I
> the Lord have spoken it, and performed it, saith the
> Lord.—Ezek. 37:11–14

Isaiah, telling of the same thing, uses the symbol of the
birth of a man-child.

> A voice of noise from the city, a voice from the
> temple, a voice of the Lord that rendereth recompence
> to his enemies. Before she travailed, she brought forth;
> before her pain came, she was delivered of a man child.
> Who hath heard such a thing? who hath seen such
> things? Shall the earth be made to bring forth in one day?
> or shall a nation be born at once? for as soon as Zion
> travailed, she brought forth her children.—Isa. 66:6–8

"Shall the earth be made to bring forth in one day?"
This is the explanation of the symbol. The man-child represents those brought forth from the earth. This symbol and
the one in Ezekiel may be better understood if we realize
what will be the condition of the Jews just prior to the return. It will be the worst experience they have ever gone
through. They will be on the very edge of annihilation. They
will say, "We are cut off for our parts," or, "It is all over
with us." The nation will be considered dead, so the sudden
return will be as a resurrection. The Bible symbol of resurrection is the birth of a man child.

At about the same time there will be another resurrection—a resurrection of the dead in Christ. The same symbol

is used. Notice the points of similarity. At the Resurrection there are three signals: the shout, the voice of the archangel, and the trump of God. Isaiah also has three: a voice of noise from the city, a voice from the temple, a voice of the Lord.

Isaiah mentions first the man-child and then the children. Before she travails she brings forth a man-child. As soon as she travails she brings forth her children. The man-child represents the first great gathering; the children, those that come after.

At the Resurrection of the dead in Christ, there is first the Rapture, the man-child, afterwards the "seed of the woman," the Tribulation Saints. In both cases the birth of the man-child represents resurrection. This establishes the meaning of the symbol. The symbol is the same in both places, only the people are different.

The balance of the chapter in Isaiah makes it abundantly clear that Israel is the subject. The balance of the chapter in Revelation makes it just as clear that the church is the subject. Nothing in Revelation 12 and 13 happened at the birth of Christ. Everything in these two chapters will happen at the Resurrection.

Micah makes mention of this same time:

> Now gather thyself in troops, O daughter of troops: he hath laid siege against us: they shall smite the judge of Israel with a rod upon the cheek. But thou, Bethlehem, Ephratah, though thou be little among the thousands of Judah, yet out of thee shall he come forth unto me that is to be ruler in Israel; whose goings forth have been from of old, from everlasting. Therefore will he give them up, until the time that she which travaileth hath brought forth: then the remnant of his brethren shall return unto the children of Israel.—Mic. 5:1–3

The whole story of the Jews is here in substance.
1. The birth of Christ in Bethlehem.

2. The rejection of Christ by the Jews. "They shall smite the judge of Israel with a rod upon the cheek."

3. Israel will be set aside temporarily. "Therefore will he give them up."

4. They will not be given up forever but only until the end of the Gentile period when "she which travaileth hath brought forth."

5. After the Resurrection (bringing forth), a remnant will return to Christ, representing the end of the time they are given up. This remnant is the 144,000. Their sealing marks the beginning of Daniel's 70th week when Israel will again be dealt with as a people. The Two Witnesses will take up where Paul left off when he said, "Lo, we turn to the Gentiles."

So in Micah also, childbirth after travail is the symbol of the Resurrection.

SEVEN HEADS. The dragon is described in Revelation 12: 3 as having seven heads and ten horns. We are dealing with consummations. The woman stands for the church of all ages. The dragon is Satan in all his power throughout all the ages. He has now reached the last days of his freedom. He has been the prince of this world and as such has dominated the world under seven typical empires. Seven is always the number of completeness.

Daniel saw four of these empires: Babylon, Persia, Greece, and Rome. There were two before Daniel: Assyria and Egypt. There will be one more under Antichrist, making up the seven.

TEN HORNS. The ten horns connect with both the sixth and seventh heads, but as we are viewing Satan in the last days, we must put the horns on the seventh head. The ten horns are the nations of the Roman Empire. This is made clear by Daniel. Daniel said they would remain until the coming of the kingdom of heaven. They are the basis of Antichrist's kingdom although Antichrist will try to dominate more territory than was in the Roman Empire.

THE THIRD PART OF THE STARS. How great an angel Satan was that in his fall he could draw to his side one-third of the angels of heaven! Satan's name was Lucifer, sun of the morning, or morning star. Angels are known as stars.

In the Bible the word "star" is used in the same sense that we use the word today, meaning either a heavenly body or a celebrity—a person of unusual ability.

Nothing more is said about these angels. They constitute Satan's government today. They are the principalities and powers in heavenly places. This kingdom of darkness will be broken up and the heavens will be cleansed. From now on there will be no more spiritual warfare; it will all center on the earth.

Revelation 12

6 And the woman fled into the wilderness, where she hath a place prepared of God, that they should feed her there a thousand two hundred and threescore days.

THE WILDERNESS. Notice the glorious position of the woman prior to the birth of the child: clothed with light, victorious over the forces of darkness, and reigning as a queen. Now compare her condition after the birth of the child: all the former glory is gone; she is persecuted, hunted, forlorn, managing to keep only one step ahead of death. All her greatness was in the child. When the child is gone, her victory is gone. She no longer stands; she runs or flies in fear and weakness. Her dwelling place is now a wilderness.

Previously she had been powerful and rich and in need of nothing. When the child is caught up to God, it takes all the glory with it. This is the most complete picture of the Rapture to be found anywhere in the Bible. Nearly every feature recorded elsewhere is found here.

The wilderness represents the conditions which the church will face upon the earth after the Rapture: the wars, the famine, the pestilence, and the persecutions of Antichrist. Antichrist will try to starve the woman by making it impossible for her members to buy or sell without the mark of the beast. It is out of this wilderness experience that the Tribulation Saints come.

Antichrist would immediately annihilate the church if he could. But there is yet to be saved a remnant of Israel and a great multitude of Gentiles from every kindred, tongue, people, and nation. Therefore the life of the church must be extended a short time.

The Holy Spirit will no longer resist Satan's attacks upon the church; but there will be other means of protection provided, and her life will be preserved for three and a half years. This has no connection with the three and a half years during which the Two Witnesses prophesy. These two distinct periods of three and a half years do not come at the same time.

Revelation 12

7 And there was war in heaven: Michael and his angels fought against the dragon; and the dragon fought and his angels,

8 And prevailed not; neither was their place found any more in heaven.

9 And the great dragon was cast out, that old serpent, called the Devil, and Satan, which deceiveth the whole world: he was cast out into the earth, and his angels were cast out with him.

10 And I heard a loud voice saying in heaven, Now is come salvation, and strength, and the kingdom of our God, and the power of his Christ: for the accuser of our brethren is cast down, which accused them before our God day and night.

11 And they overcame him by the blood of the Lamb, and by the word of their testimony; and they loved not their lives unto the death.

WAR IN HEAVEN. Satan has won and lost many battles, but they have been only skirmishes in the battle of the earth. Seemingly, Satan is continuously victorious. Just about all the world belongs to him. This will be his first disastrous defeat; for the first time he will actually lose ground.

Satan is much more powerful than we like to suppose. He is a formidable antagonist who demands and gets the respect of heaven. Even Michael, we are told, did not dare bring a railing accusation against him, but said, "The Lord rebuke thee"—Jude 9. It would be no mean personage that would attempt the temptation of Jesus. When Satan offered Him the kingdoms of the world, it would have been no temptation if Satan had not had them to give.

The church has always seemed to fight a losing battle against Satan. If he could not suppress the church from without, he would fill it with tares from within. The Resurrection of the dead is a crisis in heaven, even more so than on the earth. The earth could cast out its dead without anyone realizing what was happening. Even the catching up of the living saints will not cause more than a ripple of excitement outside of church circles. The Resurrection itself will change the earth and its ways very little, but for heaven it will be a momentous event. Untold millions will be arriving all at once. Not only that, but these new people will be the most important individuals ever to inhabit the spirit world—people for whom the angels are ministering spirits. A whole new ruling class will take over, actually sharing the throne of Christ. This will necessitate a new heaven. Whenever a new earth is mentioned, a new heaven is usually included: "And I saw a new heaven and a new earth."

These saints that are going to fill the heavens have a characteristic not shared by the angels. They are overcomers of Satan. They have met him on his own ground and have come off victorious. Such a company arriving in heaven would spell the downfall of Satan in short order. Satan must prevent the Resurrection at all costs. He occupies all the territory between earth and heaven and therefore is in a good strategic position to "devour her child as soon as it is born."

Satan and his angels occupy heavenly places. We even read of Satan having access to the throne of God (Job 1:6).[1] Whether the heavenly bodies, stars, and planets are occupied by these angels, we do not know, but we do know that things have been made and put in the sky that must be shaken out when God cleanses the heavens of things that should not be there. Haggai said:

> For thus saith the Lord of hosts; Yet once, it is a little while, and I will shake the heavens, and the earth, and the sea, and the dry land; and I will shake all nations, and the desire of all nations shall come: and I will fill this house with glory, saith the Lord of hosts.—Hag. 2:6, 7

We have an inspired commentary on this passage:

> Whose voice then shook the earth: but now he hath promised, saying, Yet once more I shake not the earth only, but also heaven. And this word, Yet once more, signifieth the removing of those things that are shaken, as of things that are made, that those things which cannot be shaken may remain.—Heb. 12:26, 27

The reason God is going to shake the heavens is that there is something there that does not belong there, and God is going to shake it out. There is going to be some house cleaning when the saints arrive. We read about this shaking in the sixth chapter of Revelation.

So the Resurrection is a crisis for Satan and his principalities and powers (organized governments). There may also be a principle involved in the Resurrection that we do not comprehend, yet we can realize that it exists. Satan cannot allow the Resurrection and still retain his position of power. He would not allow even one man to be raised if he

---

1. "Now there was a day when the sons of God came to present themselves before the Lord, and Satan came also among them" (Job 1:6).

could help it. Michael, we are told, contended with the devil over the body of Moses.

It is Michael, Daniel was told, who will stand up for the children of his people at the Resurrection. Paul mentions the voice of the archangel (Michael) at the Resurrection, and Revelation says it will be Michael who will make war against Satan and prevent him from devouring the child as soon as it is born. This war with Satan and his angels has two results: it allows the saints safe access to heaven, and it drives Satan and his angels out of heaven.

This is why the time of the Rapture must be kept so secret. It must take Satan by surprise. Jesus said He did not know the time of the Rapture. This has been explained by saying that Jesus was human as well as divine, and as a man He did not know.

This is not a very logical explanation. Jesus knew everything—even the thoughts of His hearers. He answered in detail the disciples' questions about the end of the age. The time of the Rapture was kept out of His mind so that Satan could not detect it. This is heaven's top secret. When the allied forces were poised in England ready to invade France and Germany, the German forces knew they were there. They knew that an invasion was imminent. They could read the signs, but they did not know the day and the hour, and they were taken by surprise.

Signs will be numerous. There must be great excitement in the spirit world, but the Rapture will be sudden, in the twinkling of an eye. If this were not so, the saints might be caught between two battle lines.

NOW IS COME SALVATION. Salvation is connected with the kingdom. This is not referring to the saving of individual souls but the consummation of salvation when those who are saved will receive the reward of their labors. The final and glorious phase of salvation depends upon the defeat of

Satan. The reason for this is given: he accuses them before God day and night. He never ceases to accuse them—as he did Job.

This war with Satan is not one of just brute force—such a war would be easy for Michael—but there is something else involved which is much more mysterious. There is the aspect of a court trial in which Satan shows cause why he should retain the bodies of the saints, a dispute similar to that which took place when Michael contended about the body of Moses. Satan takes up each case separately and prefers charges. He will fight over every single body. The accused answer. Again it is a court scene; they give testimony to offset Satan's accusations.

We must have the right answers. Accusation cannot be answered by accusation or excuse, or by comparing ourselves with others less virtuous, or by parading our good works. All the good works of a lifetime would not be enough to offset what Satan has against us. Many of the things people are depending on to get to heaven will be totally insufficient to counter Satan's accusations. He is a master prosecutor. We will need a lawyer—a good one.

"If any man sin, we have an advocate [lawyer] with the Father, Jesus Christ, the righteous."—I John 2:1. There is only one testimony that will win this case: "I have been redeemed by the blood of the Lamb."

Revelation 12

12 Therefore rejoice, ye heavens, and ye that dwell in them. Woe to the inhabiters of the earth and of the sea! for the devil is come down unto you, having great wrath, because he knoweth that he hath but a short time.

The American Standard Version makes slight changes in the wording of these verses, but for the most part the sense is not changed. Here the meaning is changed a little. "Inhabitant" is omitted. "Woe for the earth and woe for the sea." Not just the inhabitants but the animals, vegetation, the earth as a whole—everything will feel the effect of Satan's wrath.

THE HEAVENS ARE INHABITED. There are those who dwell (tabernacle) there. To dwell is to have a permanent residence.

Revelation 12

13 And when the dragon saw that he was cast unto the earth, he persecuted the woman which brought forth the man child.

14 And to the woman were given two wings of a great eagle, that she might fly into the wilderness, into her place, where she is nourished for a time, and times, and half a time, from the face of the serpent.

15 And the serpent cast out of his mouth water as a flood after the woman, that he might cause her to be carried away of the flood.

16 And the earth helped the woman, and the earth opened her mouth, and swallowed up the flood which the dragon cast out of his mouth.

17 And the dragon was wroth with the woman, and went to make war with the remnant of her seed, which keep the commandments of God, and have the testimony of Jesus Christ.

TRIBULATION SAINTS. When Satan finds he has lost all the true believers, he vents his wrath upon that part of the church that is left behind. This he can do without interference from the Holy Spirit, for He will have been taken out of the way—not out of the world, as some have thought, but out of the way of Antichrist (II Thess. 2: 7). The church does get some protection, but it is of a physical nature.

The earthquakes, the falling stars, the pestilences, and the plagues all hinder the dragon and help the woman. Satan sends out a flood of persecution which is designed to destroy the church completely, but the conditions on the earth and the troubles which Satan faces work out to the advantage of the church and allow it to exist for 3½ years after the Rapture. It is during this time that the Tribulation Saints are saved.

THE REMNANT OF HER SEED. The seed of the woman are those people who are saved after the Rapture, both Jew and Gentile. While we were studying these events from the standpoint of heaven, we saw these tribulation saints under the altar awaiting their resurrection. Later we saw them when they all arrived in heaven to join the whole group of saints. We were told that they were killed because of their faith and that they had gone hungry and thirsty and had passed through great tribulation. But we were not told how they were killed, or by whom, because that is purely an earthly matter.

Now we are to get the details of this persecution. We are going to see these Tribulation Saints from the earthly point of view.

Chapter Thirteen

SATAN PERSECUTES THE TRIBULATION SAINTS

Revelation 13

1 And I stood upon the sand of the sea, and saw a beast rise up out of the sea, having seven heads and ten horns, and upon his horns ten crowns, and upon his heads the name of blasphemy.

2 And the beast which I saw was like unto a leopard, and his feet were as the feet of a bear, and his mouth as the mouth of a lion: and the dragon gave him his power, and his seat, and great authority.

AND I STOOD UPON THE SAND OF THE SEA AND SAW A BEAST. The American Standard Version reads, "And he stood upon the sand of the sea, and I saw a beast." This would indicate that it was the dragon who stood on the sand of the sea and brought forth the beast. Antichrist's coming is "after the working of Satan."

The 13th chapter of Revelation is a continuation of the 12th chapter. There is no break in the story. In the 12th chapter we see Satan preparing to persecute the saints. The 13th chapter tells how he does it.

We do not have here the complete history of Antichrist but only his relationship to the saints. Revelation does not give us a connected story of Antichrist. It mentions him only as he is related to other movements.

SATAN BECOMES A MAN. There is a plain reference here to Daniel's visions of four world empires (Daniel 7), yet there is a difference. There seems to be a world of confusion in our thinking about this satanic man. Nearly all the difficulties are bound up in one fact. If we can solve this one problem, most of our difficulties would vanish. It is this: Antichrist is a man, but also Satan. It might be more accurate to say he is a man who becomes Satan. This comes close to being an incarnation, although there is one difference.

When the Son of God became flesh, He said, "A body hast thou prepared me," but there is no one to prepare a body for Satan. When he is cast out of heaven, he will be at a great disadvantage because he is only a spirit in a material world. Therefore it will be necessary for him to take over the body of a man. This man is the man commonly called Antichrist. In the Bible he is called by other names.

Daniel sees him as the man; in Revelation he is a part of the satanic trinity. This advent of Satan into the world is a direct result of his being driven out of heaven and is a fulfillment of the prophecy made to Satan in the day of his fall.

> Son of man, take up a lamentation upon the king of Tyrus, and say unto him, Thus saith the Lord God; Thou sealest up the sum, full of wisdom, and perfect in beauty. Thou hast been in Eden the garden of God; every precious stone was thy covering, the sardius, topaz, and the diamond, the beryl, the onyx, and the jasper, the sapphire, the emerald, and the carbuncle, and gold: the workmanship of thy tabrets and of thy pipes was prepared in thee in the day that thou wast created. Thou art the anointed cherub that covereth; and I have set thee so: thou wast upon the holy mountain of God; thou hast walked up and down in the midst of the stones of fire. Thou wast perfect in thy ways from the day that thou wast created, till iniquity was found in thee. By the multitude of thy merchandise they have filled the midst of thee with violence, and thou hast sinned: therefore I will cast thee as profane out of the mountain of God: and

I will destroy thee, O covering cherub, from the midst of the stones of fire. Thine heart was lifted up because of thy beauty, thou hast corrupted thy wisdom by reason of thy brightness: I will cast thee to the ground, I will lay thee before kings, that they may behold thee. Thou hast defiled thy sanctuaries by the multitude of thine iniquities, by the iniquity of thy traffick; therefore will I bring forth a fire from the midst of thee, it shall devour thee, and I will bring thee to ashes upon the earth in the sight of all them that behold thee. All they that know thee shall be astonished at thee: thou shalt be a terror, and never shalt thou be any more.—Ezek. 28:12–19

The king of Tyrus is not a type of Satan; he is Satan. This Tyre is not the ancient city but a future one. God says of Satan: "I will bring thee to ashes upon the earth." This prediction approaches its fulfillment when Satan is cast out of heaven.

The beast that rises out of the sea looks exactly like the dragon except for one detail: the crowns are on his horns instead of his heads as in the 12th chapter.

Three animals are used to describe the empire of Antichrist: a leopard, a bear, and a lion. Daniel used the same three animals as symbols of the three world empires preceding the Roman (Daniel 7). The beast was Daniel's symbol for the Roman Empire which in its final form will include all the others. When Daniel saw these empires they were still future; when John saw them they were past. Hence John mentions them in reverse order. "Sands of the sea" is a symbol of the masses of people. The rise of dictators and powerful conquerors from the common people and the revival of a strong national spirit in all countries may be the horns of the beast rising above the level of the waters. The symbol applies both to the man and his empire. This is also true of Daniel's symbols.

The dragon had crowns on his heads. Satan has always reigned over nations, but in the end time the crowns are on

the horns. The horns represent the nations that will make up
the nucleus of Antichrist's kingdom. When this beast rises
out of the sea (which usually represents humanity), six of
the seven heads are history. They no longer wear crowns.
The crowns are on the seventh head. This is the one with
which we will be dealing from now on. Something strange
happens to this head.

Revelation 13

**3 And I saw one of his heads as it were wounded
to death; and his deadly wound was healed: and all the
world wondered after the beast.**

SATAN IN PERSON. John saw one of the seven heads as
though it were wounded to death. If the seven heads represent all human government of all time, then one head would
represent human government at a given time. This head that
was wounded evidently represents the man in power at the
time that Satan is cast down to the earth. This head is
wounded to death, or at least appears to be. "As it were"
means "as though it were" wounded to death. It is a strong
expression. "He was killed dead," yet he continued to live.
This may not be a genuine resurrection from the dead, but it
is Satan's counterfeit of the Resurrection which has just
taken place. Satan draws the attention of the world away
from the wonders of the Rapture and directs it toward his
own supposed miraculous power. Daniel describes the death
of this man in these words:

> Then shall stand up in his estate a raiser of taxes in
> the glory of the kingdom: but within few days he shall
> be destroyed, neither in anger, nor in battle.—Dan. 11:20

This is a spectacular death, but it is not murder. Verse 14
indicates that the wound is to be by a sword. The purpose
of this mysterious transaction is to give Satan a body. From
this point on Satan rules in person.

THE DRAGON GAVE HIM HIS POWER, AND HIS
THRONE, AND GREAT AUTHORITY. Although Antichrist

will be Satan in the flesh and will be completely possessed by Satan, he will have a separate personality of his own. In the end, Satan will be cast into the bottomless pit, while Antichrist will be cast into the lake of fire.

There may seem to be some confusion between the man and the empire. All prophecy follows the same pattern in this respect: it starts with the history of empires showing their rise and fall till the final form of world domination is reached. Then the pronoun changes from it to he, and a man becomes the fulfillment of the symbol. This is true in Daniel as well as Revelation.

In the last days the world will be so under the complete rule of one man that he himself becomes the fulfillment of the symbol. The head that is wounded and restored is Antichrist. He already has established himself over an empire when Satan takes over his body by some process resembling death and resurrection. In the very last days before the coming of Christ, we are dealing with a man rather than an empire. There is a sort of empire, but the man is greater than the empire because his influence reaches to every part of the earth. Daniel does not recognize the empire of Antichrist, but only the man.

The death and resurrection of this man is the means by which Satan acquires a body. This is also Satan's answer to the Resurrection that has just startled the world. Satan immediately produces a resurrection of his own and thus calls attention to his own powers. This will happen right after the Rapture.

The man will have to be here and in power before Satan takes over his body. It is possible, therefore, that the rise of the beast with the crowns on his horns will precede the Rapture. According to Daniel, this man (whom Daniel calls the little horn) will rise up and conquer three nations. Daniel puts this before the heavenly scene that corresponds with

Revelation 4 and 5. So it is likely that saints living in the last days will see the rise of the man we call Antichrist.

Revelation 13

4 And they worshipped the dragon which gave power unto the beast: and they worshipped the beast, saying, Who is like unto the beast? who is able to make war with him?

5 And there was given unto him a mouth speaking great things and blasphemies; and power was given unto him to continue forty and two months.

6 And he opened his mouth in blasphemy against God, to blaspheme his name, and his tabernacle, and them that dwell in heaven.

THEY WORSHIP THE DRAGON. It is the devil who gives life and power to the beast, and that fact is known. The people actually worship Satan. The worship of a man and the worship of Satan are one and the same, as is the worship of Christ and the worship of God. When they worship Antichrist they worship the devil. The worship of man (humanism) is satanic in its conception and is the direct result of the falling away from the faith on the part of the church (modernism) (II Thess. 2:1–12).

There is only a step between the worship of man and the worship of Satan. They are the same in final result. In the last days of this age the worship of Satan will become general. It will be associated with the worship of a man and will be considered the same thing.

A newspaper reported a minister as saying, "Our attention is to be directed to man and the problems of his relation to his fellow men on the planet here and now. The Divine Element in man is the only deity we know. Man is a glorious end in himself. He is not to regard himself as a worm in the dust or as a subject before a king, but rather as a God in the making, whose potential divinity awaits unfoldment in a new social order. God helps those who help themselves, the humanists proclaim, and the God he refers to is the God in himself." Thus even the church helps to prepare the world for the worship of the beast.

FORTY-TWO MONTHS. It has been argued that Antichrist will reign only 3½ years. This is not what the Bible says. Daniel says that Antichrist will confirm a seven years' covenant with many (Jews). Therefore the reign of Antichrist must be at least seven years. How much longer, we are not told. He is actually reigning when he confirms the treaty.

The forty-two months of this chapter have nothing to do with the Jews nor with either half of that seven years mentioned by Daniel. This forty-two months is the length of time that the beast will continue to make war with the saints, for that is the subject of this chapter.

Daniel mentions the same thing in 7:25: "And he shall speak great words against the most High, and shall wear out the saints of the most High, and think to change times and laws: and they [the saints] shall be given into his hand until a time and times and the dividing of time."

A time and times and the dividing of time is the symbolic way of saying 3½ years. It is the length of time that the woman, the earthly organization called the church, is pursued by the dragon (Rev. 12:6). It is the length of time that this woman is nourished, that her life may be preserved until the Tribulation Saints have been killed (Rev. 12:14). It is the length of time that Antichrist will make war with the saints and overcome them (Rev. 13:7).

WHO IS ABLE TO MAKE WAR WITH HIM? The only reason given as to why the world will worship him is his ability to make war. This gives us some notion about the circumstances of his rise. If his ability to make war is so dramatically demonstrated that it will bring such world admiration, it must be that his rise will be against great odds. Notice also that they worshipped the dragon as well. The source of Antichrist's power will be known. They do not worship him because they think he is Christ; they are worshippers of Satan. He is Antichrist because he is against Christ. "He opened his mouth in blasphemy against God, to blaspheme his name, and his tabernacle, and them that dwell in heaven."—Rev. 13:6.

HIS TABERNACLE. Satan blasphemes those whom he cannot reach to persecute. He kills the saints within his reach and blasphemes those who have escaped him by the Rapture. There is another group that is just out of his reach, just enough to make him furious—the 144,000 on Mount Zion. They are protected from the plagues by the seal and from Antichrist by their place of abode. Mount Zion is the one place that Antichrist never reaches. It will be saved by the coming of Christ. The Psalmist says it cannot be moved but abideth forever.

The sign of God's protection and presence is the ark of the covenant in the tabernacle or temple. The tabernacle of David will be rebuilt (Amos 9:11).[1] The ark of the covenant will appear and be placed again in Mount Zion. It will be visited until its symbolism is fulfilled by the complete restoration; then it will no longer be visited (Jeremiah 3:16).[2]

The tabernacle, then, would connect with the 144,000 Israelites. There is an additional application, for there is a tabernacle in heaven containing the ark of the covenant, the originals after which the earthly ones were patterned. Antichrist as a man would not know about this, but Satan would. The ark stands for victory over God's enemies. It is the opening of the temple in heaven and the appearance of the ark that signals Satan's defeat at Armageddon. The ark connects directly with the second coming of Christ (Revelation 11:19).

---

1. "In that day will I raise up the tabernacle of David that is fallen, and close up the breaches thereof; and I will raise up his ruins, and I will build it as in the days of old" (Amos 9:11).

2. "And it shall come to pass, when ye shall be multiplied and increased in the land, in those days, saith the Lord, they shall say no more, The ark of the covenant of the Lord: neither shall it come to mind: neither shall they remember it; neither shall they visit it; neither shall that be done any more" (Jer. 3:16).

The seven vials are directed at Satan's kingdom. "And the fifth angel poured out his vial upon the seat of the beast; and his kingdom was full of darkness; and they gnawed their tongues for pain."—Rev. 16: 10. The seven angels having the seven vials come out of the tabernacle in heaven (Rev. 15: 5, 6).

Revelation 13

7 And it was given unto him to make war with the saints, and to overcome them: and power was given him over all kindreds, and tongues, and nations,

8 And all that dwell upon the earth shall worship him, whose names are not written in the book of life of the Lamb slain from the foundation of the world.

9 If any man have an ear, let him hear.

10 He that leadeth into captivity shall go into captivity: he that killeth with the sword must be killed with the sword. Here is the patience and the faith of the saints.

THE TRIBULATION SAINTS. The souls under the altar (6: 9) came out of this persecution. When they inquire how long it will last, they are told they must wait until all the others should be killed as they were. In the heaven section we saw them only as they arrived from the earth after being killed; now we learn how they were killed and by whom. We also get the answer to their question: How long? It will last 42 months, or 3½ years.

POWER OVER ALL NATIONS. As a man, Antichrist will have an empire of limited proportions, possibly no more than was covered by the four empires of Daniel. But even that will cause him trouble. His only absolute power will be over the countries symbolized by the ten horns. But as Satan he has power, at least coercive power, over all the world. As always, the faith of the saints looks not to immediate relief, but to ultimate victory.

NAMES IN THE BOOK OF LIFE FROM THE FOUNDATION OF THE WORLD. It is natural to connect the words "from the foundation of the world" with "Lamb slain" rather than with "written," but a comparison with the parallel passage in the next section makes the meaning clear. "And they that dwell on the earth shall wonder, whose names were not written in the book of life from the foundation of the world."—Rev. 17:8.

It does not mean that the Lamb was slain from the foundation of the world, but that the names of the saints were written in the book of the slain Lamb from the foundation of the world. This is a startling statement.

We are told that when God contemplated the universe of which our world is a part, the first thing He did was to write the names of the redeemed in the Book of Life. The redeemed are not an accident of history or a phase in the process of evolution. They were thought of before God's creative work. The Book of Life came first. God's purpose in making the worlds was to bring into reality the things recorded in the Book of Life. The worlds were made for the saints.

The glory promised the saints is in harmony with this conception. "And they that be wise shall shine as the brightness of the firmament, and they that turn many to righteousness as the stars forever and ever" (Dan. 12:3). "Then shall the righteous shine forth as the sun in the kingdom of their Father" (Matt. 13:43).

The great company of the saints will be the brightest thing in heaven, of whom the angels are their ministering spirits. To be known as the bride of Christ, to sit with Him on His throne, and to be the residents in the capital city of the universe where God's throne is would suggest that God has done something very special. Jesus expressed this truth in a number of parables. The parables of the pearl of great price and the treasure in the field both tell the great value of the church in the mind of God. God conceived this glorious company, wrote down their names in a book, and then set about to bring it all into being.

We cannot say how far back in this long history the angel Lucifer became Satan. We do know that demons have possessed people and still do. We also know that the spirits in the bottomless pit are, according to Revelation 9:1, turned loose on the earth during the Day of the Lord.

Chapter 13 clearly shows that the main unholy target of these evil forces are Christ's saints. Seiss says, "Many a sore trial of their patience and faith have the saints of God experienced from the persecutions of this godless world, but they will all be as nothing compared to the tribulations of the last days. Under the Antichrist, all true worshipers will be tested and tried as never before. Nor can anyone remain faithful during this Great Tribulation except he be posted and grounded beforehand in the divine teachings concerning the infernal character of such satanic powers."

In that Day the sure interference of heaven will bring speedy destruction on Antichrist and all his followers. God has His plan in place for all who lay hold on His mercy and overcome evil by their faith. God did not plan to destroy everything that He made. No, rather, he seeks to redeem all those who repent and come to Him.

In all trials and temptations, we can count on the Lord Jesus. He taught us to pray, "Lead us not into temptation but deliver us from evil." We believe that "all things work together for good to those who love Him." Even the plans and works of the devil can be used against the wicked one. Satan stirred up the leaders in both the Jewish and Roman world to destroy Jesus, but that very death of Jesus on the cross released God's great power of redemption." By the Lord's provision of grace and redemption He accomplishes two things.

First, He would by the very opposition of Satan develop a people with a strength of character and nobleness of soul such as would be impossible to create directly, because these things come out of life—not life under perfect conditions as the angels have, but under adverse conditions such as the saints have. God could have a people characterized by such rare virtues as patience, faith, hope, and love, "who loved not their lives unto the death."

Second, He could by these very people bring about a crisis in heaven that would result in the total defeat of Satan. He would have an army of overcomers who would know by firsthand experience just how to handle Satan. God would have not only a perfect world, but He would have a kingdom of priests who would know how to run that world.

All this and more is involved in those simple words, "from the foundation of the world." The book of Revelation is the consummation of what God had in mind when He wrote those names in the book of life. Is it any wonder that He says, "He that hath an ear let him hear"?

Revelation 13

11 And I beheld another beast coming up out of the earth; and he had two horns like a lamb, and he spake as a dragon.

12 And he exerciseth all the power of the first beast before him, and causeth the earth and them which dwell therein to worship the first beast, whose deadly wound was healed.

13 And he doeth great wonders, so that he maketh fire come down from heaven on the earth in the sight of men,

14 And deceiveth them that dwell on the earth by the means of those miracles which he had power to do in the sight of the beast; saying to them that dwell on the earth, that they should make an image to the beast, which had the wound by a sword, and did live.

15 And he had power to give life unto the image of the beast, that the image of the beast should both speak, and cause that as many as would not worship the image of the beast should be killed.

16 And he causeth all, both small and great, rich and poor, free and bond, to receive a mark in their right hand, or in their foreheads:

17 And that no man might buy or sell, save he that had the mark, or the name of the beast, or the number of his name.

18 Here is wisdom. Let him that hath understanding count the number of the beast: for it is the number

of a man; and his number is Six hundred threescore and six.

THE BEAST OUT OF THE EARTH. There has been some dispute as to whether the beast out of the earth or the beast out of the sea is Antichrist. There is no point to the argument because the name Antichrist is not applied directly to either one in the Bible. The term Antichrist appears only four times in the Bible, all in I and II John. John applies the word to anyone who opposes Christ. In this sense it can be applied to either or both of these individuals the Revelation calls beasts.

The dragon and the two beasts are a trinity of evil, one in spirit and purpose, and there is no reason for separating them in our thinking. Satan will counterfeit the Trinity. There will be three personalities in one satanic head. They are Antichrist. Even the people recognize this when they worship both the beast and the dragon. Even this beast out of the earth has characteristics like the dragon.

He has horns and he speaks like the dragon. It says his horns are like a lamb. The word lamb is not capitalized. It does not refer to Christ. It means that his horns are small as compared with those of the beast out of the sea. They probably stand for two religious-political powers which have yet to identify themselves with Antichrist.

THE MARK OF THE BEAST. He will make a law that all must have the mark of the beast in the palms of their hands or upon their foreheads. No man will be allowed to buy or sell anything without this mark. Those who refuse will be killed or allowed to starve to death. This is the law, but its enforcement will be hindered by the judgment sent from heaven. It is impossible to enforce an unpopular law. Many people will avoid the mark.

SIX HUNDRED AND SIXTY-SIX. Six is the number of evil. This triple six represents a trinity of evil: devil, Antichrist, and false prophet. It also indicates a certain man. It is a means of identification. However, it is not too apparent. Only those with understanding may count the number. This understanding is probably not a knowledge of the arts, sciences, and languages but rather an understanding of the Word of God.

Many commentators have attempted to discover the name denoted by this number by attaching to each letter of the name its numerical value, the total of which should equal the number 666. However, there is no assurance that that is the proper method of interpretation. Hebrew, Greek, and Latin letters each have a numerical value. We use the numerical value of certain Latin letters in our Roman numerals. So by substituting the number in place of the letter of a person's name, many commentators thought they had discovered the identity of Antichrist. The attempt has universally failed to establish any truth.

It is surprising the number of names which in the hands of ingenious students may be made to equal 666. Here are a few: Nero Caesar, Pope Benedict the Ninth, Mohammed, Martin Luther, John Calvin, and Napoleon Bonaparte.

Here is a formula by which any man's name may be made to add up to 666. It is this: First try it in Latin. If that does not work, try it in Greek. If that does not work, try it in Hebrew. If that does not work, add a title. If that does not work, do not be too particular about the spelling. It usually takes all five to make it come out right. Surely this is not the way Scripture is to be interpreted. This mark will appear only after the Rapture. Some of the sixes may be involved in the name or insignia of Antichrist when he first appears, although that would not be necessary.

Chapter Fourteen

THE GOSPEL IN THE TRIBULATION

Firstfruits of the Kingdom

Revelation 14

1 And I looked, and, lo, a Lamb stood on the mount Sion, and with him an hundred forty and four thousand, having his Father's name written in their foreheads.

2 And I heard a voice from heaven, as the voice of many waters, and as the voice of a great thunder: and I heard the voice of harpers harping with their harps:

3 And they sung as it were a new song before the throne, and before the four beasts, and the elders: and no man could learn that song but the hundred and forty and four thousand, which were redeemed from the earth.

4 These are they which were not defiled with women; for they are virgins. These are they which follow the Lamb whithersoever he goeth. These were redeemed from among men, being the firstfruits unto God and to the Lamb.

5 And in their mouth was found no guile: for they are without fault before the throne of God.

ONE HUNDRED AND FORTY-FOUR THOUSAND. The sealing of the 144,000 Israelites was noted in the 7th chapter, together with the company of Tribulation Saints who are raised from the dead. The Resurrection is not seen in this section as it does not concern the earth. The 144,000 remain here so they appear also in the earth history. The seal is evidently the name of God in their foreheads.

Normally they would be a part of the church since they were saved at the same time as the Tribulation Saints. The reason they are not among the saved in heaven is that they were not killed. It would not be supposed that Antichrist would be killing Jews in Palestine at the same time he is confirming the covenant with them.

In this scene they join the other saints from heaven in a song. The redeemed Israelites on earth sing to the accompaniment of music played in heaven. All the saved in heaven and on earth join in a service of worship.

VIRGINS. The employment of the figure of adultery and fornication to denote spiritual unfaithfulness is common in the Bible. The opposite would denote faithfulness. "Virgin" is a word equally applicable to men and women. Paul uses the word in the same sense: "I have espoused you to one husband, that I may present you as a chaste virgin to Christ." It implies freedom from impurity and unfaithfulness.

There is another thought in this term if we take it literally, as some expositors insist that we should. They were not defiled with women. This does not mean that they were not married, for that is not defilement. The outstanding evil that marked the days of Noah before the flood was defilement with women. It was the cause of the flood. Jesus said the last days would be as it was in the days of Noah. We may have here a view of the moral conditions of the times, so to be undefiled with women would be synonymous with being a Christian.

FIRSTFRUITS. Jesus was the firstfruits of the Resurrection. These 144,000 are the firstfruits of redeemed Israel. Their sealing marks the beginning of Daniel's 70th week. They will be the earthly nucleus here to receive the King when He returns.

How the Gospel Is Preached During the Tribulation

Revelation 14

6 And I saw another angel fly in the midst of heaven, having the everlasting gospel to preach unto them that dwell on the earth, and to every nation, and kindred, and tongue, and people,

7 Saying with a loud voice, Fear God, and give glory to him; for the hour of his judgment is come: and worship him that made heaven, and earth, and the sea, and the fountains of waters.

THE EVERLASTING GOSPEL. There is only one gospel. Paul speaks of "my gospel," but it was not another gospel. He said, "But though we, or an angel from heaven, preach any other gospel unto you than that which we have preached unto you, let him be accursed."—Gal. 1:8. This angel from heaven does not preach any other gospel. There may be various adaptations to conditions and times, but the gospel, whether it be the gospel of the kingdom, the gospel of grace, my gospel, or the everlasting gospel, is the good news of salvation based upon faith in Jesus Christ.

The everlasting gospel will be preached all the time that Antichrist is persecuting the saints. It is through this preaching that the saints are multiplied in the earth. No preaching is done by the apostate church. No missionary work is done by those who are saved. That would be impossible under the conditions. The preaching is done by the redeemed in heaven.

They seem like "angels" from the earth. The word angel means messenger. These messengers can reach every part of the earth in a short time. Then will be fulfilled the words of Jesus, "This gospel of the kingdom shall be preached in all the world . . . then shall the end come."—Matt. 24:14.

The message is adapted to the times. It is a warning of the judgments that are coming and of the penalty of receiv-

ing the mark of the beast. It has in it the elements of old-
fashioned hell-fire preaching.

These angels are sent out from heaven immediately after
the Rapture, when the first seal is broken. In heaven it appeared to be a white horseman going forth conquering and
to conquer. From the earth it seems like angelic messengers.

THE FIRST MESSENGER announces the near approach
of judgment and calls upon the people of the earth to worship
the God who made heaven and earth and the sea and the
foundations of waters. Science has prepared the world for
the worship of Antichrist. The theory of evolution allows for
no God except a kind of deity that is itself the product of
the same evolution. The arrival of a superman, Antichrist,
will be hailed as the "emergence of Deity on a new level."

Now the angel announces that the God who made heav-
en, earth, the sea, and the fountains of waters is about to
bring judgment upon this unbelieving world. The angel mentions specifically four things that God has made. These are
the first four things to be affected when the judgment comes.

The first angel warns the people that they are living in
a world that God has created; that there is above them a
heaven where God is; and that He is about to send terrible
plagues upon those who corrupt the earth, the sea, and the
fountains of water.

Revelation 14

**8 And there followed another angel, saying, Babylon
is fallen, is fallen, that great city, because she made all
nations drink of the wine of the wrath of her fornication.**

THE SECOND MESSENGER announces the fall of Babylon. This is also prophetic. The fall of Babylon occurs just
prior to the coming of Christ. "Babylon is fallen" is the Bible
method of announcing in advance the coming event (Isa.
21:9).

Revelation 14

9 And the third angel followed them, saying with a loud voice, If any man worship the beast and his image, and receive his mark in his forehead, or in his hand,

10 The same shall drink of the wine of the wrath of God, which is poured out without mixture into the cup of his indignation; and he shall be tormented with fire and brimstone in the presence of the holy angels, and in the presence of the Lamb:

11 And the smoke of their torment ascendeth up for ever and ever: and they have no rest day nor night, who worship the beast and his image, and whosoever receiveth the mark of his name.

THE THIRD MESSENGER warns the people concerning the beast. The whole world will hear this warning and probably thousands of people who never actually become Christians will, by some means, avoid the mark of the beast.

Revelation 14

12 Here is the patience of the saints: here are they that keep the commandments of God, and the faith of Jesus.

13 And I heard a voice from heaven saying unto me, Write, Blessed are the dead which die in the Lord from henceforth: Yea, saith the Spirit, that they may rest from their labours; and their works do follow them.

THE FAITH OF JESUS. From heaven, this messenger appeared as a horseman. Now we see the work of the rider on the white horse as it appears to the people on the earth. The world does not see the living ones or the horsemen. They are heavenly institutions who appear to the people on the earth as angels flying through the sky. The time is the tribulation, just after the Rapture. This preaching results in the saving of a host of people from every kindred, tongue, people, and nation. Here is the steadfastness of the "faith of Jesus." The gospel they preach is the same as we preach today—salvation by faith in Christ.

During the tribulation thousands will die in the Lord. In this section we see them die; in the heaven section we saw them raised. This mighty preaching by the saints who have gone to heaven will produce a world-wide revival, even though to confess Christ means almost certain death.

The preaching during the tribulation must all be done from heaven. The reason is obvious. There will be no churches holding services during the reign of Satan; there will be no preaching in halls or on street corners; there will be no missionaries to far-off countries; yet the whole world must be warned and enlightened in 3½ years' time. The preaching from heaven will probably cover the whole world at once.

It seems strange that so many should insist that the 144,000 will do the preaching in that day. They connect with Israel, otherwise they could not be the firstfruits. Christ is the firstfruits of the church. If these Jews ventured out of Palestine, they would be killed instantly. There is not a single word in Revelation to indicate that these 144,000 Israelites · ever preach the gospel to Gentiles. Some of them may preach in Palestine. Revelation does not mention it because Revelation is not concerned with the Jews. But when Jesus sent out His disciples on a missionary tour, He gave them instructions that could apply only to some future time. "But when they persecute you in this city, flee ye into another: for verily I say unto you, Ye shall not have gone over the cities of Israel, till the Son of man be come."—Matt. 10:23.

Revelation 14

14 And I looked, and behold a white cloud, and upon the cloud one sat like unto the Son of man, having on his head a golden crown, and in his hand a sharp sickle.

15 And another angel came out of the temple, crying with a loud voice to him that sat on the cloud, Thrust in thy sickle, and reap: for the time is come for thee to reap; for the harvest of the earth is ripe.

16 And he that sat on the cloud thrust in his sickle

on the earth; and the earth was reaped.

17 And another angel came out of the temple which is in heaven, he also having a sharp sickle.

18 And another angel came out from the altar, which had power over fire; and cried with a loud cry to him that had the sharp sickle, saying, Thrust in thy sharp sickle, and gather the clusters of the vine of the earth; for her grapes are fully ripe.

19 And the angel thrust in his sickle into the earth, and gathered the vine of the earth, and cast it into the great winepress of the wrath of God.

20 And the winepress was trodden without the city, and blood came out of the winepress, even unto the horse bridles, by the space of a thousand and six hundred furlongs.

VISIONS OF ARMAGEDDON. This is a part of the preaching of the messengers. It is prophetic and also visual. The sky is the screen, and a great moving picture of the events ahead is portrayed for all to see. This is powerful preaching, yet it is what might be expected when the saints have every means at their command and do not have to count the cost.

The fulfillment of this prophecy is the pouring out of the vials that is immediately to follow. They culminate in what has come to be known as the battle of Armageddon (Rev. 16:16), although Armageddon is only the place of mobilization. There may be some fighting there, but the decisive battle is "without the city" (Jerusalem).

Sixteen hundred furlongs is about 170 miles. This is a part of the moving picture in the sky. It is highly symbolic, but it will be understood by the viewers. There are many Old Testament references to this climax of world history. A very similar one is found in Isaiah.

Who is this that cometh from Edom, with dyed garments from Bozrah? this that is glorious in his apparel, travelling in the greatness of his strength? I that speak in righteousness, mighty to save. Wherefore art thou red in thine apparel, and thy garments like him that treadeth in the winefat? I have trodden the winepress alone;

and of the people there was none with me: for I will tread them in mine anger, and trample them in my fury; and their blood shall be sprinkled upon my garments, and I will stain all my raiment. For the day of vengeance is in mine heart, and the year of my redeemed is come. And I looked, and there was none to help; and I wondered that there was none to uphold: therefore mine own arm brought salvation unto me; and my fury, it upheld me. And I will tread down the people in mine anger, and make them drunk in my fury, and I will bring down their strength to the earth.—Isa. 63:1–6

See Ezekiel 39 and Joel 3: 9–16, also the first chapter of Zephaniah.

Chapter Fifteen

PREPARATION
FOR THE SEVEN LAST PLAGUES

Revelation 15

1 And I saw another sign in heaven, great and marvellous, seven angels having the seven last plagues; for in them is filled up the wrath of God.

2 And I saw as it were a sea of glass mingled with fire: and them that had gotten the victory over the beast, and over his image, and over his mark, and over the number of his name, stand on the sea of glass, having the harps of God.

3 And they sing the song of Moses the servant of God, and the song of the Lamb, saying, Great and marvellous are thy works, Lord God Almighty; just and true are thy ways, thou King of saints.

4 Who shall not fear thee, O Lord, and glorify thy name? for thou only art holy: for all nations shall come and worship before thee; for thy judgments are made manifest.

Each new phase of the program of redemption is preceded by a service of worship. You will notice if you compare the two sections that if details are supplied in one, they are omitted in the other. This worship service is reported in greater detail in this section. The parallel is Revelation 8: 1–6. The seven vials contain the fulfillment of the wrath of God. When they are over, the Millennium has arrived. This same thing was said of the seven trumpets (10:7). Here is another verification of our structure and also of the use of the number seven as expressing totality.

TRIBULATION SAINTS. Their resurrection was reported in chapter 7. Now we see them conducting the meeting in heaven. This verse should be troublesome to those expositors who put the tribulation in the last half of Daniel's 70th week, just before the return of Christ. They have the Tribulation Saints in heaven before they are saved. Again this supports our interpretation. We saw them saved, we saw how they were saved; we saw them killed, we saw how they were killed; we saw them raised from the dead, now we see them active in heaven, preparing to send out the seven last plagues.

THE SONG OF MOSES. There are two recorded songs of Moses. The occasion of the first one was the crossing of the Red Sea. The second was in connection with Moses' final instruction to the congregation. Both songs (Exodus 15, Deuteronomy 32) are prophetic and both would apply to this time of judgment. Here are excerpts from these songs:

> The Lord is my strength and song, and he is become my salvation: he is my God, and I will prepare him an habitation; my father's God, and I will exalt him. The Lord is a man of war: the Lord is his name.—Ex. 15:2, 3

> Thy right hand, O Lord, is become glorious in power: thy right hand, O Lord, hath dashed in pieces the enemy. And in the greatness of thine excellency thou hast overthrown them that rose up against thee: thou sentest forth thy wrath, which consumed them as stubble.—Ex. 15:6, 7

> He is the Rock, his work is perfect: for all his ways are judgment: a God of truth and without iniquity, just and right is he.—Deut. 32:4

> They have moved me to jealousy with that which is not God; they have provoked me to anger with their vanities: and I will move them to jealousy with those which are not a people; I will provoke them to anger with a foolish nation. For a fire is kindled in mine anger, and shall burn unto the lowest hell, and shall consume the earth with her increase, and set on fire the foundations

of the mountains. I will heap mischiefs upon them; I will spend mine arrows upon them. They shall be burnt with hunger, and devoured with burning heat, and with bitter destruction: I will also send the teeth of beasts upon them, with the poison of serpents of the dust. The sword without, and terror within, shall destroy both the young man and the virgin, the suckling also with the man of gray hairs. I said, I would scatter them into corners, I would make the remembrance of them to cease from among men.—Deut. 32:21–26

See now that I, even I, am he, and there is no god with me: I kill, and I make alive; I wound, and I heal: neither is there any that can deliver out of my hand. I lift up my hand to heaven, and say, I live for ever. If I whet my glittering sword, and mine hand take hold on judgment; I will render vengeance to mine enemies, and will reward them that hate me. I will make mine arrows drunk with blood, and my sword shall devour flesh; and that with the blood of the slain and of the captives, from the beginning of revenges upon the enemy. Rejoice, O ye nations, with his people: for he will avenge the blood of his servants, and will render vengeance to his adversaries, and will be merciful unto his land, and to his people.—Deut. 32:39–43

KING OF THE NATIONS. Nowhere else in the Bible is Jesus called King of saints, and this translation is obviously erroneous. The expression does not occur in any of the manuscripts. Some read *King of nations*, and some *King of the ages*. King of the nations is more in keeping with the Bible use of King. Jesus is King of kings, and Lord of lords.

Revelation 15

5 And after that I looked, and, behold, the temple of the tabernacle of the testimony in heaven was opened:

6 And the seven angels came out of the temple, having the seven plagues, clothed in pure and white linen, and having their breasts girded with golden girdles.

7 And one of the four beasts gave unto the seven angels seven golden vials full of the wrath of God, who liveth for ever and ever.

8 And the temple was filled with smoke from the
glory of God, and from his power; and no man was able
to enter into the temple, till the seven plagues of the
seven angels were fulfilled.

THE TABERNACLE IN HEAVEN. In these words God
commanded Moses to build the tabernacle:

And let them make me a sanctuary; that I may dwell
among them. According to all that I shew thee, after
the pattern of the tabernacle, and the pattern of all the
instruments thereof, even so shall ye make it.—Ex.
25:8, 9

The pattern was the heavenly tabernacle and ark.

Who serve unto the example and shadow of heavenly
things, as Moses was admonished of God when he was
about to make the tabernacle; for, See, saith he, that
thou make all things according to the pattern shewed to
thee in the mount.—Heb. 8:5

A large portion of the symbolism of the tabernacle and
ark was fulfilled in the atonement—but not all. The ark was
symbolic of victory and possession of the land. The ark could
not go into its place of rest in the temple until all the enemies
had been put down and peace prevailed. Now all the symbolism is to be fulfilled.

At the crucifixion, the temple on earth was opened by the
rending of the veil. A few years later the temple itself was
destroyed, but the ark had been put in a place of safekeeping
many years before. It held no symbolism for this age except
that which was fulfilled on Calvary. Now at the beginning
of Daniel's 70th week, when God will again deal with Israel
as a nation, the tabernacle is opened in heaven. The word for
tabernacle here means holy of holies. That is where the ark
was kept. The nations are to be restored to the people of
God, and the kingdom to David.

And say unto them, Thus saith the Lord God; Behold,
I will take the children of Israel from among the heathen,
whither they be gone, and will gather them on every side,

and bring them into their own land: and I will make them one nation in the land upon the mountains of Israel; and one king shall be king to them all: and they shall be no more two nations, neither shall they be divided into two kingdoms any more at all: neither shall they defile themselves any more with their idols, nor with their detestable things, nor with any of their transgressions: but I will save them out of all their dwellingplaces, wherein they have sinned, and will cleanse them: so shall they be my people, and I will be their God. And David my servant shall be king over them; and they shall have one shepherd: they shall also walk in my judgments, and observe my statutes, and do them.—Ezek. 37:21-24

Chapter Sixteen

ARMAGEDDON

(See also chapters 8 and 9. The new features in this chapter are found in verses 12–17.)

Revelation 16

12 And the sixth angel poured out his vial upon the great river Euphrates; and the water thereof was dried up, that the way of the kings of the east might be prepared.

13 And I saw three unclean spirits like frogs come out of the mouth of the dragon, and out of the mouth of the beast, and out of the mouth of the false prophet.

14 For they are the spirits of devils, working miracles, which go forth unto the kings of the earth and of the whole world, to gather them to the battle of that great day of God Almighty.

15 Behold, I come as a thief. Blessed is he that watcheth, and keepeth his garments, lest he walk naked, and they see his shame.

16 And he gathered them together into a place called in the Hebrew tongue Armageddon.

KINGS OF THE EAST. The exact names of all the countries designated by "kings of the east" are nowhere given in the Bible because these nations did not exist in Bible times. Some names are given, however, to show the general location of these countries. These kings of the east are one group, which must be considered with the three other groups indicated by the three spirits, like frogs, that proceed from the satanic trinity, to assemble those nations that are directly under the control of Antichrist.

Four is the world number. Whenever four is used in this special sense, the whole world is in view. The three spirits, like frogs, go out in three directions to work on three groups of nations.

There is another group making up the four, somewhat independent, yet they send forces into Palestine for some other reason than the summons of Antichrist. This fourth group is known in Revelation as the kings of the east. The world is round and every nation is east of Palestine. These do not have to be countries that we in America would think of as eastern lands. Nebuchadnezzar was called the king from the north (Ezek. 26:7), not because Babylon was north of Palestine, but because the Babylonians entered Palestine from the north.

Kings of the east are nations anywhere in the world that enter Palestine from the east. Antichrist will have Palestine surrounded until this break comes, symbolized by the drying up of the Euphrates. Then a way will be opened so that other nations can come in from the east.

A more detailed account of this invasion is found in Ezekiel 38 and 39. There also we find four groups of nations, three under Antichrist and one independent. The first group is represented by Meshech and Tubal; the second by Persia, Ethiopia and Libya; and the third by Gomer and Togarmah. The second group—Persia, Ethiopia, and Libya—are named because they are the same today as they were in Ezekiel's day. The first and third groups represent nations that were not in existence in Ezekiel's day. The names are grandsons of Noah, who in a general way peopled the countries that Ezekiel desired to indicate. Gomer and Togarmah are the nations of Europe. Meshech and Tubal are north of Palestine and probably represent countries that will eventually be carved out of southern Russia, around the Black and Caspian Seas. This is exactly the territory covered by the four visions of Daniel and symbolized by the lion, the bear, the leopard, and the beast and repeated in Revelation 13.

That pretty well settles the identity of the nations under Antichrist. Ezekiel adds: "And many people with thee." This would include scattered satellites in other parts of the world.

Then Ezekiel has a fourth group, quite independent, that even sends a note of protest when the invasion of Israel is threatened. This corresponds with the fourth group in Revelation. Ezekiel, therefore, describes the kings of the east as follows:

> Sheba, and Dedan, and the merchants of Tarshish, with all the young lions thereof, shall say unto thee, Art thou come to take spoil? hast thou gathered thy company to take a prey? to carry away silver and gold, to take away cattle and goods, to take a great spoil?—Ezek. 38:13

Sheba and Dedan are named first. They are not important countries today. Their locations are not known with any degree of exactness, but the general location would be in Arabia and Africa. They will become powerful nations, and they will be leaders in a group which will include the merchants of Tarshish and the young lions thereof. Tarshish is Gibraltar. It never has been a nation. Ezekiel is referring to some country or empire in the Atlantic that is also a merchant country. The young lions would be the offshoots of that empire.

Today there is only one such country—Britain. The young lions would be America, Canada, Australia and other members of the Commonwealth, or which were once members of the Commonwealth. This would be true even though a war should force the moving of the capital to some other land, for Ezekiel mentions only the merchants of Tarshish.

EUPHRATES DRIED UP. A river is not a barrier to modern armies. It might slow them down, but it would not stop them. The Euphrates may actually dry up after three and a half years of no rain; but much more than that is meant, possibly much more than we can understand. The two hundred million evil spirits that were imprisoned there have been turned loose. The river represents more than the city of Babylon; it takes in all the nation. Its fall would render it incapable of preventing foreign armies from passing through.

When Ezekiel lists the countries involved in this battle, he conspicuously omits two important ones—Babylon (now Iraq) and Egypt. Egypt will become a great empire. However, Egypt is to be totally destroyed so that there will be neither man nor beast in the land. When the nations gather at Armageddon, there will be no Egypt. This is expressed in Ezekiel by a reference to the rivers:

> Behold, therefore I am against thee, and against thy rivers, and I will make the land of Egypt utterly waste and desolate, from the tower of Syene even unto the border of Ethiopia. No foot of man shall pass through it, nor foot of beast shall pass through it, neither shall it be inhabited forty years.—Ezek. 29:10, 11

The Sudan is included with Egypt, all the way to Ethiopia. The destruction of Babylon will take place just before Armageddon, so there will be no Babylon when the armies assemble. This is expressed in Revelation by the same terms that Ezekiel uses—the drying up of the river.

BEHOLD, I COME AS A THIEF. This is the only direct connection with the parallel section, but an important one. The action takes place between the sixth and seventh vials which correspond to the sixth and seventh trumpets. There the length of time is given—$3\frac{1}{2}$ years.

How does Satan know when to gather his armies? Why the great emergency? Why so large a force—the whole world—against a few unarmed Jews? To take a spoil may be the incentive given the nations, but Satan's reason is to prevent the coming of Christ and the saints. It is told in detail in the 19th chapter. At this time we see only the mobilization of the armies.

The circumstances that throw Satan's kingdom into a frenzy are recorded in the 10th chapter, between the sixth and seventh trumpets. Christ, with the authority of the open book, takes formal possession of the earth and the sea. This is an invasion from outer space, and the rulers of the world react as would be expected if their power is threatened by a common enemy. The nations of the world would forget their differences and unite against an outside force.

WORKING MIRACLES. Satan always imitates God. The Egyptian magicians duplicated the plagues imposed by Moses. Satan will produce a resurrection to offset the Rapture. When God sends down the Two Witnesses working miracles, Satan sends out devils or devilish spirits also working miracles. This contest goes on until Satan suddenly succeeds in killing the Two Witnesses who have been standing him off. Just as soon as this happens—and it will be hailed as a great victory for Satan, showing his invincible power—the armies will gather at great speed. They will come like a whirlwind, Isaiah says (Isa. 5: 26–30).[1]

ARMAGEDDON. The American Standard Version reads: "They gathered them together." That is, the evil spirits who were sent out gathered the armies together. The correct reading is Har-Magedon (Hebrew), meaning mountain of Megiddo. It probably refers to Carmel, at the foot of which extends the plain of Megiddo, an ancient gathering place for armies.

---

1. "And he will lift up an ensign to the nations from far, and will hiss unto them from the end of the earth: and, behold, they shall come with speed swiftly: none shall be weary nor stumble among them; none shall slumber nor sleep; neither shall the girdle of their loins be loosed, nor the latchet of their shoes be broken: whose arrows are sharp, and all their bows bent, their horses' hoofs shall be counted like flint, and their wheels like a whirlwind: their roaring shall be like a lion, they shall roar like young lions: yea, they shall roar, and lay hold of the prey, and shall carry it away safe, and none shall deliver it. And in that day they shall roar against them like the roaring of the sea: and if one look unto the land, behold darkness and sorrow, and the light is darkened in the heavens thereof" (Isa. 5:26–30).

Revelation 16

17 And the seventh angel poured out his vial into the air; and there came a great voice out of the temple of heaven, from the throne, saying, It is done.

IT IS DONE. This is the end as the angel said.

> But in the days of the voice of the seventh angel, when he shall begin to sound, the mystery of God should be finished, as he hath declared to his servants the prophets.—Rev. 10:7

The fire is out, the evil spirits have been disposed of, the seals have been opened, the trumpets have blown, the great mass of prophecy has been fulfilled. There remains one earthquake and one war. Both the earthquake and the war are the greatest in the world's history. The earthquake comes before the final battle.

There have been earthquakes before. Revelation records some big ones before this, but there is a difference. Most earthquakes are caused by a movement of rock formations within the earth. This last one is caused by the whole earth suddenly shifting its position. To put it in Isaiah's words, "The earth shall reel to and fro like a drunkard."—Isa. 24:20.

The earth is inclined on its axis 23½ degrees. This is what causes the extreme cold at the poles and most of the storms and cyclones. This will be changed. High mountains connect with colder weather. Revelation 16:20 says "Every island fled away and the mountains were not found." This earthquake will make the earth more level—like it originally was. Mountains will move into the sea. The great hailstones, weighing over 60 pounds, may be caused by the ice at the poles being thrown high into the air when the earth moves to and fro.

Chapter Seventeen

BABYLON

<table>
<tr><td>

Fifth Room

SATAN'S CHURCH

Satan's Kingdom

Satan's Prosperity

Destruction of Those
Things Which Cannot be
Redeemed

FROM THE RAPTURE TO
THE RETURN OF CHRIST

Chapters 17 & 18

</td></tr>
</table>

Again we will start back in the room called *The Churches*. The final exit from that room is a passageway leading from the wicked woman Jezebel of the Thyatira Church. This was the type of the church of the dark ages when Romanism had almost extinguished the light of God's Word. There came a reformation in the Sardis era which started the church again on its way to fulfill its destiny.

Prophecy does not show the Protestant Church as coming out of the Romish Church but Romanism as growing up within the church as a parasite which had to be cast out. Jezebel is the type of this parasite. She did not cease to exist after the church was cleansed. She became Satan's grand counterfeit of the church. In the last days she bears the same relationship to the beast that the church does to Christ. This is not something new in the world.

Satan has always had his mock religion. Jezebel of the Old
Testament was a type of the same satanic religion. Now we
are to look at this woman in the last days of her existence
when she will probably take unto herself all false religions
and many apostate churches.

Revelation 17

1 And there came one of the seven angels which
had the seven vials, and talked with me, saying unto me,
Come hither; I will shew unto thee the judgment of the
great whore that sitteth upon many waters:
2 With whom the kings of the earth have committed
fornication, and the inhabitants of the earth have been
made drunk with the wine of her fornication.
3 So he carried me away in the spirit into the
wilderness: and I saw a woman sit upon a scarlet col-
oured beast, full of names of blasphemy, having seven
heads and ten horns.
4 And the woman was arrayed in purple and scarlet
colour, and decked with gold and precious stones and
pearls, having a golden cup in her hand full of abominations and filthiness of her fornication:
5 And upon her forehead was a name written,
MYSTERY, BABYLON THE GREAT, THE MOTHER OF
HARLOTS AND ABOMINATIONS OF THE EARTH.

THE SCARLET WOMAN. This woman is in every way
the opposite of the sun-clad woman of the 12th chapter. Here
is the struggle for supremacy of two great systems: on the
one hand, God (the Father, Son, and Holy Spirit) and the
Church; on the other hand, the devil (Dragon, Antichrist,
and False Prophet) and the Anti-church.

The scarlet woman rides on a scarlet-colored beast
having seven heads and ten horns. This fits either the description of the dragon or of Antichrist (Rev. 12:3; Rev. 13:1).

The Beast is a composite symbol of:

1. All the world empires of all time—the seven heads.
2. The world empire of the last days—the ten horns.

3. The real head of all human governments—the prince of this world, the devil.
4. The human head of the last world empire—Antichrist, the carnal manifestation of Satan.

Historically, this woman dates from the time the mighty hunter (rebel) Nimrod built a city in defiance of God and called it Babel. It was the beginning of the first world empire (beast), and it was the beginning of idolatrous worship (the mother of harlots).

The woman known as *"Babylon the Great"* is Satan's own ecclesiastical system. She is the mother of the "abominations of the earth." All idolatrous systems are her harlot daughters.

In the days of the early church, the seat of control of the devil's system had shifted from Babylon to Pergamos "where Satan's seat is"; thence to Rome, and Rome became "that great city which reigneth over the kings of the earth." In the last days Babylon will again become the center of a world religious system.

SITTETH UPON MANY WATERS. The interpretation of this is given in verse 15, where the waters are stated to be "peoples, and multitudes, and nations and tongues." Her influence reaches around the world, and she exercises authority over many widely scattered people.

FORNICATION. To commit fornication spiritually is to worship idols. Symbolically, it is a league, union, or working agreement with an idolatrous or false religious system— the prostituting of spiritual values for material gain. Governments of whatever nature are called "kings." This so-called church exercises authority over kings and receives certain advantages in return for material gain.

MYSTERY BABYLON. The word "mystery" means "what is known only to the initiated." The true church has its secrets which are very carefully guarded. The unregenerate cannot know the things of the Spirit because they are spiritually discerned.

The Anti-church, Babylon, will also have its mysteries. The devil's mysteries are "lying wonders." But God has made known the secrets of Satan. "And the angel said unto me, Wherefore didst thou marvel? I will tell thee the mystery of the woman, and of the beast that carrieth her, which hath the seven heads and ten horns."—Rev. 17:7.

Joseph Seiss, the author of *The Apocalypse*, makes these valuable remarks as to the symbols of the seven heads or *"the seven mountains on which the woman sits."*—Rev. 17:9. Of these seven regal mountains, John was told *"the five are fallen,"* dead, passed away, their day over; *"the one is,"* that was standing, at that moment, was then in sway and power; *the other is not yet come, and when he shall come, he must continue a little time."*

By these seven great powers then, filling up the whole interval of this world's history, this great harlot is said to be carried. On these she rides according to the vision. It is not upon one alone, nor upon any particular number of them, but upon all of them, the whole seven-headed beast, that she sits. These seven powers, each and all, support the woman as their joy and pride; and she accepts and uses them, and sways their administrations, and rides in glory by means of them. They are her devotees, lovers, and most humble servants; and she is their patronizing and most noble lady, with a mutuality of favors and intercommunion belonging to her designation.

This is the picture as explained by the angel. But to say that the Romish Papacy was thus carried, nurtured, and sustained by the ancient empires of Greece, Persia, Babylon, Assyria, and Egypt would be a great lie on history. It was not so. In the nature of things it could not be so. By no means then can this harlot be judged as "an errant" papacy alone,

as maintained by all *"respectable interpreters."* Furthermore,
it is a matter of fact, that as surely as Rome in John's day,
and Greece, Persia, Babylon, Assyria, and Egypt before Rome,
existed and bore sway on earth as regal mountains, so surely
and conspicuously were they each and all ridden by this great
harlot. *They were each and all the lovers, supporters, and
defenders of organized falsehood in religion, the patrons of
idolatry, the foster friends of all manner of spiritual harlotry.*
Nimrod, the hunter of the sons of men and author of despotic
government, established his idolatrous inventions as the crown
and glory of his empire, and intertwined the worship of idols
with the standards of his power.

It was the same with Egypt, whose colossal remains,
unfading paintings, and mummy scrolls confirm the Scripture
portraitures of her disgusting devotions, and tell how the
priests of these abominations were honored by the throne, of
which they were the chief advisers. It was so with Assyria as
the exhumations of Nineveh abundantly attest. It was so with
the Babylon of Nebuchadnezzar, as Daniel, who lived amid
it all, has written. It was so with Greece, as her own most
cherished poets sung, her mightiest orators proclaimed, and
all her venerated artists and historians have set forth. It was
so with Rome, as all her widespread monuments still show,
and all the Christian testimonies, with her own, render clear
and manifest as the sun. And it will be so with the last, which
is yet to come, as declared in the apocalyptic foreshowings
and in all the prophecies in the Book of God upon the subject.
It requires but a glance at history to see that spiritual harlotry
has ever been the particular pet and delight of all the beast-
powers of time. If ever the worship and requirements of the
true God won their respect and patronage, they soon corrupted
it to their own selfish and ambitious ends, or never were easy
until freed from the felt restraint.

True religion and an uncorrupted church have never
suited the representatives of power or pleased them long.

Dragon agencies are ill-at-ease without some form of Dragon worship. Only what will dignify, if not deify, lust and selfishness is in accord with their spirit. They simply favor and honor their own when they favor and cherish the base woman. Her gaudiness and pomp, her gaiety and ready compliances, her ennoblement of "the lust of the flesh, the lust of the eyes, and the pride of life," enamor them and make them glad to bear her on their shoulders. It is a sad commentary on humanity, *but* it is the truth, and *all* the great world-powers, from first to last, are the paramours and props of the harlot woman."

Revelation 17

6 And I saw the woman drunken with the blood of the saints, and with the blood of the martyrs of Jesus: and when I saw her, I wondered with great admiration.

7 And the angel said unto me, Wherefore didst thou marvel? I will tell thee the mystery of the woman, and of the beast that carrieth her, which hath the seven heads and ten horns.

8 The beast that thou sawest was, and is not; and shall ascend out of the bottomless pit, and go into perdition: and they that dwell on the earth shall wonder, whose names were not written in the book of life from the foundation of the world, when they behold the beast that was, and is not, and yet is.

WAS, AND IS NOT, AND YET IS (i.e., is to come). This is explained in the verses that follow. The beast symbol is explained by giving its history. The beast is the devil. He is the one who will come out of the bottomless pit and go into perdition (Rev. 20:1, 2, 7, 10). He is also prince of this world, and as such, has an earthly history symbolized by the seven heads.

The seven heads are the seven great world empires: Egypt, Assyria, Babylon, Persia, Greece, Rome, and the one that is yet to come.

There is a space of years between the fall of Rome and this last empire. In that sense the beast is not, yet he is, because the devil has a certain power over the nations and will succeed in forming another empire.

Revelation 17

9 And here is the mind which hath wisdom. The seven heads are seven mountains, on which the woman sitteth.

10 And there are seven kings: five are fallen, and one is, and the other is not yet come; and when he cometh, he must continue a short space.

SEVEN MOUNTAINS. Some have thought these seven mountains refer to the seven hills of Rome, but the angel said specifically that the seven mountains, the seven heads, are symbols of the seven kings; that is, the seven world empires of history.

Five are fallen: Egypt, Assyria, Babylon, Persia, Greece. One is: the Roman, which existed in the time of John. The other is not yet come: the new empire of Antichrist. This must continue a short time.

Revelation 17

11 And the beast that was, and is not, even he is the eighth, and is of the seven, and goeth into perdition.

THE EIGHTH. The eighth is the devil in the person of Antichrist. Satan himself will not create an empire. He will assume control of an empire already in existence when he makes his miraculous appearance. In other words the empire will be formed by a conqueror, and although it will be in effect a revival of the Roman empire, it will be new and counted as the seventh. At the time of the Rapture, Satan will take over this empire, probably arrange the kingdoms into ten, and extend its power to the ends of the earth. He is the eighth but is of the seven.

Revelation 17

12 And the ten horns which thou sawest are ten
kings, which have received no kingdom as yet; but receive power as kings one hour with the beast.

13 These have one mind, and shall give their power
and strength unto the beast.

14 These shall make war with the Lamb, and the
Lamb shall overcome them: for he is Lord of lords, and
King of kings: and they that are with him are called, and
chosen, and faithful.

THE TEN KINGS. This is the same beast that we saw
rise out of the sea in Revelation 13. It represents Satan's control of the kingdoms of the earth. The ten horns represent
the world empire of the last days. The ten kings "have received no kingdom as yet; but receive power as kings one
hour with the beast." This suggests how the last empire is
to be formed—by a union of ten nations. The beast himself
will set his own kings over these nations. Their reign will be
short. "One hour" indicates a brief time, probably a few
years.

ONE MIND. The unseen mind is Satan. In yielding their
power to one man they are following the plan of Satan. Both
Daniel and Revelation indicate that there will be more than
one head to this last empire. First there will be the man who
brings the empire into existence. This is to be the seventh of
the world empires which are represented by the seven heads
of the beast. When Antichrist is revealed as the incarnation
of Satan, he will take over this empire, set up his own kings
over the nations, and so become an eighth but really only a
continuation of the seventh.

WAR WITH THE LAMB. These nations have one policy
which is dictated by the beast. At the coming of Christ they
will be lined up against Him. This "war with the Lamb" is
known as the battle of Armageddon and is described in the
19th chapter.

This is the part of Revelation that deals with the destruction of those things that cannot be redeemed. These items are taken up systematically, and in each case their end is mentioned. The woman is the main subject, and her end comes in the next chapter. The devil will ascend out of the bottomless pit, where he will be cast at the beginning of the Millennium, and will go into perdition. The seventh world empire will continue but a short time, when Antichrist will take it over. Antichrist will also go into perdition. The ten kingdoms will make war with the Lamb, and the Lamb will overcome them.

Revelation 17

15 And he saith unto me, The waters which thou sawest, where the whore sitteth, are peoples, and multitudes, and nations, and tongues.

16 And the ten horns which thou sawest upon the beast, these shall hate the whore, and shall make her desolate and naked, and shall eat her flesh, and burn her with fire.

17 For God hath put in their hearts to fulfil his will, and to agree, and give their kingdom unto the beast, until the words of God shall be fulfilled.

18 And the woman which thou sawest is that great city, which reigneth over the kings of the earth.

The angel announces the subject of this chapter—the fall of Babylon. The Old Testament prophets likewise were interested in the fall of Babylon. It is the same city in each case. Babylon will have to rise to the heights from which it falls. Is there any time before the Rapture when conditions might be right for the growth of so much wealth?

The Laodicean Church reflects such a condition. It is rich and increased with goods. Churches exist on the surplus of their members, so a rich church means a rich membership. Satan's most ambitious counterfeit seems to be a false millennium. By it he will deceive the whole world. Daniel says, "By peace he will destroy many." It is when they say, "Peace and safety," that the sudden destruction comes upon them.

The sudden destruction is after the Rapture; the false peace and safety come before. That is why the first thing God does after the Rapture is to take peace from the earth. Satan's false millennium will end in disaster.

THE WATERS. We now have the angel's explanation of the symbols. The scarlet woman was said to sit upon many waters and also to be carried by the beast. The waters refer to a vast multitude beyond the limits of the ten kingdoms. This woman exerts her wicked influence over all the earth. It is a universal or catholic church.

THE TEN HORNS SHALL BURN HER WITH FIRE. There has always been contention between the Roman Church and the kingdoms of the world. As the power of the Roman Church increases and as the power of dictators increases, the friction between them will become more pronounced. Although the church needs the beast and to a large extent the beast will profit by the commercial activities of the church, they will hate each other. This hatred will break out in persecution until the woman herself and her city will be destroyed.

THE GREAT CITY. This woman who represents a great religious commercial system of the last days, goes by the name of the city where her throne is located. The only city in the world which has ever claimed to exercise spiritual and temporal sovereignty over the kings of the earth is Rome. At the present time this verse could apply to no other city.

The woman does not come suddenly into existence. She has been carried by the beast throughout its history. She represents the devil's ecclesiastical system of this world and of all ages from the building of the tower of Babel. The central city of Satan's church has not always been Rome. Once it was Babylon. Revelation 2:13 mentions it as being Per-

gamos. Today it is Rome, but it may not always remain so.
There is much Bible evidence that the city of Babylon will
be rebuilt and become "that great city which reigneth over
the kings of the earth."

Satan's Peace and Prosperity

During a Billy Sunday revival campaign, the churches
attempted to forestall adverse criticism by placing large signs
in conspicuous places which read, "Never Judge an Unfinished Work." Such judgment might be unfair. God never
judges an unfinished work. The judgment is the harvest.
When the tares were discovered among the wheat, the angels wanted to weed them out at once, but the King said,
"Nay; lest while ye gather up the tares, ye root up also the
wheat with them. Let both grow together until the harvest."
—Matt. 13:29, 30.

That which is to be judged is first allowed to come to
maturity. "The mystery of iniquity doth already work: only
he who now letteth will let, until he be taken out of the
way. And then shall that Wicked be revealed."—II Thess.
2:7, 8.

He who hinders the working of iniquity is the Holy Spirit in the church. In the last days the influence of the Holy
Spirit and the church will be withdrawn and iniquity will develop to its limit. The harvest of modernism is humanism,
the worship of man, and finally the worship of a man. The
evils of modernism are not always visible to the naked eye,
but God will allow it to reach its logical end; then He will
judge it.

God will judge the nations, but first He will give them a
free hand that they may demonstrate their real character.
There will be no question in that day as to the justice of His
judgment. God will judge "the root of all evil"—the love of
gold—but not till He has given gold its day.

Gold was plentiful in the days of Nebuchadnezzar, and he made a golden image and commanded all people to worship it. Gold will be plentiful again in the days of Antichrist, and Babylon will be decked with it. People will worship it.

Babylon will yet be the center of a great commercial system that will bring wealth to the world. Gold heads the list (Rev. 18:12). The merchants of the earth will wax rich through the abundance of her delicacies. The governments of the earth will make unholy alliances (commit fornication) with her in order to have a part in her great wealth. The world will get drunk on gold. They will think, yea, the preachers will preach that they have at last arrived at a time when war and poverty will be abolished and the curse of work will be lifted.

Along with wealth and leisure go immorality and all kinds of wickedness, even "as it was in the days of Noah." Judgment will be swift and complete. Babylon never again will be inhabited but will remain forever "as when God overthrew Sodom and Gomorrah."

The time of this judgment is after the Rapture and before the return of Christ. The announcement of the fall comes directly after the Rapture. The fall itself comes suddenly, as an act of God, just prior to the revelation of Christ.

Chapter Eighteen

BABYLON

(Continued)

Revelation 18

1 And after these things I saw another angel come down from heaven, having great power; and the earth was lightened with his glory.

2 And he cried mightily with a strong voice, saying, Babylon the great is fallen, is fallen, and is become the habitation of devils, and the hold of every foul spirit, and a cage of every unclean and hateful bird.

3 For all nations have drunk of the wine of the wrath of her fornication, and the kings of the earth have committed fornication with her, and the merchants of the earth are waxed rich through the abundance of her delicacies.

It is remarkable that so much space should be given to Babylon. It must be that it will assume much more importance than any other city or religion has ever enjoyed. The world has never seen anything like what is described here. Herein lies the reason for the difficulty of understanding these words. Nothing like it, or anywhere near it, has ever happened before.

AFTER THESE THINGS. This chapter begins a new vision, but the subject is the same. Then why a new vision? The 17th chapter gives us the form of Satan's religious enterprise through the years; the 18th chapter shows the form it will take at the very end. Then it is not Rome; it is Babylon.

Rome is not so situated that it could fulfill the terms of the prophecy, yet today it is only Rome of whom it could be said, "In her was found the blood of prophets, and saints, and of all that were slain upon the earth." *We are going to see some sensational changes in Bible lands.*

There is another unusual feature found in this chapter. It is true that there are many references to the Old Testament in Revelation—many more than is usually supposed—but nowhere are they so numerous as here. Almost every verse has its parallel in the Old Testament. We are dealing here with a major subject of prophecy.

One reason for its prophetic importance is that it is physical; it is tangible; it can be seen. There can be no question about it when it happens, so it will be a very significant sign. We can watch it all the way. Great commercial centers do not come overnight. It will take time for the world to become dependent on one city. The merchants of the earth, the rulers, industrial czars, the shipping companies, the office buildings, the manufacturing plants, the distribution centers, the great selling organizations, factory representatives, advertising agencies, and all the side businesses that go with such a vast industrial empire will come by degrees. It will have to be built up, and the conditions for such expansion of wealth must be very favorable.

Babylon, the center of all this activity, is now a sandy waste in a too-hot country that for generations has known nothing but poverty and tribal wars, a land that naturally resists the encroachment of outside culture.

Babylon is also a religious center. From it stems a world religion like that which came out of it before the confusion of tongues. When we look at Babylon from the religious point of view, it is still more astounding. Mohammedanism and Romanism are ancient enemies. It would take powerful forces to bring them together. A common hatred or a common enemy might do it.

When will all this happen? It could not very well happen during the preparation for Armageddon; that is the beginning of the end. It could not come during the fire of the first four trumpets. Babylon could not reach such heights of grandeur and wealth while the wars and famines are in progress that come under the first five seals. There is not time between the Rapture and the return of Christ when such a city and world system as Babylon could be built. It might exist through such times, but it could not come into existence in times like that. Such wealth and worldly glory could not be built up in a time of trouble such as never was since there was a nation.

Jesus gave us the first signs of the approaching end of the age: the rise of many false Christs, saying, "the time draweth near." But Jesus said, "The end is not yet." Wars and rumours of wars must come before the time of the end. A time of peace and prosperity on a grand scale will follow the wars and rumors of wars.

We learn also that the eighth head (Satan) is a continuation of the seventh. The eighth head comes by a death and resurrection of the man who is the seventh head of the beast. In that case, the seventh head, which we call Antichrist, must be here when Satan takes over. Putting all this together we arrive at a sequence of events something like this:

World-wide wars and commotions
Coming of the man we call Antichrist
Peace and prosperity on a vast scale
Building of Babylon and other cities

Because of the emergency of wars, new things are brought forth in a crash program that normally would require years of development. In the recent past, wars have opened backward countries to world progress. There are no more dark continents. All peoples are aware of world trends.

President Truman once said that if we should attempt to raise the standard of living of India by ten percent, it would keep our factories busy day and night for ten years. The nations are rich in natural resources and they all need what other nations produce. When the big push comes to give all people a high standard of living, Babylon will be at the crossroads of world trade.

BABYLON THE GREAT. Babylon starts as a universal religious system with its headquarters in a city that would almost have to be Rome. It ends as a universal, religious commercial system with its headquarters in a new city called Babylon. Actually the Romish system started in Babylon; it is only fitting that it should meet its doom there.

Zechariah tells of such a move from one place to another:

> Then the angel that talked with me went forth, and said unto me, Lift up now thine eyes, and see what is this that goeth forth. And I said, What is it? And he said, This is an ephah that goeth forth. He said moreover, This is their resemblance through all the earth. And, behold, there was lifted up a talent of lead: and this is a woman, that sitteth in the midst of the ephah. And he said, This is wickedness. And he cast it into the midst of the ephah; and he cast the weight of lead upon the mouth thereof. Then lifted I up mine eyes, and looked, and, behold, there came out two women, and the wind was in their wings; for they had wings like the wings of a stork: and they lifted up the ephah between the earth and the heaven. Then said I to the angel that talked with me, Whither do these bear the ephah? And he said unto me, To build it an house in the land of Shinar: and it shall be established, and set there upon her own base. —Zech. 5:5–11

The ephah is the largest unit of dry measure. In this case it is a container. The thing it contains is a universal system of some kind. "This is their resemblance through all the earth." This system is represented by a woman—a wicked woman. A woman in prophetic symbolism is a church—in this case Satan's church because it is called wickedness. These two women, the one in Revelation and the one in Zechariah, are identical. Zechariah describes a moving day when this woman moves her headquarters from one city to another. She moves by air. "between the earth and the heaven."

The purpose of the move is to establish the church on a new base. The reason for the sudden move is not told. It has some of the marks of a rescue. The modern name for Babylon is Iraq; the ancient name was Shinar. It is there that the new city will be built. Many astonishing things will happen there.

Babylon will be rebuilt by a church. The church whose idolatrous worship started there, will return there, and there come to its end. Who are the two women that carry the ephah to the land of Shinar? We are not told. Being women, they probably represent churches. If Babylon is to be a center of a universal religion, Satan will have to unite the great false religions of the world.

This is going to be something new, something that has never happened before. The whole world will join one great religion which is able to make it rich. This is in every respect the opposite of true Christianity. Jesus said, "Thou shalt have treasure in heaven." Not very many people are interested in that. Satan offers riches right here and now. They will believe the lie. Notice the angel says, "All nations have drunk." This city will be operating for some time before it is destroyed.

Revelation 18

4 And I heard another voice from heaven, saying, Come out of her, my people, that ye be not partakers of her sins, and that ye receive not of her plagues.

5 For her sins have reached unto heaven, and God hath remembered her iniquities.

6 Reward her even as she rewarded you, and double

**unto her double according to her works: in the cup which
she hath filled fill to her double.**

**7 How much she hath glorified herself, and lived de-
liciously, so much torment and sorrow give her: for she
saith in her heart, I sit a queen, and am no widow, and
shall see no sorrow.**

**8 Therefore shall her plagues come in one day,
death, and mourning, and famine; and she shall be utterly burned with fire: for strong is the Lord God who
judgeth her.**

Jeremiah has the same word of warning:

And I will punish Bel in Babylon, and I will bring
forth out of his mouth that which he hath swallowed
up: and the nations shall not flow together any more
unto him: yea, the wall of Babylon shall fall. My people,
go ye out of the midst of her, and deliver ye every man
his soul from the fierce anger of the Lord.—Jer. 51:44,
45

Who are these people who are warned to come out of
Babylon? The 144,000 are safely on Mount Zion. The Tribulation Saints are either killed or in prison or in hiding. They
would not have freedom of movement. The Lord may have
people we do not know about.

However, we do not have to place this warning as applying to a time after the Rapture. The angel has just said that
the nations have been waxing rich and corrupt as a result
of this city. This warning could apply to people living when
this city first rises. This could be before the Rapture. Many
people would be attracted there because of its rapid expansion.

Babylon is seen here in Revelation at the time of its destruction, but it recognizes the fact that Babylon will have a
history.

Revelation 18

**9 And the kings of the earth, who have committed
fornication and lived deliciously with her, shall bewail**

her, and lament for her, when they shall see the smoke of her burning.

10 Standing afar off for the fear of her torment, saying, Alas, alas, that great city Babylon, that mighty city! for in one hour is thy judgment come.

11 And the merchants of the earth shall weep and mourn over her; for no man buyeth their merchandise any more.

HER TORMENT. They stood afar off for fear of her torment. There is something about the burning city that is dangerous to be near. There is considerable evidence that the destroyers of Babylon are the soldiers of Antichrist. Babylon will not be destroyed by some stroke from heaven, but by armies on earth. In the previous chapter we are told: "And the ten horns which thou sawest upon the beast, these shall hate the whore, and shall make her desolate and naked, and shall eat her flesh, and burn her with fire."—Rev. 17:16.

It is therefore possible that the sudden destruction is the result of an atomic bomb. The torment that the kings of the earth are afraid of may be fallout.

This chapter should be read in its entirety. It presents a most amazing spectacle. Nothing like it has ever happened before; no city like this ever existed before. The building of Babylon and the world system that stems from it will fulfill such precise prophecies that it cannot help but jar the religious world. Even the articles of trade are itemized. They come from every part of the world.

Revelation 18

12 The merchandise of gold, and silver, and precious stones, and of pearls, and fine linen, and purple, and silk, and scarlet, and all thyine wood, and all manner vessels of ivory, and all manner vessels of most precious wood, and of brass, and iron, and marble,

13 And cinnamon, and odours, and ointments, and frankincense, and wine, and oil, and fine flour, and wheat, and beasts, and sheep, and horses, and chariots, and slaves, and souls of men.

14 And the fruits that thy soul lusted after are departed from thee, and all things which were dainty and goodly are departed from thee, and thou shalt find them no more at all.

15 The merchants of these things, which were made rich by her, shall stand afar off for the fear of her torment, weeping and wailing,

16 And saying, Alas, alas that great city, that was clothed in fine linen, and purple, and scarlet, and decked with gold, and precious stones, and pearls!

17 For in one hour so great riches is come to nought. And every shipmaster, and all the company in ships, and sailors, and as many as trade by sea, stood afar off.

18 And cried when they saw the smoke of her burning, saying, What city is like unto this great city!

19 And they cast dust on their heads, and cried, weeping and wailing, saying, Alas, alas that great city, wherein were made rich all that had ships in the sea by reason of her costliness! for in one hour is she made desolate.

20 Rejoice over her, thou heaven, and ye holy apostles and prophets; for God hath avenged you on her.

21 And a mighty angel took up a stone like a great millstone, and cast it into the sea, saying, Thus with violence shall that great city Babylon be thrown down, and shall be found no more at all.

22 And the voice of harpers, and musicians, and of pipers, and trumpeters, shall be heard no more at all in thee; and no craftsman, of whatsoever craft he be, shall be found any more in thee; and the sound of a millstone shall be heard no more at all in thee;

23 And the light of a candle shall shine no more at all in thee; and the voice of the bridegroom and of the bride shall be heard no more at all in thee: for thy merchants were the great men of the earth; for by thy sorceries were all nations deceived.

The angel acts out the scene. He drops a bomb from the sky. Using a great stone, the angel says, "This is the way it will be done."

Babylon will not be the only city to be built during a period of world prosperity. Ezekiel also laments over the city of Tyre which will rival Babylon in splendor and influence (Ezek. 26, 27). These cities reflect a world prosperity on a scale never before dreamed of.

The Laodicean Church reflects a similar prosperity. The whole world is included in this boom. Prophecy deals only with the destruction of these cities, but they have to be built and prosper for some time; we do not know how long.

Both Babylon and Tyre are centers of world trade, indicating a world-wide common market. All nations are rich in natural resources and talent. A world market unhindered by tariff walls would be enough to bring about vast wealth to all peoples. Antichrist will have a mouth speaking great things. He will show the world how to get rich. His great commercial empire will collapse when God takes peace from the earth. Old antagonisms will come to life with violence— nation against nation, race against race. It is when they say "peace and safety" that the sudden destruction comes upon them. Satan's false millennium will suddenly come to an end.

Revelation 18

24 And in her was found the blood of prophets, and of saints, and of all that were slain upon the earth.

BLOOD OF MARTYRS. This may be taken in two ways. Rome has always been a killer of prophets and saints, but this woman represents more than Rome. The Roman Church is only the present phase of Satan's religion. This woman represents Satan's false church of all ages. Jezebel of the Old Testament was a part of this system. All the prophets and saints that have been killed owe their death to this woman.

This may also be applied to the tribulation. The speed and thoroughness with which Satan causes the Tribulation Saints to be killed is due to the fact that he has an organization, world-wide, whose purpose and ambition is to get rid of Protestants. This church will be Satan's ready and willing agent in the program of wiping out the Protestant Church.

Chapter Nineteen

THE RETURN OF CHRIST

Sixth Room

KINGDOM

Satan Chained

Kingdom of
Christ and the Saints

FROM THE RETURN
OF CHRIST TO THE END
OF THE 1000 YEARS

Chapters 19 & 20

Revelation 19

1 And after these things I heard a great voice of much people in heaven, saying, Alleluia; Salvation, and glory, and honour, and power, unto the Lord our God:

2 For true and righteous are his judgments: for he hath judged the great whore, which did corrupt the earth with her fornication, and hath avenged the blood of his servants at her hand.

3 And again they said, Alleluia. And her smoke rose up for ever and ever.

4 And the four and twenty elders and the four beasts fell down and worshipped God that sat on the throne, saying, Amen; Alleluia.

5 And a voice came out of the throne, saying, Praise our God, all ye his servants, and ye that fear him, both small and great.

6 And I heard as it were the voice of a great multitude, and as the voice of many waters, and as the voice of mighty thunders, saying, Alleluia: for the Lord God omnipotent reigneth.

Then the heaven and the earth, and all that is therein,
shall sing for Babylon: for the spoilers shall come unto
her from the north, saith the Lord.—Jer. 51:48

Usually at the beginning of a new series of events, there
is a worship service in anticipation of what is about to happen. This time the rejoicing is because of what has already
happened. The destruction of this church and world system
is of great concern in heaven. The marriage of the Lamb
seems to wait for the destruction of this rival woman.

THE BLOOD OF HIS SERVANTS. Again reference is
made to the part this church plays in the persecution of the
saints. This is not a new role for the Catholic Church, but it
will be the first time that she is able to do in all the world
what she always does in countries where she is in control of
the government.

Marriage of the Lamb

Revelation 19

7 Let us be glad and rejoice, and give honour to
him: for the marriage of the Lamb is come, and his wife
hath made herself ready.

8 And to her was granted that she should be arrayed in fine linen, clean and white: for the fine linen is
the righteousness of the saints.

9 And he saith unto me, Write, Blessed are they
which are called unto the marriage supper of the Lamb.
And he saith unto me, These are the true sayings of God.

There is a great rejoicing in heaven over the judgment
of Babylon. It means the end of wickedness in the world. It
means the Kingdom of God is about to come.

And there were great voices in heaven, saying, The
kingdoms of this world are become the kingdoms of our
Lord, and of his Christ; and he shall reign forever
and ever. And the four and twenty elders which sat
before God on their seats [thrones], fell upon their
faces, and worshipped God, saying, We give thee

thanks, O Lord God Almighty, which art, and wast,
and art to come; because thou hast taken to thee
thy great power, and hast reigned. And the nations
were angry, and thy wrath is come, and the time of the
dead, that they should be judged, and that thou shouldest
give reward unto thy servants the prophets, and to the
saints, and them that fear thy name, small and great;
and shouldest destroy them which destroy the earth.—
Rev. 11:15–18

THE MARRIAGE OF THE LAMB. Although this subject is common to both Old and New Testaments, there is
little positive information about it. Many questions will come
up which cannot be answered completely.

THE BRIDEGROOM. On this point there is not much
room for misunderstanding. He is called the Lamb. The Lamb,
a type of Christ in the Old Testament, became a name for
Christ in the New when John the Baptist said, "Behold the
Lamb of God." The Old Testament church is represented as
betrothed to God, anticipating a glorious union with Him
in due time. Psalm 45 unmistakably refers to this subject.
The Song of Solomon must be understood as referring to
Christ and His Bride.

Christ represented himself as the Bridegroom. He speaks
of the Kingdom of Heaven being "like unto a certain king
which made a marriage for his son," and those called by the
gospel as "bidden to the marriage."—Matt. 22: 1–14.

John the Baptist spoke of Christ as the Bridegroom, and
Paul compared the earthly marriage relationship to that of
Christ and His church (Eph. 5: 32).

THE BRIDE. Who is the bride? Upon this question we
do not have very much positive knowledge. In a general way
it may be said that the bride will be the Lord's true and faithful people who were saved by His blood. But in addition to
the bride, we find mentioned "friends of the bridegroom,"
virgins waiting for the bridegroom, "companions" of the

queen and "the virgins her companions that follow her."—
Ps. 45:14.

The bride is made up of those who have immortal bodies,
that is, those who have been raised from the dead or translated into heaven. Believers living on the earth might con-
ceivably attend the wedding, but they could not be the bride.
The 144,000 Israelites will still be living on the earth. They
are called virgins (Rev. 14:4).

We do not know what the immediate results of the work
of the Two Witnesses are. Their ministry is primarily to the
Jews and no details are given. Revelation is about the church
and the work of the saints in the reclamation of the earth,
and all we know about the work of the Two Witnesses is
what the angel told John in heaven. There are many possi-
bilities for guests and attendants at the wedding which are
not recorded in the story of Revelation.

Revelation 19
10 And I fell at his feet to worship him. And he said
unto me, See thou do it not: I am thy fellowservant, and
of thy brethren that have the testimony of Jesus: worship
God: for the testimony of Jesus is the spirit of prophecy.

"The same thing happens again in 22:8, 9, and this
makes it improbable that St. John imagined the angel to be
Christ. More probably, St. John was so overwhelmed with the
tremendous character of the revelation just made to him, that
in his humility he pays undue reverence to the angel who
had communicated it to him."—Pulpit Commentary.

The angel said, "I am a fellowservant with thee and
with thy brethren." If one of the angels that administered
the trumpets and vials was a fellow servant, we may assume
the others were also. This is in keeping with God's announced
plan that the saints should have charge of the redemption
processes. Here is a telling reason why the Rapture must
come before any of these things start. The saints are the
ones who start them and carry them to completion.

THE TESTIMONY OF JESUS. Revelation is the testimony of Jesus. That in itself makes it an important book, one that we must not disregard. The fact is that all the teachings of Jesus have a prophetic character. Very little that Jesus said was understood by the people of His time. He almost always spoke with the future in mind. It was for the joy that was set before Him that He endured the cross. This joy was ever before Him and tempered everything He said. His testimony is always the spirit of prophecy.

Second Coming of Christ

Revelation 19

11 And I saw heaven opened, and behold a white horse; and he that sat upon him was called Faithful and True, and he doth judge and make war.

12 His eyes were as a flame of fire, and on his head were many crowns; and he had a name written, that no man knew, but he himself.

13 And he was clothed with a vesture dipped in blood: and his name is called The Word of God.

14 And the armies which were in heaven followed him upon white horses, clothed in fine linen, white and clean.

15 And out of his mouth goeth a sharp sword, that he should smite the nations: and he shall rule them with a rod of iron: and he treadeth the winepress of the fierceness and wrath of Almighty God.

16 And he hath on his vesture and on his thigh, a name written, KING OF KINGS, AND LORD OF LORDS.

THE SECOND COMING OF CHRIST. This is a major subject in the Bible. It is told in song, in story, in parable, in direct prophecy. To treat the subject exhaustively would require a commentary on the whole Bible. What follows is a brief summary of the Bible teaching on the second coming of Christ.

It must be remembered that the prophets of old saw the events of the future but did not always see them in the order in which they were to come. They saw the prophesied events as great mountain peaks, but they did not always see the valley between. Sometimes the prophets saw the first coming and the second coming as if they were one event.

The Second Advent is in two parts: (1) The coming of Christ *for* His church and (2) the coming of Christ *with* His church. His coming for His church is the Rapture. His coming with His church is His revelation. It is then that He comes to the earth and remains to reign.

THE MIGHTY CONQUEROR. He comes out of heaven in fulfillment of the promise He made when He ascended into heaven: "This same Jesus, which is taken up from you into heaven, shall so come in like manner as ye have seen him go into heaven."—Acts 1: 11.

Isaiah spoke of this event when he said,

> Oh that thou wouldest rend the heavens, that thou wouldest come down, that the mountains might flow down at thy presence, as when the melting fire burneth, the fire causeth the waters to boil, to make thy name known to thine adversaries, that the nations may tremble at thy presence! When thou didst terrible things which we looked not for, thou camest down, the mountains flowed down at thy presence. For since the beginning of the world men have not heard, nor perceived by the ear, neither hath the eye seen, O God, beside thee, what he hath prepared for him that waiteth for him.—Isa. 64:1-4

HE RIDES UPON A WHITE HORSE. His followers, the saints, also ride upon white horses. White connects with righteousness. When Christ broke the first seal, a rider was sent out from heaven upon a white horse. Many of those who now come with Christ are there because of the work of the white horseman.

HE IS FAITHFUL AND TRUE. This is in sharp contrast to the beast who is a deceiver and a liar.

IN RIGHTEOUSNESS HE DOTH JUDGE AND MAKE WAR. The wars of Antichrist have been for selfish purposes.

Now there will be a war that will have a righteous aim. To the world in armed rebellion, He comes as the mounted warrior, the minister of righteousness, and the destroyer of all that is evil.

HIS EYES WERE AS A FLAME OF FIRE. Men have been killed by the look of kings. What sinful man could face the piercing glance of omniscient perception?

ON HIS HEAD ARE MANY CROWNS. The popes wear a triple crown, emblematic of three sovereignties united in one. The dragon has seven diadems on his seven heads, as the possessor of the seven great world-powers (chap. 12:3). The beast has ten diadems on his ten horns, as combining ten sovereignties, (chap. 13:1). In all these cases the accumulation of crowns expresses accumulated victory and dominion. It is the same in this case. Christ comes against the beast and his confederates as the conqueror on many fields, the winner of many battles, the holder of many sovereignties secured by His prowess and power. He comes as the One anointed, endowed of heaven with all the sovereignties of the earth as His rightful due and possession.

HE HAD A NAME WRITTEN, THAT NO MAN KNEW, BUT HE HIMSELF. Notice how much the saints are like their Lord. The promise is, "When we see him, we shall be like him." He rides a white horse. They ride white horses. He has a name too wonderful for any man to understand, for He has a name which is above every name. The saints are also promised a new name. "To him that overcometh will I give ... a new name, which no man knoweth save he that receiveth it."—Rev. 2:17.

HE WAS CLOTHED WITH A VESTURE DIPPED IN BLOOD. These are stains from the blood of the enemy slain. It has been remarked that these stains appear before the battle, but this is not the first battle in which Christ has been engaged. There was a war in heaven in which the dragon and his angels were cast out. However, this description of the blood stains may be in anticipation of the battle that is to take place, the great battle of Armageddon. Isaiah describes this same scene.

> Who is this that cometh from Edom, with dyed garments from Bozrah? this that is glorious in his apparel, travelling in the greatness of his strength? I that speak in righteousness, mighty to save. Wherefore art thou red in thine apparel, and thy garments like him that treadeth in the winefat? I have trodden the winepress alone; and of the people there was none with me: for I will tread them in mine anger, and trample them in my fury; and their blood shall be sprinkled upon my garments, and I will stain all my raiment. For the day of vengeance is in mine heart, and the year of my redeemed is come.—Isa. 63:1-4

OUT OF HIS MOUTH GOETH A SHARP SWORD. Isaiah said, "He shall smite the earth with the rod of his mouth, and with the breath of his lips shall he slay the wicked."— Isa. 11:4. He speaks and it is done. Something like this happened when the armed mob came forth against Him in Gethsemane. When Jesus said to them, "I am he," they went backward and fell to the ground (John 18:6). If so mild an utterance prostrated His enemies, then what will it be when He girds himself for the "battle of the God Almighty"—when He comes with all the cavalcade of heaven to tread the winepress of the fierceness of Jehovah's anger?

"The word of God is quick, and powerful, and sharper than any two-edged sword, piercing even to the dividing asunder of soul and spirit, and of the joints and marrow"— Heb. 4:12; and when that Word goes forth in execution of almighty wrath upon those in arms against His throne, what a flow of blood, and wilting of life, and tornado of deadly disaster must it work! He is King of kings and Lord of lords, not now in name only, but by actual possession and by a personal and literal reign, for "the law of the Lord shall go forth of Zion, and the word of the Lord from Jerusalem."

The seventh trumpet of the *heaven* section brought forth the announcement: "The kingdoms of this world are become the kingdoms of our Lord and of his Christ: and he shall reign for ever and ever." The final world-shaking earthquake and the great hail bring to an end the seven last plagues.

The *earth* section also ended with the same signs of the immediate return of Christ: namely, the mighty earthquake and the great hail. Just before this seventh plague, we saw Satan gathering the armies of the world together at Armageddon, preparing for the battle for the possession of the earth. The story was interrupted to tell of the destruction of Satan's church and kingdom. Now it is resumed. The *heaven* history unites with the *earth* history because the saints which were in heaven return with Christ to rule on the earth.

Armageddon

Revelation 19

19 And I saw the beast, and the kings of the earth, and their armies, gathered together to make war against him that sat on the horse, and against his army.

20 And the beast was taken, and with him the false prophet that wrought miracles before him, with which he deceived them that had received the mark of the beast, and them that worshipped his image. These both were cast alive into a lake of fire burning with brimstone.

21 And the remnant were slain with the sword of him that sat upon the horse, which sword proceeded out of his mouth: and all the fowls were filled with their flesh.

ARMAGEDDON. These few verses describe an event that actually is the climax of world history and comprises a large section of Old Testament prophecy. In the Old Testament it is the Jews rather than the saints that are in view. The saints, the Jews and the nations are involved in this battle. The armies are gathered against Jerusalem.

Behold, the day of the Lord cometh, and thy spoil shall be divided in the midst of thee. For I will gather all

nations against Jerusalem to battle; and the city shall be
taken, and the houses rifled, and the women ravished;
and half of the city shall go forth into captivity, and the
residue of the people shall not be cut off from the city.
Then shall the Lord go forth, and fight against those
nations, as when he fought in the day of battle. And his
feet shall stand in that day on the mount of Olives, which
is before Jerusalem on the east, and the mount of Olives
shall cleave in the midst thereof toward the east and
toward the west, and there shall be a very great valley;
and half of the mountain shall remove toward the north,
and half of it toward the south. And the Lord shall be
king over all the earth: in that day shall there be one
Lord, and his name one.—Zech. 14:1–4, 9

Ezekiel's description is almost word for word like that
of Revelation except that it gives the location of the battle
and tells the effect it has on Israel. Ezekiel speaks from the
standpoint of the Jews, Revelation from the standpoint of
the saints who are with Christ.

And, thou son of man, thus saith the Lord God;
Speak unto every feathered fowl, and to every beast of
the field, Assemble yourselves, and come; gather yourselves on every side to my sacrifice that I do sacrifice
for you, even a great sacrifice upon the mountains
of Israel, that ye may eat flesh, and drink blood. Ye shall
eat the flesh of the mighty, and drink the blood of the
princes of the earth, of rams, of lambs, and of goats,
of bullocks, all of them fatlings of Bashan. And ye shall
eat fat till ye be full, and drink blood till ye be drunken,
of my sacrifice which I have sacrificed for you. Thus
ye shall be filled at my table with horses and chariots,
with mighty men, and with all men of war, saith the
Lord God. And I will set my glory among the heathen,
and all the heathen shall see my judgment that I have
executed, and my hand that I have laid upon them. So the
house of Israel shall know that I am the Lord their God
from that day and forward.—Ezek. 39:17–22

Joel paints a remarkable picture of this scene, and again
it is from the standpoint of the Jews.

Proclaim ye this among the Gentiles; Prepare war, wake up the mighty men, let all the men of war draw near; let them come up: beat your plowshares into swords, and your pruning hooks into spears: let the weak say, I am strong. Assemble yourselves, and come, all ye heathen, and gather yourselves together round about: thither cause thy mighty ones to come down, O Lord. Let the heathen be wakened, and come up to the valley of Jehoshaphat: for there will I sit to judge all the heathen round about. Put ye in the sickle, for the harvest is ripe: come, get you down; for the press is full, the vats overflow; for their wickedness is great. Multitudes, multitudes in the valley of decision: for the day of the Lord is near in the valley of decision. The sun and the moon shall be darkened, and the stars shall withdraw their shining. The Lord also shall roar out of Zion, and utter his voice from Jerusalem; and the heavens and the earth shall shake; but the Lord will be the hope of his people, and the strength of the children of Israel. So shall ye know that I am the Lord your God dwelling in Zion, my holy mountain: then shall Jerusalem be holy, and there shall no stranger pass through her any more. And it shall come to pass in that day, that the mountains shall drop down new wine, and the hills shall flow with milk, and all the rivers of Judah shall flow with waters, and a fountain shall come forth of the house of the Lord, and shall water the valley of Shittim.—Joel 3:9–18

This battle will do more for Israel than for any other people. It is the fulfillment of all their hopes and prophecies, the beginning of the promised kingdom. None of this is seen in Revelation. As usual, Revelation is concerned only with the saints. It sees the armies gathered against the Lord and those that are with Him. Both views are true. Satan's purpose in bringing the armies of the nations together is to prevent the reign of Christ and the saints. The kings of the earth are more interested in taking a spoil from the Jews. That is the bait that Satan uses to gather the nations.

And thou shalt say, I will go up to the land of unwalled villages; I will go to them that are at rest, that dwell safely, all of them dwelling without walls, and having neither bars nor gates, to take a spoil, and to take a prey; to turn thine hand upon the desolate places that are now inhabited, and upon the people that are gathered out of the nations, which have gotten cattle and goods, that dwell in the midst of the land.—Ezek. 38:11, 12

Chapter Twenty

THE KINGDOM

Satan Chained

Revelation 20

1 And I saw an angel come down from heaven, having the key of the bottomless pit and a great chain in his hand.

2 And he laid hold on the dragon, that old serpent, which is the Devil, and Satan, and bound him a thousand years,

3 And cast him into the bottomless pit, and shut him up, and set a seal upon him, that he should deceive the nations no more, till the thousand years should be fulfilled: and after that he must be loosed a little season.

SATAN CHAINED. Satan is not cast into the lake of fire yet, but he is put in a place of confinement where he can no longer tempt the people or deceive the nations. Then will follow one thousand years of perfect government.

This marks the beginning of a new dispensation. This thousand-year reign of Christ is not the beginning of a new world, but the end of an old. What the Jewish Sabbath is to the week, the Millennium is to the ages. There is a perfect government during this reign of Christ and His saints, but there is not a perfect world until the end.

The plagues, the earthquakes, the great hail, and the fire have destroyed the works of man. The earth is in ruins. It will require seven months to bury the dead after the Battle of Armageddon (Ezek. 39:12).[1]

Then will begin the work of reconstruction under the personal supervision of Christ. This work will be carried on until perfection is attained. That which man had failed to accomplish—lasting peace and universal prosperity with no cycles of depression—Christ will bring to pass. Long life is restored during these days, but death, "the last enemy," still prevails until the end of the thousand years.

Judgment

Revelation 20

4 And I saw thrones, and they sat upon them, and judgment was given unto them: and I saw the souls of them that were beheaded for the witness of Jesus, and for the word of God, and which had not worshipped the beast, neither his image, neither had received his mark upon their foreheads, or in their hands; and they lived and reigned with Christ a thousand years.

5 But the rest of the dead lived not again until the thousand years were finished. This is the first resurrection.

6 Blessed and holy is he that hath part in the first resurrection: on such the second death hath no power, but they shall be priests of God and of Christ, and shall reign with him a thousand years.

WHO WILL ENTER THE KINGDOM? (1) The saints will, those who have immortal bodies. They will reign with Christ for one thousand years and then go to their eternal home, New Jerusalem, which is the heavenly city; (2) the Jews living on the earth; (3) the Gentiles that survive.

The population of the earth will be greatly reduced, especially the man-power, so that "in that day seven women shall take hold of one man, saying, We will eat our own

1. "And seven months shall the house of Israel be burying of them, that they may cleanse the land" (Ezek. 39:12).

bread, and wear our own apparel: only let us be called by thy name, to take away our reproach."—Isa. 4:1.

God told Isaiah concerning that day, "I will punish the world for their evil, and the wicked for their iniquity. I will make a man more precious than fine gold; even a man than the golden wedge of Ophir."—Isa. 13:11, 12.

Afterwards the population will increase with great rapidity. "A little one shall become a thousand, a small one a strong nation. I, the Lord will hasten it in his time."—Isa. 60:22. "And of the increase of his government and peace there shall be no end."—Isa. 9:7.

THE JUDGMENT OF THE LIVING NATIONS. Christ is the judge and ruler. But John said, "I saw thrones, and they sat upon them, and judgment was given unto them." The saints, the bride of Christ, will reign with Him and assist in the judgment of the nations. This judgment is not described here in detail. It is a judgment according to works. It will determine who of the living nations may enter the eternal kingdom. Jesus described such a judgment in Matthew 25:31–46.

THE FIRST RESURRECTION. There will be no resurrection of saints at the Second Coming of Christ. The first resurrection mentioned in verse five is identified in verse four. It comprises first those who occupy the thrones. They are mentioned in the same way in chapter 4. They are those who have part in the Rapture. Also, the first Resurrection includes those who were saved during the tribulation and did not receive the mark of the beast, but were killed for the witness of Jesus.

There is no record or suggestion here that the earth is to be destroyed by fire at the end of the Millennium. It is God's purpose to redeem the earth, not to destroy it. That which is redeemed is not destroyed. The reign of Christ for 1000 years will not end in such failure that His kingdom will have to be destroyed by fire. Instead, we are told that He will deliver up to God a perfect work.

> Then cometh the end, when he shall have delivered up the kingdom of God, even the Father; when he shall have put down all rule and all authority and power. For he must reign till he hath put all enemies under his feet. The last enemy that shall be destroyed is death.— I Cor. 15:24–26

Some have supposed that the references to fire and the destruction of the earth in II Peter 3 teach that the earth is to be destroyed at the end of the Millennium. But everything that Peter says in this chapter is fulfilled by the seven last plagues, all of which carry fire so that all the green grass and one-third of the trees of the earth are burned up.

First comes destruction. This all comes in the Day of the Lord. Next comes restoration and redemption. This is the work of Christ and the saints during the kingdom reign. Then comes eternity. The work of redemption will be complete at the end of the 1000 years, but the kingdom will last forever.

THE REST OF THE DEAD. Revelation mentions a first resurrection and a second death. It does not mention a second resurrection. When the dead come forth for judgment, it is not called a resurrection. Jesus mentioned a resurrection of damnation. When Revelation says the dead lived not again until the thousand years were finished, it is natural to connect this event with the second death mentioned in the next verse. But it might also be connected with the preceding verse so that it would read, "They lived and reigned with Christ a thousand years . . . . The rest of the dead lived not again until the thousand years were finished." This would suggest that there are some who will be raised to eternal life after the Millennium. Who could they be?

The great white throne judgment is recorded at the end of the 1000 years, but it may have been going on all through that time. Even though two events were happening at the same time, they would have to be recorded one after the other. A judgment on so vast a scale would take considerable time, and the new heaven and the new earth must follow the Millennium immediately.

The great white throne judgment could start with the return of Christ and end at the same time the Millennium does. In fact, we have a direct statement to this effect.

> And the nations were angry, and thy wrath is come, and the time of the dead, that they should be judged, and that thou shouldest give reward unto thy servants the prophets, and to the saints, and them that fear thy name, small and great; and shouldest destroy them which destroy the earth.—Rev. 11:18

This would include all the dead. All those who are not raised to immortality are in the great white throne judgment. However, there will be death during the Millennium. Life will be long, but death will not be done away with until after the 1000 years. Isaiah tells about the new heaven and the new earth in the 65th chapter. He saw the kingdom not in its perfection but in its process. The reign of Christ and the saints is the process by which the earth is made new. This is what Isaiah recorded:

> For, behold, I create new heavens and a new earth: and the former shall not be remembered, nor come into mind. But be glad and rejoice for ever in that which I create: for, behold, I create Jerusalem a rejoicing, and her people a joy. And I will rejoice in Jerusalem, and joy in my people: and the voice of weeping shall be no more heard in her, nor the voice of crying. There shall be no more thence an infant of days, nor an old man that hath not filled his days: for the child shall die a hundred years old; but the sinner being a hundred years old shall be accursed. And they shall build houses, and inhabit them; and they shall plant vineyards, and eat the fruit of them. They shall not build, and another inhabit; they shall not plant, and another eat: for as the days of a tree are the days of my people, and mine elect shall long enjoy the work of their hands.—Isa. 65:17-22

It is only after the 1000 years that there is no more death. The people who die during the 1000 years will not be raised until the end. The same was true of the Tribulation Saints; they were not raised one at a time but all at once. Nothing more is said about these saved people who die during the Millennium. It is quite evident they do not belong with those who inhabit the Holy City. There are many groups of people who are not cast into the lake of fire but whose future place is not revealed. There are kingdoms besides the ones on the earth and in the Holy City. There is no limit to God's resources.

Revelation 20

7 And when the thousand years are expired, Satan shall be loosed out of his prison,

8 And shall go out to deceive the nations which are in the four quarters of the earth, Gog and Magog, to gather them together to battle: the number of whom is as the sand of the sea.

9 And they went up on the breadth of the earth, and compassed the camp of the saints about, and the beloved city: and fire came down from God out of heaven, and devoured them.

10 And the devil that deceived them was cast into the lake of fire and brimstone, where the beast and the false prophet are, and shall be tormented day and night for ever and ever.

THE FINAL CLEANSING. It should be remembered that during this 1000 years we do not have a perfect world or a perfect people but only a perfect government. The Millennium is not the beginning of a new order, but the ending of an old. Although Satan himself will be without power, sin will not have been eradicated from the human race. This will require one more cleansing. Even the judgment of the nations mentioned by Christ may be a process lasting many years, in which case many people will enter the kingdom age who will obey Christ only because they have to. At the end of the 1000 years all such people will be segregated and destroyed from the earth. The method of separating them is simple. Satan will be loosed and will immediately set about to gather his own kind together against the Lord. They will be destroyed, and Satan will be cast into the lake of fire from which no one ever comes back.

The kingdom does not come to an end at the end of the thousand years. There is a change, but the Kingdom of God is everlasting. *The 1000 years is not the length of the kingdom but the length of time Satan is chained.*

There is no such thing as the end of the world. The Bible speaks of "the end of the age" (sometimes translated "world"), but it does not teach that the world will come to an end. The kingdom of David is everlasting—"world without end" (Isa. 45: 17) .[1]

This was God's promise to David: "He shall build an house for my name, and I will establish the throne of his kingdom for ever before thee: thy throne shall be established for ever."—II Sam. 7: 13, 16.

This was God's revelation to Daniel:

> And there was given him dominion, and glory, and a kingdom, that all people, nations and languages should serve him; his dominion is an everlasting dominion, which shall not be destroyed. But the saints of the most High shall take the kingdom, and possess the kingdom forever.—Dan. 7:14, 18

See also Daniel 4: 3.[2]

This was God's promise to Mary: "He shall be great and shall be called the Son of the Highest: and the Lord God shall give unto him the throne of his father David: and he shall reign over the house of Jacob forever; and of his kingdom there shall be no end."—Luke 1: 32, 33.

---

1. "But Israel shall be saved in the Lord with an everlasting salvation: ye shall not be ashamed nor confounded world without end" (Isa. 45:17).
2. "How great are his signs and how mighty are his wonders! his kingdom is an everlasting kingdom, and his dominion is from generation to generation" (Dan. 4:3).

GOG AND MAGOG. These names are found also in
Ezekiel where the meaning is the same (Ezek. 38, 39). Magog
is the name of a man (Gen. 10:2); Gog is not. Gog is Satan
and Magog is the man whom Satan possesses. When Satan
is personally operating in the world, he is known as Gog and
Magog. This will happen twice, once before the Millennium,
and once at the end. When Satan is cast out of heaven and
takes up his position in the body of a man, Ezekiel calls him
by the term Gog and Magog. Then at the end of the Millennium, when Satan is again turned loose and begins to operate
on the earth, Revelation calls him Gog and Magog.

Revelation 20

11 And I saw a great white throne, and him that
sat on it, from whose face the earth and the heaven fled
away; and there was found no place for them.

12 And I saw the dead, small and great, stand before
God; and the books were opened: and another book was
opened, which is the book of life: and the dead were
judged out of those things which were written in the
books according to their works.

13 And the sea gave up the dead which were in it;
and death and hell delivered up the dead which were
in them: and they were judged every man according to
their works.

14 And death and hell were cast into the lake of
fire. This is the second death.

15 And whosoever was not found written in the
book of life was cast into the lake of fire.

At the end of one thousand years of the reign of Christ,
the final judgment is completed. It is the end of the seven
dispensations or cycles of world history. Sin and death are
to be no more. The whole plan of redemption is now complete.
The time of the judgment of the dead has come. This judgment does not take place on earth. The people on the earth
have no part in it. Neither do those who have previously been
raised. "Blessed and holy is he that hath part in the first
resurrection: on such the second death hath no power."—

Rev. 20: 6. The subjects of this judgment are the dead who were not saved by the blood of Christ.

John was suddenly taken from the earth so fast that it seemed to speed out of sight behind him, and he beheld the great judgment throne of God, before which all the dead would be judged. No place was found in the judgment for those who inhabit the earth and the heavens. This does not mean that the earth and the heavens went out of existence, but only that they had no place in this final judgment.

There are two sets of books and there are two classes of people in this judgment. First there are "the books." In these books are written the record of the lives of all those who have lived on the earth. This is a judgment according to works.

It is the only basis for judgment for those who have never heard of Christ or who have had no opportunity of being saved by faith. The greater part of the people in this judgment are in that class. They have had no opportunity for the exercise of faith. They are judged according to their works.

But there is another book and another class of people. It is called the book of life. Those not found in the book of life are cast, without further ceremony, into the lake of fire. It contains the names of those born into the world, but some names have been crossed out. Those who have rejected Christ are not judged according to their works. They are judged on the basis of faith, or the lack of it. Only those whose names have not been thus crossed out of the book of life are judged according to their works. Jesus taught a similar doctrine (John 5: 25–29).[1]

---

1. "Verily, verily, I say unto you, The hour is coming, and now is, when the dead shall hear the voice of the Son of God: and they that hear shall live. For as the Father hath life in himself; so hath he given to the Son to have life in himself; and hath given him authority to execute judgment also, because he is the Son of man. Marvel not at this: for the hour is coming, in the which all that are in the graves shall hear his voice, and shall come forth; they that have done good, unto the resurrection of life; and they that have done evil, unto the resurrection of damnation" (John 5:25-29).

First there is the resurrection when those who hear the call of God will respond and come out of their graves. Later, all that are in the graves will come forth, "they that have done good, unto the resurrection of life; and they that have done evil, unto the resurrection of damnation." In this judgment they are judged by what they have done. It is a judgment according to works. It must, therefore, refer to the judgment of the great white throne.

Not all of those who stand before the great white throne are cast into the lake of fire. What the future is of those whose works have been good is not revealed. It is evident that they will not enter the holy city.

Chapter Twenty-one

THE HOLY CITY

A New Heaven and a New Earth

Seventh Room

HOLY CITY

Eternal Home of
Immortals

Capital of the Universe

FROM THE 1000 YEARS
FOREVER

Chapters 21 & 22

Revelation 21

1 And I saw a new heaven and a new earth: for the first heaven and the first earth were passed away; and there was no more sea.

A NEW HEAVEN AND A NEW EARTH. The new heaven and the new earth are not the result of some unrecorded catastrophe, happening between the 20th and 21st chapters. They are the result of the process of redemption and the reign of Christ for one thousand years. It is unthinkable that the redemptive work of Christ, culminating in the reign of Christ, should result in. such failure that total destruction would be necessary.

This is a retrospect on the part of John. "Old things are passed away. Behold all things are become new." With the final cleansing of the earth and the judgment of the great white throne, redemption is complete. For a thousand years

Christ and the saints have been working at the task of restoring all things. The result is recorded in this verse.

This verse completes the story of redemption that began in the Garden of Eden. Every effort of man to restore
the earth has failed. Every civilization has in it the germs of
its own destruction. There is one hope and only one, the
blessed hope (Titus 2: 13) .[1]

Imagine, if you can, the condition on this earth after
the seven last plagues and the battle of Armageddon. Then
imagine the changes that would come in a thousand years of
reconstruction under the personal supervision of Christ. If
you could imagine that, then you would see what John saw—
"a new heaven and a new earth; for the first heaven and the
first earth were passed away."

There is nothing in the word "pass" or in the word
"away" that suggests any kind of destruction. We speak of
our loved ones as having passed away. They have passed into
a new realm and eventually are forgotten here. *Passed away*
is a redemption expression. Paul, after his conversion, said,
"Old things are passed away, behold, all things are become
new." The same is true of the redeemed earth. "The former
things are passed away." "Behold, I make all things new."

AND THERE WAS NO MORE SEA. This does not mean
that there will be no more water but that the land and the
water will be more evenly divided, doing away with all barren
land and making every spot on the earth a Garden of Eden.
This change in the earth's surface will probably be one of the
results of the mighty earthquakes so frequently mentioned in
the prophecies concerning the last days.

Again, this is retrospect. John was summing up. He had
seen the world as it is today. He had seen the destruction in
the Day of the Lord—the earthquakes, the falling stars, the
fire, and the hail. He had seen every wall fall to the ground

---

1. "Looking for that blessed hope, and the glorious appearing of the great God and
our Saviour Jesus Christ" (Tit. 2:13).

and the mountains moved into the sea, bringing whole new continents into being. He had seen the surplus water disappear.

Regeneration is restoration to the original state. The heavens and the earth as they were before the fall are described in Genesis.

This was also a remaking, as the earth has been here for a long time. We may learn something of the restored heaven and earth by looking at the former one.

> And God said, Let there be a firmament in the midst of the waters, and let it divide the waters from the waters. And God made the firmament, and divided the waters which were under the firmament from the waters which were above the firmament: and it was so. And God called the firmament Heaven ... And God said, Let the waters under the heaven be gathered together into one place, and let the dry land appear: and it was so. And God called the dry land Earth; and the gathering together of the waters he called Seas.—Gen. 1:6–10

The word for seas in both the Hebrew and the Greek may be used of bodies of water large or small. The meaning must be gathered from the context. The original seas could have been large enough for whales and still not be larger than the Mediterranean. On the other hand, there could have been a great number of seas, all connected. Whole new continents could rise in the oceans and still there would be plenty of water.

When John said "there was no more sea," he could have meant that the great oceans were filled with new expanses of land so that we would have the "seas" of Genesis rather than the "sea" or ocean of the present time.

If, then, there was less water at the first and more dry land, where was this extra water? Genesis tells us. The firmament called heaven is the sky—the atmosphere above the earth. This firmament was in the midst of the waters so that it divided the waters from the waters. Genesis suggests that the division was somewhat equal. There was a great amount of water above the sky. This water that was above the sky was not then upon the earth. Instead of being three quarters water and one quarter land, the surface of the earth might have been more land than water. The animals that God created could easily have migrated to all parts of the earth where their remains have been found.

Even the remote islands of the sea could have been connected to the mainland, as must have been the case. The great earthquake described in Revelation 16 will bring awesome changes over the terrain of the whole earth.

But what about the water above the firmament? There is no such water there now. Water at that height would be almost transparent. The sun, moon, and stars could be seen, although possibly not with the same clarity.

Dr. Vail, one of the scientists who first brought out this theory of water around the earth, thought that this water was in the form of a ring somewhat like the rings around Saturn, only wider. The rings, he thought were wide enough to produce the sifting of the cosmic rays but not wide enough to hide the entire sky. However, this ring theory is not necessary to conform to Genesis. Water in some forms is quite transparent; so are some forms of vapor. Pure water itself is quite transparent at a distance.

But life on the earth would be quite different. Life would be impossible now if it were not for the layer of strange gas that sifts out certain lethal rays from the sun. Water would sift out other rays, possibly those which allow decay and fermentation. Life would be much longer. Food would not spoil as quickly. The temperature would probably be more even and the light softer. Such a water canopy might have the effect of air conditioning, making the whole earth a paradise.

This seems to have been the condition between the time of the Garden of Eden and the flood. The canopy of water above the firmament would provide a vast amount of water needed for the flood. Rain clouds, as we know them today, would not be a sufficient source of water for a flood that covered the earth to the tops of the mountains.

Clouds are formed by the evaporation of water so that the total amount remains constant. But at the flood, the amount of water on the earth was suddenly increased. This extra water seems to have come from two sources.

In the six hundredth year of Noah's life, in the second month, the seventeenth day of the month, the same day were all the fountains of the great deep broken up and the windows of heaven opened.—Gen. 7:11

Dr. Vail thought the great deep was the reservoir of water above the earth. In that case the breaking up of the windows of heaven would be the same thing.

However, water may have come from two directions: up from the ground and down from the heavens. The water that came out of the ground may have gone back into the ground after the flood. The water that came down from the sky did not return but evidently rushed to the poles. Some remained, so that large amounts of land never appeared again, but stayed under water and will so remain as long as this surplus water stays on the earth.

There must have been an enormous tidal wave when that flood water rushed to the polar regions of the earth. It would certainly have swept back around the earth had it not been instantly stopped and held there by freezing.

If, therefore, the poles suddenly became cold, and if that cold has caused the tipping of the earth, then the earth must have tipped suddenly. This could have been caused by the rush of water to the poles. In fact, it must have been caused by the rush of water to the poles because animals have been found there imbedded in the ice.

When the earth suddenly tipped, it suddenly became dark at the poles and remained dark for six months of the year. This is all eloquently expressed in Job:

> Who shut the sea with doors, when it brake forth, as if it had issued out of the womb? when I made the cloud a garment thereof, and thick darkness a swaddling-band for it, and established my decree upon it [margin], and set bars and doors, and said, Hitherto shalt thou come, but no further: and here shall thy proud waves be stayed.—Job. 38:8-11

This has been applied to Genesis, when God separated the waters into seas. But there is no indication there of any such turmoil or breaking forth with a mighty rush. There were no clouds in the Genesis story. In fact, it says that it had not rained upon the earth, but a mist went up and watered the land. There is no mention of rain till the flood.

That canopy of water surrounding the earth might have had some surprising effects, especially as the sun set, producing a refracted light of gorgeous colors. Even now we can sometimes see the sun after it has set if the atmosphere is just right. The rays are bent by the water in the sky. A complete canopy of water might bring a long twilight. Maybe it never would get absolutely dark. But when the sky cleared and the earth tipped, thick darkness prevailed. God made the thick darkness a swaddling, as He told Job.

Geologists tell us that normal climatic times on the earth are times of low relief. High mountains connect with cold weather. The great mountain ranges could all have been raised up since the flood. That accounts for the fact that the mountains will move into the sea as a result of the final earthquake. God is restoring the earth to its original form.

The heat of the seven last plagues would melt the ice but it would also evaporate the water, drawing it unto the sky. Then there would be water above the firmament and water below the firmament. The water below the firmament would be in seas, rather than great oceans. This would restore the heavens and the earth to their original state.

Holy City

Revelation 21

2 And I John saw the holy city, new Jerusalem, coming down from God out of heaven, prepared as a bride adorned for her husband.

3 And I heard a great voice out of heaven saying, Behold, the tabernacle of God is with men, and he will dwell with them, and they shall be his people, and God himself shall be their God.

4 And God shall wipe away all tears from their eyes; and there shall be no more death, neither sorrow, nor crying, neither shall there be any more pain: for the former things are passed away.

5 And he that sat upon the throne said, Behold, I make all things new. And he said unto me, Write: for these words are true and faithful.

6 And he said unto me, It is done. I am Alpha and Omega, the beginning and the end. I will give unto him that is athirst of the fountain of the water of life freely.

This chapter is in two parts: (1) the new heaven, (2) the new earth. The only feature of the new heaven that is in view is the Holy City. This feature dominates the scene, but a few verses are given to the new earth.

THE NEW EARTH. Here again we do not have the whole picture. Most of what the Old Testament prophets saw applies to the Millennium (Isaiah 35). Isaiah 60:17-22 seems to look beyond the Millennium into eternity. It suggests that the Holy City will remain over the earthly Jerusalem and be its light, so there will be one place on the earth that will never get dark.

For brass I will bring gold, and for iron I will bring silver, and for wood brass, and for stones iron: I will also make thy officers peace, and thine exactors righteousness. Violence shall no more be heard in thy land, wasting or destruction within thy borders; but thou

shalt call thy walls Salvation, and thy gates Praise. The
sun shall be no more thy light by day; neither for brightness shall the moon give light unto thee: but the Lord
shall be unto thee an everlasting light, and thy God thy
glory. Thy sun shall no more go down; neither shall
thy moon withdraw itself: for the Lord shall be thine
everlasting light, and the days of thy mourning shall be
ended. Thy people also shall be all righteous: they shall
inherit the land for ever, the branch of my planting, the
work of my hands, that I may be glorified. A little one
shall become a thousand, and a small one a strong
nation: I the Lord will hasten it in his time.—Isa.
60:17-22

ALL THINGS NEW, not all new things. To make all new
things would be to start over again; it would not be redemption. The things that God made and called good are not to
be destroyed; they are to be purged by fire, hail, and earthquake and then made new. This is true of all redeemed things.
Even our immortal bodies are raised from the dead. Only
those who have mortal bodies can have immortal bodies (on
whom the second death hath no power). Satan and his angels
are cast into the lake of fire, which is the second death, but
the lake of fire would have no power over an immortal body
such as the saints have. Redeemed bodies are old bodies made
new. They are of a different nature than mere spirit bodies.
Their possessors can become the bride of Christ. Redeemed
things have a higher place in heavenly values than directly
created things, however good.

The glory of the Holy City lies in the fact that it is the
city of the redeemed—those who were once lost, people made
new. "Then shall the righteous shine forth as the sun in the
kingdom of their father." God is the Creator of the angels
but the Father of the saints. Only those who have been made
new may be adopted into the family of God and become joint
heirs with Christ. God never made an angel worthy of that
honor. Only those redeemed by His blood will be glorified
with Him.

The earth will be a redeemed planet; that makes it different from all worlds that have ever been made or will be made. The Bible suggests that it will be the seed plot from which God will people many worlds. The idea of going from one planet to another is no longer strange; it is even being seriously planned, but God is way ahead of man in His planning.

The earth is not big enough to hold all the things that God talks about. There is not enough room here to fulfill all the promises in the Bible. A people made new occupy the capital city of the spiritual universe, and the earth made new will occupy the central place in an ever-expanding kingdom.

IT IS DONE. This is the third time Christ has said this, marking off the three main divisions in the process of redemption:

1. John 19:30. "It is finished"—the words of Christ on the cross. The redemption price had been paid.

2. Rev. 16:17. "It is done"—the voice from the throne at the seventh vial; the Second Coming of Christ.

3. Rev. 21:6. "It is done"—spoken by Him that sits on the throne at the time that He delivers up to God the perfected kingdom.

Revelation 21

7 He that overcometh shall inherit all things; and I will be his God, and he shall be my son.

8 But the fearful, and unbelieving, and the abominable, and murderers, and whoremongers, and sorcerers, and idolaters, and all liars, shall have their part in the lake which burneth with fire and brimstone: which is the second death.

The fearful are probably those who were not overcomers because of fear. The others are outright sinners who cannot be reclaimed. In the previous chapter it merely says that those who were not found in the book of life were cast into the lake of fire. It did not explain further. Here we find the kind of people who have been crossed out of the book of life.

Revelation 21

9 And there came unto me one of the seven angels which had the seven vials full of the seven last plagues, and talked with me, saying, Come hither, I will shew thee the bride, the Lamb's wife.

10 And he carried me away in the spirit to a great and high mountain, and shewed me that great city, the holy Jerusalem, descending out of heaven from God,

11 Having the glory of God: and her light was like unto a stone most precious, even like a jasper stone, clear as crystal;

12 And had a wall great and high, and had twelve gates, and at the gates twelve angels, and names written thereon, which are the names of the twelve tribes of the children of Israel:

13 On the east three gates; on the north three gates; on the south three gates; and on the west three gates.

14 And the wall of the city had twelve foundations, and in them the names of the twelve apostles of the Lamb.

15 And he that talked with me had a golden reed to measure the city, and the gates thereof, and the wall thereof.

16 And the city lieth foursquare, and the length is as large as the breadth: and he measured the city with the reed, twelve thousand furlongs. The length and the breadth and the height of it are equal.

17 And he measured the wall thereof, an hundred and forty and four cubits, according to the measure of a man, that is, of the angel.

18 And the building of the wall of it was of jasper: and the city was pure gold, like unto clear glass.

19 And the foundations of the wall of the city were garnished with all manner of precious stones. The first foundation was jasper; the second, sapphire; the third, a chalcedony; the fourth, an emerald;

20 The fifth, sardonyx; the sixth, sardius; the seventh, chrysolyte; the eighth, beryl; the ninth, a topaz; the tenth, a chrysoprasus; the eleventh, a jacinth; the twelfth, an amethyst.

21 And the twelve gates were twelve pearls; every several gate was of one pearl: and the street of the city was pure gold, as it were transparent glass.

22 And I saw no temple therein: for the Lord God Almighty and the Lamb are the temple of it.

23 And the city had no need of the sun, neither of the moon, to shine in it: for the glory of God did lighten it, and the Lamb is the light thereof.

24 And the nations of them which are saved shall walk in the light of it: and the kings of the earth do bring their glory and honour into it.

25 And the gates of it shall not be shut at all by day: for there shall be no night there.

26 And they shall bring the glory and honour of the nations into it.

27 And there shall in no wise enter into it any thing that defileth, neither whatsoever worketh abomination, or maketh a lie: but they which are written in the Lamb's book of life.

THAT GREAT CITY. It is called "the bride, the Lamb's wife." It is the home of the bride. The marriage of the Lamb, the ceremony that forever unites Christ and His saints, is mentioned in the 19th chapter, just prior to the return of Christ to the earth. Nothing is said about when this ceremony takes place, but it is only after the Millennium that the bride goes to live in her especially prepared city and home.

ORIGIN. John sees it coming down out of heaven from God. The saints themselves are the workmanship of God. The city is the home of "the bride, the Lamb's wife." It is the complete fulfillment of the promise of Christ: "In my Father's house are many mansions. I go to prepare a place for you."— John 14:2.

LOCATION. The location is not specifically told. It is near the earth, but not a part of the earth. The nations of the earth walk in the light of it. It is above them.

SPLENDOR. Here the details are numerous, but they are read with difficulty. The world knows no such splendor as is here described. All the precious stones of earth brought together fail to describe the glory of New Jerusalem. A jasper stone is wavy with the various colors of the rainbow, but it is translucent. This city is like a jasper stone, crystal clear.

We have no such gold as is here pictured—transparent gold, like the most perfect glass. Maybe it is the brightness of the light that makes the gold transparent, "for the glory of God did lighten it, and the Lamb is the light thereof."

SIZE. The city is twelve thousand furlongs (about 1400 miles) square and twelve thousand furlongs high. It is a cube; it is foursquare (vs. 16).

LIGHTING. It does not need the sun nor any artificial light. It is light. It gives light. "Then the moon shall be confounded, and the sun ashamed, when the Lord of hosts shall reign in Mount Zion and in Jerusalem, and before his ancients gloriously."—Isa. 24:25. The glory of the Lord is the light of Jerusalem.

TEMPLE. There is no temple in the Holy City, for the Lord God himself is the temple. There is no need of special forms or times or places of worship.

The city is noted for its size, beauty, light, river, trees, and inhabitants.

A WALL GREAT AND HIGH. The wall, however, is not as high as the city. 144 cubits is slightly more than 250 feet. The entrances to the city are through gates in the wall. Each gate is guarded by an angel and is named after one of the tribes of Israel.

TWELVE FOUNDATION STONES. The wall has twelve foundations, named after the twelve apostles. The Church (the New Testament saints) will have a part in the Holy City.

TWELVE GATES. The twelve gates are twelve pearls. On these pearls are written the names of the twelve tribes of Israel (vs. 12). The Old Testament saints will also have their part in the Holy City.

A pearl is a product of a living organism. It is the result of injury. A particle of sand injures the oyster and a pearl is the result. It is the answer of the injured to the injury done.

The Holy City and its inhabitants are the result of an injury inflicted upon Christ. The Jews did not consider the pearl a precious stone. It was never mentioned among their valuable possessions.

> A pearl is found beneath the flowing tide.
> And there is held a worse than worthless thing.
> Spoiling the shell-built home where it must cling,
> Marring the life near which it must abide.

This is emblematic of the sin of Israel, resulting in the crucifixion of her Lord. But out of it comes the pearl of greatest price, and in that day each one of the gates upon which the names of the twelve tribes of Israel are written will be of pearl. And then the pearl will be Israel's most precious stone.

Chapter Twenty-two

ETERNITY

Revelation 22

1 And he shewed me a pure river of water of life, clear as crystal, proceeding out of the throne of God and of the Lamb.

2 In the midst of the street of it, and on either side of the river, was there the tree of life, which bare twelve manner of fruits, and yielded her fruit every month: and the leaves of the tree were for the healing of the nations.

3 And there shall be no more curse: but the throne of God and of the Lamb shall be in it; and his servants shall serve him.

RIVER OF WATER OF LIFE. This river is in the Holy City, New Jerusalem, not on the earth. This life-giving stream flows from the throne and forms a part of a great park-like boulevard comprising the main street of the city. It runs through the center of the boulevard. The street is on each side. There are two rows of trees planted by the river which bring forth their fruit in their season. These trees grow on each side of the river, midway between the river and the street.

New Jerusalem, the city of the redeemed, is the capital city of the universe, for the throne of God is in it. Its citizens are all kings and priests. They dispense to the world the ben-

efits of the water of life and the leaves of the tree of life,
which are for the healing of the nations.

People on the earth can live forever only as they have
access to the tree of life. But the tree of life will not again
be planted upon the earth. The nations will be dependent
upon the Holy City for its benefits. Therefore the kings of the
earth "do bring their glory and honor into it."

The people will receive spiritual as well as material bless-
ings from the Holy City, for "the nations of them which are
saved shall walk in the light of it."

The city will have a kingly and priestly supervision over
the activities of the earth. People who live in temples of flesh
and blood will always need supernatural assistance. The Holy
City is God's perfect provision for this eternal need.

It is not to be supposed that the redeemed will be kept
as prisoners within the confines of the four walls. It is the
home, the eternal city of the redeemed, but it does not follow
that we will always be at home. In Christ the saints are heirs
to "all things."

Revelation 22

**4 And they shall see his face; and his name shall
be in their foreheads.**

**5 And there shall be no night there; and they need
no candle, neither light of the sun; for the Lord God
giveth them light: and they shall reign for ever and ever.**

AND THEY SHALL SEE HIS FACE. This is a rare privi-
lege, but the full meaning cannot be comprehended until that
day. It is, however, the natural sequence of 21:2: "And I John
saw the holy city, new Jerusalem, coming down from God
out of heaven, prepared as a bride adorned for her husband."
The relationship between Christ and the redeemed will be
as intimate as that of bride and groom. No created being can
ever aspire to greater position or power or experience.

HIS NAME SHALL BE IN THEIR FOREHEADS. This
would not be a distinction if the redeemed were never to

leave the Holy City, for they would all have the same mark. But out in the universe, wherever they go this signet will be a mark of distinction as belonging only to those who have been redeemed by the blood of Christ; who lived victoriously in Satan's realm; who silenced the music of the angels with their songs of redemption; who are citizens of the glorious Holy City; and who see His face.

NO NIGHT THERE. The gates will never be shut. They will be open all day and there is no night. Inasmuch as no one may enter the city except those for whom it was prepared, the open gates must be for those inhabitants who desire to come and go.

Isaiah saw this day as one standing on the earth and looking up, beholding the Holy City with its open gates and its inhabitants coming and going. Isaiah asks in wonderment, "Who are these that fly as a cloud, and as doves to their windows?"—Isaiah 60:8.

THE LORD GOD GIVETH THEM LIGHT. "The Lamb is the light thereof." "The glory of God did lighten it." Light is associated with life. There could be no darkness in the presence of One who has the power of an endless life. "For in him was life, and the life was the light of men."

Only those cleansed will be allowed to pass through the gates into the Holy City, for the slightest sin, though concealed in the innermost thought, would be immediately detected in that light. "Wherefore, beloved, seeing that ye look for such things, be diligent that ye may be found of him in peace, without spot, and blameless."—II Peter 3:14.

Revelation 22

6 And he said unto me, These sayings are faithful and true: and the Lord God of the holy prophets sent his angel to shew unto his servants the things which must shortly be done.

7 Behold, I come quickly: blessed is he that keepeth the sayings of the prophecy of this book.

8 And I John saw these things, and heard them. And when I had heard and seen, I fell down to worship before the feet of the angel which shewed me these things.

9 Then saith he unto me, See thou do it not: for I am thy fellowservant, and of thy brethren the prophets, of them which keep the sayings of this book: worship God.

10 And he saith unto me, Seal not the sayings of this book: for the time is at hand.

THE SAYINGS OF THE PROPHECY OF THIS BOOK are a sacred trust committed unto us till our Lord comes. They are today a powerful weapon in the hands of the Christian.

God gave Moses a message for the children of Israel. God gave the prophets, each in turn, a message for their day. In those long years in the wilderness, God gave John the Baptist the message peculiarly suited to his day. Likewise, the apostles and their successors, the leaders of the Great Reformation, the evangelists and missionaries of all ages—all have received from God the particular message for their times.

God has a message for this day. The man who is equipped with this knowledge is equipped for this day. To know and proclaim this message is to wield the sword of the Spirit with the peculiar power of the mighty men of old. God's special message for the *last days* is in the *last book* of His Word. The time is at hand; seal not this book. Publish it, proclaim it, teach it, for "blessed is he that keepeth the sayings of the prophecy of this book."

Revelation 22

11 He that is unjust, let him be unjust still: and he which is filthy, let him be filthy still: and he that is righteous, let him be righteous still: and he that is holy, let him be holy still.

12 And, behold, I come quickly; and my reward is with me, to give every man according as his work shall be.

13 I am the Alpha and Omega, the beginning and the end, the first and the last.

14 Blessed are they that do his commandments, that they may have right to the tree of life, and may enter in through the gates into the city.

15 For without are dogs, and sorcerers, and whoremongers, and murderers, and idolaters, and whosoever loveth and maketh a lie.

NO MORE CHANGE. There is an air of finality about these words. We have reached a changeless state. This will be a new experience for us. Throughout our whole existence change has been the controlling factor. As we grow, our bodies change. We are always changing styles, acquaintances, environment. We sometimes have a change of heart, a change of mind, a change of plans. This is the way of the world. The poet expressed in a song:

"Change and decay in all around I see;
O Thou who changeth not, abide with me."

The new world is the world of Him who changes not. It is important that we understand this situation now; because, if there is no change, we will have to spend eternity in the same condition we go into it. If we are not satisfied with the state of our heart or mind, now is the time to change. It is in this life that we must attain righteousness and holiness.

REWARDS ACCORDING TO WORKS. Jesus will come quickly. He did not mean that He would come immediately. He was not talking about the time but the manner of His coming. We should not separate these two statements: "Behold, I come quickly"; "My reward is with me."

The suddenness of His coming will not allow time to build up rewards. If people realized that the time for rewards had come, they would rush out and do something. But no such opportunity will be given; He will come quickly. Rewards are accumulated over a lifetime. We cannot, as some people seem to plan on, hurry out to build up some rewards when the signs of His coming begin to appear, for He will come quickly.

BLESSED ARE THEY THAT DO HIS COMMAND-MENTS. The American Standard Version reads: "Blessed are they that wash their robes." The Vulgate adds: "in the blood of the Lamb," which is, of course, the meaning. The best manuscripts support the American Standard. These blessed ones have a right to the tree of life. That is: they have authority over it. They can dispense its benefits as well as partake of the fruit. The leaves are for the healing of the nations but the tree grows only in the Holy City. Only those who may enter through the gates into the Holy City may administer the benefits of the tree of life.

There are some who have no right to any of the benefits of the tree of life; they are "the dogs." This is a term used in the Eastern countries to mean that which is most degraded. The reference seems to be to people who are too wicked even to be judged by their works. They have not only missed all the benefits of the tree of life; they cannot even have the leaves. They are, in fact, so far beyond hope that even the Great White Throne Judgment would be too good for them.

Revelation 22

16 I Jesus have sent mine angel to testify unto you these things in the churches. I am the root and the offspring of David, and the bright and morning star.

17 And the Spirit and the bride say, Come. And let him that heareth say, Come. And let him that is athirst come. And whosoever will, let him take the water of life freely.

18 For I testify unto every man that heareth the words of the prophecy of this book, If any man shall add unto these things, God shall add unto him the plagues that are written in this book:

19 And if any man shall take away from the words

of the book of this prophecy, God shall take away his part out of the book of life, and out of the holy city, and from the things which are written in this book.

COME. Here is a double invitation: an invitation to Christ to come, and an invitation to all who thirst to take freely of the water of life that flows like a great river from the throne of God. "The Spirit and the bride say, Come." Jesus says, "Behold, I come quickly." The Bride responds, "Even so, come, Lord Jesus." All the hopes and aspirations of all the followers of Christ are contingent upon His second coming. It is the "blessed hope" of the church. And because of the fulfillment of this hope, all the redeemed "whosoever will" may take the water of life freely. This is not an invitation to sinners to accept Christ. It is an invitation to the redeemed, for only those who are saved by the blood of Christ and live in the Holy City may come down to the banks of the river of the water of life.

How Jesus does plead with His church concerning this truth. "I Jesus have sent mine angel to testify unto you these things in the churches." This is the one book that is specifically appointed to be read in the churches. It is the only book that contains a description of Jesus. It is the only book that contains a word from Jesus after His ascension. He said, "I go to prepare a place for you," and after He had gone, He sent back this message telling about the place.

Seven times He repeats, "He that hath an ear let him hear what the Spirit saith unto the churches." To scorn this book is to scorn Jesus. And yet the church is today treating this message in the same fashion that the scribes and Pharisees treated Jesus when He was upon earth. There is great tenderness in these closing verses. One can almost hear the quiver in His voice as He pleads with His church concerning His coming, even as He pled with Israel at the end of His earthly ministry: "O Jerusalem, Jerusalem, thou that killest the prophets, and stonest them which are sent unto thee, how often would I have gathered thy children together, even as a hen gathereth her chickens under her wings, and ye would not! Behold, your house is left unto you desolate. For I say unto you, ye shall not see me henceforth, till ye shall say, Blessed is he that cometh in the name of the Lord."— Matt. 23: 37–39.

The last promise in the Bible is *"surely I come quickly."* The last prayer in the Bible is *"even so, come, Lord Jesus."*

INDEX TO SCRIPTURE REFERENCES

INDEX

331